Palgrave Studies in Classical Liberalism

Series Editors
David F. Hardwick
Department of Pathology and Laboratory Medicine
The University of British Columbia
Vancouver, BC, Canada

Leslie Marsh
Department of Pathology and Laboratory Medicine
The University of British Columbia
Vancouver, BC, Canada

This series offers a forum to writers concerned that the central presuppositions of the liberal tradition have been severely corroded, neglected, or misappropriated by overly rationalistic and constructivist approaches.

The hardest-won achievement of the liberal tradition has been the wrestling of epistemic independence from overwhelming concentrations of power, monopolies and capricious zealotries. The very precondition of knowledge is the exploitation of the epistemic virtues accorded by society's situated and distributed manifold of spontaneous orders, the DNA of the modern civil condition.

With the confluence of interest in situated and distributed liberalism emanating from the Scottish tradition, Austrian and behavioral economics, non-Cartesian philosophy and moral psychology, the editors are soliciting proposals that speak to this multidisciplinary constituency. Sole or joint authorship submissions are welcome as are edited collections, broadly theoretical or topical in nature.

More information about this series at
http://www.palgrave.com/gp/series/15722

Alessandro Roselli

Economic Philosophies

Liberalism, Nationalism, Socialism: Do They Still Matter?

palgrave
macmillan

Alessandro Roselli
City, University of London
London, UK

ISSN 2662-6470 ISSN 2662-6489 (electronic)
Palgrave Studies in Classical Liberalism
ISBN 978-3-030-53316-8 ISBN 978-3-030-53317-5 (eBook)
https://doi.org/10.1007/978-3-030-53317-5

This Palgrave Macmillan imprint is published by the registered company Springer Nature Switzerland AG
The registered company address is: Gewerbestrasse 11, 6330 Cham, Switzerland

Our concern is the widespread belief that the economic analysis can exist as some kind of socially disembodied study

Robert Heilbroner, William Milberg

50 years ago, economists and philosophers talked to one another

Angus Deaton, Nobel laureate

Preface

This essay calls for an explanation about its purpose and plan. Recent literature devoted to the philosophy of economics deals mainly with economics as a "science", which is regarded as similar to physical sciences, where laws are discovered, or models created, according to logical and experimental methodologies. Economic philosophers explore and test the methodology and logical structure of the economic science, in the same way as a physical scientist would do. My purpose is different, because the essay focuses on the ideological, or pre-analytical, side of the economic discipline. To clarify this point: I try to show the ideological underpinning of the economist's work, and the ideological perspectives here examined are those that have largely prevailed in the last couple of centuries.

This is a study of liberalism, nationalism, socialism. The extension of these ideologies goes well beyond the economic dimension, but this essay focuses on this dimension only. It's indeed on the strength of these unifying principles—liberalism, nationalism, socialism—that systems of political economy have been constructed.

"Ideology" is a term often accompanied by a negative connotation. Hayek, as Pareto and Schumpeter (and maybe others), tracks to Napoleon the origin of the derogatory meaning attributed to the word: Napoleon "gave currency to the word 'ideologue' in its new sense by using it as a favourite expression of contempt for all those who ventured to defend freedom against him".[1] This instrumental use of the word is testified by the fact that social sciences' writers often tend to consider their theory as the only "true" one, and qualify others' theories as "ideologies", implying that these theories do not deserve "scientific" attention.

To find the dividing line between what is "scientifically true" and what is "ideological" in social science is particularly challenging. For instance, Marx saw his vision as "scientific"—the scientific socialism, as opposed to other more or less utopian forms of socialism—, and was blind to the ideological element of his own thinking. The drivers of the historical process—he observed—are the society's evolving structures, based on different modes of production, while any system of ideas that prevails at a certain time and in a certain social group is a "superstructure", the ideology of the prevailing class. As a consequence, according to him, the mainstream economic science of his time—the Classical School and, even more so, the emerging neo-classical economics—was the ideology of the bourgeoisie, the prevailing class. Schumpeter observes: "The temptation is great to avail oneself of the opportunity to dispose at one stroke of a whole body of propositions one does not like, by the simple device of calling it an ideology".[2]

Since these two concepts are central to this book, a key should be given to the reader on the meaning that I assume for them and their inter-relations. In this regard, I broadly follow the approach of an Italian philosopher, Norberto Bobbio,[3] who in turn very much relies on the work of Vilfredo Pareto. The starting point is that science and ideology belong to separate fields; they are inspired by two different criteria of truth. In science, it is true what is empirically verified; in an ideology, what is in accordance with one's own sentiments.[4]

The word "ideology", in its highest meaning, can be viewed as a worldly vision (*Weltanschauung*) that is implicit in all the expressions of individual and collective life, and therefore also in the economic activity.[5]

What is to be avoided is to exchange a value judgement—which is ideological—for a factual assertion. A "false ideology" is an ideology disguised as fact. But this does not mean that ideology and science cannot be linked, in the field of social sciences. In reality, they always are.

Sometimes, when discussing economics as a discipline, rather than using the word Ideology, in order to distance themselves from the term, writers mention Value judgements as revealing one's ideology but avoid being identified with it; or they allude to Visions or Intuitions, or Set of assumptions, as perceptions and pre-analytical acts that antedate any scientific effort, or as an understanding of social processes to which the economist applies his analysis[6]; or other similar terms. This sort of partition may be justified in the context of certain discourses aiming at finding a dividing line between science on one side, and the ways we inevitably "see" things, on the other; but it tends to create in most cases an unnecessary complication. For this reason I have preferred to write, more generally, of "(economic) philosophy", as a set of more or less defined ideas underpinning, or having an influence on economic reasoning. I shall consider how, and to what extent, some philosophical assumptions, or value judgements, have influenced the theoretical constructions—including formal models—of a few important economists. The central theme of this book is therefore an attempt to penetrate the "veil"[7] of economic theorizing, to show the economic philosophy that lies behind the economist's thought, and the assumptions of the social philosophy[8] that the economist draws from his theory.

To make this point more explicit, I have to rely on the widely accepted distinction in the economic discipline between positive economics and normative economics. Both are bodies of systematized knowledge, but they have an opposite approach to value judgements in economics. Positive economics is in principle independent of any particular ethical position or normative judgements and its performance has to be judged by precision, scope and "conformity with experience of the predictions it yields"[9]; it wants to be an objective science in precisely the same sense as any of the physical sciences, to which it is often compared. Normative economics, "the art of economics" in the words of Milton Friedman, is instead a body of systematized knowledge discussing ways of bringing about what ought to be.

While practising economists are greatly occupied with normative economics (it is sufficient to cite Piketty's works on capitalism and its ideology), the modern philosophy of economics generally neglects it. We read, in recent books on this subject, that "we do not cover normative issues…We take very seriously the naturalistic insistence that philosophy of science is continuous with science itself".[10]

However, the problem of normative economics, which the philosophy of economics as philosophy of science has been reluctant to deal with, resurfaces whenever subjective elements, or value judgements cannot be avoided in facing certain themes, in particular those related to public welfare: for instance, any macroeconomic perspective poses the question about "how science ought to be done from studying how science is actually done".[11] And, it should be added, how economic science ought to be done means implicitly to call in question "philosophy" in a different perspective, that is in the perspective of the underlying vision of the economist.

One relevant point (which I shall try to develop in the course of this book), is that even the "positive" approach of economics, which points directly to ruling out any value judgement in gathering evidence and formulating theories, is inevitably conditioned by biases that can be explained only in "normative", ideological terms. No social scientist, and no economist, should claim to stand "upon the rock of truth, the unbiased judge of all things human".[12] If there is a dividing line between scientific inquiry and ideology, it is certainly very thin.

Whether specific economic theories—or economics in general—can be defined as "science" on Bobbio's, or Pareto's, definition, I shall not dwell upon. Indeed, I shall not discuss them in detail, even though some reflections on the theme of economics as a science will be presented in the course of this essay. I'll rather argue that it is hard to disentangle economic theory from its explicit or implicit ideological assumptions. What I would like to stress is that this book is not an attempt to write a sort of history of economic thought, but an attempt to identify the ideological underpinnings of the larger socio-economic framework.

The plan of this essay follows, broadly speaking, a chronological and thematical path. Economic liberalism constituted, and probably still constitutes, the underlying philosophical assumption of the mainstream of the economic discipline, influenced by the prevailing liberal ideology that extends well beyond the economic discipline. However, economic liberalism has taken different shapes in its development through time, leaning originally towards an unhindered laissez-faire, other times—in particular in the central decades of last century—towards a wider role of the State in the economic system, influenced by the competing socialist ideology.

A philosophical notion of liberalism that took shape in early twentieth century saw the liberal idea as a supreme reference point in human actions, disentangled from specific economic organizations of the society. The notion of a non-necessary identification of the liberal idea with economic liberalism gained ground, and then apparently receded in more recent decades. After the decline of what may be called a "Keynesian consensus", a series of efforts have been done to re-establish an individualistic approach to issues of income determination and wealth distribution, going under the catch-all term of neoliberalism.

But the proposition that more than one single economic theory can be coherent with the liberal idea is currently the object of a renewed reflection, stimulated by recurring economic crises and by the difficulties to adopt appropriate economic policies to get rid of them, even less to prevent them.

Nationalism was, politically and economically, a driving force in the nineteenth century. It was behind the movements for freedom and consolidation of national entities. While mainstream economics followed economic liberalism, and then turned towards a "scientific", individualistic approach relying on the new positivist philosophy, protectionist policies were however very much present and influential, as instrumental to what was perceived as the national interest. The confrontation, in the end a military confrontation, between liberal Britain and authoritarian and protectionist Germany, can be read not only as a clash of power politics and of economic interests, but also of philosophies. Italian corporativism of the interwar period may have appeared as the last gasp of nationalistic philosophies, given the overwhelming political and economic hegemony of liberalism, after the Second World War, under the widespread wings of American power. However, the decline of nationalism, and its resurgence in recent times, show that history is far from ended. And it is unclear what shape this nationalism is taking from an economic and political point of view. This is particularly obscure in the case of that specific form of nationalism that is called populism. Its Rousseauian origin, and the affirmation of the "general will", does not bode well for any form of liberalism, and the result appears to be an affirmation of incoherent, anti-liberal economic policies.

Socialism, in its wider meaning, penetrated liberal societies and influenced liberalism, contributing to its metamorphoses in the twentieth century. Marx's vision, his historical materialism—materialistic because the structure (modes of production) precedes the superstructure (the institutional organization and culture of a society), and historical because modes of production and superstructures change over time—had a major impact on the twentieth century. The authoritarian communism of the Soviet Union was sometimes greeted as a "new civilization"; but was followed by decline and collapse. That collapse can perhaps be explained also in a Marxian perspective: Marxists failed to recognize the relevance of changes in the structure. Evolving modes of production meant that small bourgeoisie, far from becoming part of a widening proletariat, became the numerically prevailing class, while capitalistic creative destruction—far from determining the final obsolescence of the entrepreneurial class (Schumpeter)—gave it further strength, reinforcing its prevailing role.

The essential contrast between ownership of means of production and labour remains, however, well entrenched, while taking different forms.

The question about whether liberalism—disembodied of its ethical underpinning, attacked by nationalism's new strength and hit by the enduring contradictions of capitalism—will survive, remains open.

London, UK Alessandro Roselli

Notes

1. Hayek (1955, p. 116). See also Schumpeter (1949, p. 347); Pareto (1963, p. 1244).
2. Schumpeter (1954, p. 36).
3. Bobbio (1971, pp. 79–107).
4. "Ideologies are not simply [scientific] lies: They are truthful statements about what a man thinks he is": Schumpeter (1949, p. 349).
5. I like this definition by Antonio Gramsci. See Gramsci (1947–1971).
6. Heilbroner (1988, p. 183).
7. To use Heilbroner's word.
8. J. M. Keynes titles the final chapter of his *General Theory: "Concluding Notes on the Social Philosophy Towards which the General Theory Might Lead"*.
9. See Friedman, M.: The Methodology of Positive Economics [1953], in Hausman (2008, pp. 145–178).
10. Kinkaid, H., & Ross, D. (2009, p. V).
11. Hausman (2007, p. 3).
12. Schumpeter (1954, p. 37).

References

Bobbio, N. (1971). Pareto e la critica delle ideologie. In *Saggi sulla scienza politica in Italia*. Roma-Bari: Laterza.

Friedman, M. (2007). The Methodology of Positive Economics [1953]. In D. Hausman (Ed.), *The Philosophy of Economics. An Anthology*. Cambridge: Cambridge University Press.

Gramsci, A. (1947–1971). Il materialismo storico e la filosofia di Benedetto Croce, 1948. In *Opere di Antonio Gramsci*. Torino: Einaudi.

Hausman, D. (2007). *The Philosophy of Economics: An Anthology*. Cambridge: Cambridge University Press.

Hayek, F. (1955). *The Counter-Revolution of Science: Studies in the Abuse of Reason*. New York: The Free Press.

Heilbroner, R. (1988). *Behind the Veil of Economics: Essays in the Wordly Philosophy*. New York and London: W.W. Norton.
Kinkaid, H., & Ross, D. (2009). *Oxford Handbook of Philosophy of Economics.* New York: Oxford University Press.
Pareto, V. (1963 [1935]). *A Treatise on General Sociology*. New York: Dover Publications.
Schumpeter, J. A. (1949). Science and Ideology. *American Economic Review, 39.*
Schumpeter, J. A. (1954). *History of Economic Analysis*. New York: Oxford University Press.

Acknowledgements

I am extremely grateful to several people who provided comments, suggestions and generous assistance while I was engaged in this research. In particular, I have been fortunate to try the arguments of this book with William (Bill) Allen and Robert Pringle. They have closely followed the entire project and their invaluable comments and criticism have been fundamental to put things in the right perspective. Also, I really benefitted from the insights and encouragement of Richard Hitchman. But I am also indebted to the following persons: Piero Barucci, Pierluigi Ciocca, Oliviero Pesce, Alberto Mingardi, Aldo Montesano, Roberto Morozzo della Rocca, Vera Negri Zamagni, Pedro Schwartz, Geoffrey Wood. Their comments and sometimes critical observations confirmed my idea that any issue can be seen from different sides, and each of them can have its own reasonable motivation. A particular thank you to Lavanya Devgun for her careful editorial assistance.

Contents

CHAPTER 1

Ideologies and Political Economy in the Nineteenth Century

1.1 Schumpeter: At the Origin of Political Economy

Joseph Alois Schumpeter has been one of the few critical minds that have tried to go to the core of economic science. In an essay he wrote more than a century ago, he observed that "the science of economics, as it took shape towards the end of the 18th century, had grown from two roots which must be clearly differentiated from one another". The first root originated in the study of philosophy, specifically in that strand of philosophy which considered social activities as the fundamental problem, as the essential element of the world vision. The other root reflected the views of "people of various types" whose interest was focussed on actual, practical matters of their daily lives.[1]

Regarding the first stream of thought the social world—until then accepted either as evident in itself and therefore not deserving special attention, or as a mystery explicable only in supernatural, religious terms—was seen in a different perspective, as an intellectual problem to be dealt with natural, not supernatural, methods, based on empirical observation and factual analysis.[2] For a true understanding of the social world, it had to be explained in rational terms, that is by means of a cause–effect relation in human behaviour. Moral philosophy, as a unity that resulted from these reflections, included Theology, Ethics, Jurisprudence and Economics. "In this organic unity one element affects all the others,

A. Roselli, *Economic Philosophies*,
Palgrave Studies in Classical Liberalism,
https://doi.org/10.1007/978-3-030-53317-5_1

almost every thought is of importance for Economics as well". And at this point Schumpeter names Locke and Hume: "Never again was philosophy to such an extent a social science as at this period".[3]

Regarding the other root, the interest in practical, daily matters meant that, differently from the first, it did not see human activity as, *per se*, problematic. Thinkers belonging to this second stream, on one side rich in business experience, were on the other side devoid of scientific background and reluctant to raise philosophical questions. One can understand why—Schumpeter adds—some excellent beginnings did not have any meaningful follow-up, because, if the immediate, practical problem had been solved, no need was felt of additional and deeper reflection. This sort of literature revealed its freshness and fruits in the direct observation of the social world, but remained fruitless beyond that. However, this "vulgar" economy (the adjective is Schumpeter's, and was previously used by Marx, however in a slightly different meaning[4]), based as it was on the reality of the business life, gave an important contribution to the rising political economy. Over time, mostly in England, the experience of practical life started being fertilized by a mental habit of a scientific kind: for instance, "Great progress was made when the 'bullionist' conception was given up, and people realized instead that exchange rates and balance of trade were correlated".[5]

This sort of cross-fertilization of practical behaviour and theoretical thinking assumed different character in different countries. In England, political conditions related to parliamentarism favoured an open debate in the public opinion and a pressing need for economic analysis. Elsewhere, autocratic governments discouraged these discussions of political economy. In Germany, the low level of a rational discussion on economics was the result of years of religious wars and reflected a lack of free discussion. There, the adoption of foreign models hindered any original development of economic science. On the other side, in no country as in Germany the State became the object of inexhaustible interest: the State as an essential factor of the process of civilization. "The German not only thought much more about the State than anybody else did but he understood something quite different by the term 'State'…than Englishmen or Frenchmen [understood]".

For the British, their story was about making society free from an oppressive monarch, while for the Germans it meant the affirmation of a strong State from a backward-looking feudalism. Administrative law took in Germany the same place that political economy had taken in England.

In England, merchants discussed among themselves in the same way civil servants discussed in Germany. If in England they discussed about economy, this became economic theory; while in Germany this took the shape of political science of the economy. Schumpeter quotes a work by the German neo-cameralist Johann von Justi (1756), whose plan and aim are the same as Adam Smith's *Wealth of Nations* (1776): not so distant in terms of time, but "as regards clarity and insight the two works are separated by the labours of a century".[6] As valuable is von Justi's book in the field of the technique of administration, in economic matters it lacks approaches and methods which were already well available. Von Justi's practical judgements reveal common sense, but the analytical structure of his work is flawed. It has been recently observed by Werner Plumpe that von Justi shared with Smith the view that common well-being depends on the sound working of the market, but von Justi thought that it is up to the State the duty to channel properly the private interest so that the well-being can be reached by the market. Differently from the Scottish Enlightenment, in the German semantics the role of the State is of fundamental importance. While, according to Smith, the interest of the bourgeoisie was implicitly addressed to the common good through the free exchange on the market (the "invisible hand"), the German tradition thought that the State must be the visible hand that creates that common good.[7] In Germany, Law acquired the same standing that Economics was playing in Britain; and a doctrine of State economy meant that "the individual problem is never an object of treatment for its own sake but only as part of the whole".[8] This systematic approach has characterized economics in Germany "to this [Schumpeter's] day", he writes. One may wonder whether this is true up to our own days.

Schumpeter saw well the philosophical roots of the economic science, that is the ideological framework that influences the theoretical choices of the economist, his "wordly philosophy", to use Robert Heilbroner's words.[9]

What has just been said about the different attitude that the discussion on economic matters took in Britain and Germany, had a decisive influence on the development of the discipline of economics. The first attitude is focussed on an individualistic point of view, centred on the individual as a rational agent, and therefore assuming that any "unreasonable" action should be seen as a philosophical curiosity if not an uninteresting aberration; the second turns to the State and sees public interest as not necessarily coincident—sometimes in opposition—to the private one.

These philosophies are the premise, often undisclosed, of every economic reasoning that goes beyond what Schumpeter defines as the "vulgar" economy.[10]

However, if in their common philosophical origin we make a distinction between the two, it is easy to notice that the first—the vision centred on the rational individual—met fruitfully with the vulgar economy, based as it was on the immediate self-interest in human actions; while the second made more complicated any relation between the rational State and the individual. Indeed, if we put society, or the State as its representative, as the embodiment of rationality, the individual actions do not deserve to be put at the centre of the analyst's attention. To the extreme, in a sort of ranking, the individual comes always second, after the State. From this perspective, the detachment of the philosophical root (which sees the State as the embodiment of rationality) from the individualistic approach (which looks at the specific person who aims to his personal satisfaction) is certainly wider.

We shall deal first with the approach based on the rational individual (Sects. 1.2–1.5), and then with the one centred on the rational State (Sects. 1.6–1.11). Our reference period in this chapter is mainly the nineteenth century.

1.2 Radical and Moderate Enlightenment: Adam Smith and David Ricardo

Liberalism of the nineteenth century can be seen as centred on the individual, and demanding a new standard governing the relationship between the individual and the State. This standard was based on three main requirements: non-intrusion, non-exclusion, non-obstruction.[11] The first requirement implied securing the individual and his property, his property rights, primarily through the legal system, from interference by State, market, society; the second, mostly moral and originally rooted in religion, was based on the recognition of human dignity, but knew—when transposed to politics—some not irrelevant limits; the third gave economic leverage to the full development of human capabilities, to be kept unstifled by obstacles of any kind.

Individualism as a centrepiece of liberalism was a common denominator, which unified liberals against authoritarianism, rules dictated by tradition, and by invoking primacy of man's freedom and responsibility. But liberalism took specific shapes, tilting sometimes towards equality and solidarity, other times towards seeing the liberal man and society as a "join-if-you-wish-club" (Fawcett). This point can be better understood if we keep in mind that the immediate antecedent of liberalism is Enlightenment, through its insistence on individual freedom and on the restrained power of the sovereign.

In the field of the economic discipline Enlightenment shows the fruitful results of the intermingling of philosophy focussed on the rational individual, with the vulgar view of the individual looking for satisfaction of his daily needs. "Adam Smith [and other thinkers] were indisputably the key pioneers of this new science, but to study their economic ideas in isolation from their general philosophy, moral ideas, and social concepts – as is usual – risks reducing economics emergence to something extraneous and detached from its age".[12] Jonathan Israel observes that "to be properly grasped in its historical context, classical economics must be situated against the background of struggle between Radical and Moderate Enlightenment thought".[13]

A common background between Radical and Moderate thinkers can be found in their shared conviction that a liberal, commercial society offers a superior form of freedom: that of liberty under law. But the substance of the moral base upon which society rests is—in these two approaches—different.

In the Radical vision of a democratic, even republican, political culture—as expressed by authors as diverse as Diderot, d'Holbach, Helvétius, Condorcet and others,—tolerance and the unconditioned quest for liberty of thought and expression are closely linked to the concept of social and political equality. The non-violent revolution, in the name of freedom, which, for instance, Diderot and d'Holbach aimed at, was directed to make equality as the supreme moral principle of the social organization.

It was therefore subverted Locke's theological conception of equality, which deemed individuals spiritually equal before Christ but not equal in civil status: a society ranked by different classes,[14] even admitting slavery, in a sort of philosophical dualism that distinguished between body and soul. Locke was "A philosopher who clearly favoured steeply stratified social hierarchy and wide property inequality; there was undeniably an element of hesitation, even perhaps contradiction, in his comments on slavery".[15] Locke, after having defined a slave as a captive taken in a just war, writes: "as a slave he has lost all his goods, and as a slave he is not capable of having any property; so he can't in his condition of slavery be considered as any part of civil society, the chief purpose of which is the preservation of property".[16] A similar—if less extreme—vision of morality, which is inclusive of "preservation of property", would then be promoted by the Scottish philosophers of the Moderate Enlightenment, but these philosophers would be belittled by the Radical thinkers as "moral sense" theologians, who restricted the scope of reason. "The Anglo-Scottish conception of ethics was [by them] outright rejected".[17]

In this quest for equality, Radical thinkers of the French revolution period observed that the "great vice of our social system ...is the monstrous inequality of fortunes". "The rich understand the resentment this causes but will not tolerate a genuinely democratic republic, knowing sooner or later this will deprive them of some of their wealth". "*Le capitaliste* was [by them] identified as antisocial, selfish, and damaging, able to subvert government in his own interest. Montagnards[18] ...also thought in terms of imposing new egalitarian lifestyle norms through education and public instruction".[19]

An inspiration to the Montagnards was the Swiss Jean Jacques Rousseau, and his radically egalitarian strand of thought. Indeed, among the Radical thinkers, a specific, extreme place is occupied by him. His doctrine of the "General Will", according to which popular sovereignty cannot be delegated, would be in opposition even to other Radical exponents, who advocated a regime of parliamentary representation.

This parliamentarian regime was indeed seen by them—nor only by French Enlightenment thinkers, but also by the American founding fathers—as a revolutionary step that would eliminate hereditary or privileged access to any national assembly, take control of public finances in the interest of the State, and hinder attempts by the sovereign to use them for personal purposes: a representative democracy.[20]

What, on the contrary, did the republican Rousseau write? "[T]he activity of private interest, the vastness of states, conquest and the abuse of government, suggested the method of having deputies or representatives of the people in the national assemblies...[but] Sovereignty, being nothing less than the exercise of the General Will, can never be alienated, and...the Sovereign, who is no less than a collective being, cannot be represented except by himself[21] ...[T]here is no intermediate possibility. The deputies of the people, therefore, are not and cannot be its representatives: they are merely its agents, and can't settle anything by themselves. Any 'law' that the populace hasn't ratified in person is null and void – it isn't a law".[22] And Rousseau adds: "The people of England regards itself as free, but it is grossly mistaken: it is free only during the election of members of parliament. As soon as they are elected, slavery overtakes it".[23] Few years after, Voltaire would write a book full of admiration for the British constitution.[24]

In his *Discourse* which follows the *Social Contract*, Rousseau explores some ideas on political economy, with strong egalitarian accents. He emphasises public education organised by the State, necessary to reach conformity in the General Will, and a system of very progressive taxation that will also discourage luxury: "the populace would be ready to adore a Minister who went to Council on foot, because he sold off his carriages to supply a pressing need of the State".[25]

The absence of parliamentarian representation, the prevalence of the general will, and Rousseau's egalitarian views, are further discussed in Chapter 4 of this essay, in dealing with populist ideology.

Along similar lines, the Italian political thinker Melchiorre Gioja saw monarchy as equivalent to ignorance and stupidity, believed in a free republic for his country, with a democratic constitution and, following the economic ideas of the Radical Enlightenment, criticized Adam Smith's free trade doctrines (see below), contending that "philosophy has declared war on inequality" and favouring scrupulous State regulation of industry and commerce.[26]

Classical economic thinking takes shape mainly through the philosophy of Moderate Enlightenment. It is based on a reconciliation of ethics and utilitarianism, and on the preservation of social order to enhance economic growth. The validity of this thought is seen as universal, independent from time and place. Institutionally, its economic doctrine rests on a self-regulating market and on a sound monetary system; its political design, on a liberal State that permits the private sector of the economy to flourish and develop.

The Scottish philosophers "ground[ed] their moral thought in what is ultimately a theological and socially deferential stance". There is an "inextricable entwining of [Adam] Smith's moral philosophy and, later, economics with notion of divine providence and his (and Hume's) defence of existing social order".[27] Smith, in his *Wealth of Nations*, does not spend many words on monarchy. According to him: "Though monarchs, in making treaties, act like individuals in making bargains, there is a great difference with regard to their adhering to the contract. Individuals act under the control of law, and are, therefore, obliged to adhere to their engagements; but monarchs keep them no longer than suits their purposes".[28] Smith's deferential stance narrowed the scope of reason and tended to prioritize sentiment and tradition. Defending inequality as a necessary condition for the social order, the Irish thinker Edmund Burke would then reject "compulsory equalizations. They pull down what is above. They never raise what is below. And they depress high and low together beneath the level of what was originally the lowest"[29]: a statement that, interestingly, we find almost unchanged in "marginalist" thinking of a century later (see Sects. 1.4 and 1.5).

Which can be the "moral" base of this inequality? Adam Smith finds this base in the necessity to preserve the social order. In the *Wealth of Nations* Smith's assumption is the acknowledgement of different social classes, each having its own role: the capitalists, the landowners, the labourers; and in the *Theory of Moral Sentiments* (which was published in 1759, before *The Wealth*), he observes: "The peace and order of society, is of more importance than even the relief of the miserable…Moralists warn us against the fascination of greatness. This fascination, indeed, is so powerful that the rich and the great are too often preferred to the wise and the virtuous. Nature has wisely judged that the distinction of ranks, the peace and order of society, would rest more securely upon the plain and palpable difference of birth and fortune, than upon the invisible and often uncertain difference of wisdom and virtue".[30]

The Moderate Enlightenment provided the most fertile ground on which economic liberalism—and the classical political economy of the free market—could flourish and develop. This development couldn't happen without linking morality to a pronounced utilitarian perspective.

Here, we have to bear in mind that that concept of "utility" is one of the most used, and abused, in the entire body of political economy. Any time this term is central to a writer of political economy, we must necessarily link it to its begetter's ideology.

Classical economists' vision of utility is rather far from the "scientifically" calculated utility of successive neo-classical thinking. This point needs some clarification. In late eighteenth century, the most comprehensive formulation of the concept is in Jeremy Bentham's *Principles of Morals and Legislation* (1789). What does Bentham mean by the "utility principle"? It is "the principle that approves or disapproves of every action according to the tendency it appears to have to increase or lessen the happiness of the person or group whose interest is in question". The immediate pursuit of this objective differentiates, according to Bentham, utilitarianism from asceticism, which belongs to the moralists (who are driven by hope, that is by a prospect of pleasure) and to the "religionists" (who are driven by fear, that is by a prospect of pain). However, moral or religious behaviour can, itself, give rise to happiness. Therefore, happiness is not necessarily of a physical nature, it can well be of a political or moral nature (when it is stimulated by persons connected to the individual in a spontaneous, not coercive disposition), or of a religious nature (when it comes from the hand of a superior invisible being).[31] In summary, utilitarianism has not to be identified necessarily with the pursuit of material happiness, it means only that the individual has his own scale of values that should not be subject to any external constraints.[32] We are well far from the mathematically measurable, "marginal utility" of the Neo-classical School.

Given this definition of utility as instrumental to pursue happiness—which, it should be repeated, can well be of a political, moral and even religious nature,—Bentham writes that Ethics is "the art of directing men's action to the production of the greatest possible quantity of happiness, on the part of those whose interest is in view". This is the "art of self-government, or private ethics". Importantly, if happiness is the end (purpose) of private ethics, "legislation can have no other". Legislator's duty is just to favour private ethics. "The art of legislation teaches how a multitude of men, composing a community, may be disposed to pursue that course which upon the whole is the most conducive to the happiness of the whole community".[33] Here is the link between individual's and community's happiness.

In the British Enlightenment, any dialectic relation between Utility, Ethics and Social Order is therefore resolved by considering the individual as pursuing his self-interest and, at the same time, as a morally motivated subject in a society. It is a morality which is more focussed on person's honesty and perhaps on charity (reliant on individual initiative, differently from public welfare initiatives), than on discussing the existent social order. The British Enlightenment relies more on individually driven feelings of wealth, and on an apt institutional system, than on requirements of equality, as French Enlightenment does.[34] "Early Enlightenment philosophers endowed ethics with a new and hopefully sounder basis in psychology. Morality had traditionally been cast as an objective system of divine laws…increasingly, virtue was refigured as a matter of heeding inner promptings – goodness lay…in harnessing motives…passions were naturally benign…and pleasure had to be derived from sympathy".[35] "Lecturing to young Scots, Smith elevated the ego of commercial man above the civic virtues of the classical republican, dwelling particularly on the wealth, freedom and political wisdom needed to sustain a commercial polity".[36] There is, in Smith's political economy, a sentiment of sympathy that links human behaviour and makes trust as the basis of social and economic relations. The concept of trust is recurrent in his *Wealth*: a trust that must start from the legislator: "But the law ought always to trust people with the care of their own interests, as in their local situations they must generally be able to judge better of it than the legislator can do".[37]

On the basis of the natural freedom and of the utilitarian principle as the driver of men's actions, the central proposition of Smith's Moderate Enlightenment is that society can correct its own disequilibria and make progress if market can work unhindered by constraints; and that this can happen without destroying the hierarchy principles, the class ranking, by which society is governed.

The class ranking is relevant, and the capitalist class is at the centre of the economic system. Progress is the result of the proper working of a free market, which allows profit to be created. "Economic growth is assured by the surplus, or net product, which becomes the engine that generates further wealth by giving the means through which production is increased, technique refined, trade stimulated".[38] The capitalistic class is therefore the true engine of economic growth, differently from the idle rentiers, who are only consumers, and from the labourers, too poor to save or invest (the dislike of the unproductive class of rentiers is a constant of classical economists, but is also shared by Keynes, and obviously by Marx).

There is not a better synthesis of the meaning of *Wealth of Nations* than the one written several years ago by the political economist Herbert Stein, who says: "Starting the treatise with the simple, homely description of a pin factory was a brilliant stroke. At first one wonders what that is doing there. But then it becomes clear that Smith is leading us to understand and appreciate the division of labor. And the division of labor leads us inexorably to the idea of exchange as the natural and efficient way to organize an economy. At that point the battle is half over: the rest is drawing out the implications of the fact that a modern economy is an exchange system...The Wealth of Nations is full of well-crafted sentences. The most famous...is probably: 'It is not from the benevolence of the butcher, the brewer, or the baker, that we expect our dinner, but from the regard to their own interest'[39]...The people who wear Adam Smith tie are not doing so to honor the literary genius. They are doing so to make a statement of their devotion to the idea of free market and limited government...[even though Smith] was prepared to accept or propose qualifications to that policy in the specific cases where he judged that their net effect would be beneficial and would not undermine the basically free character of the system".[40]

There is only one thing to add: by quoting shopkeepers, Adam Smith gives evidence of the fruitful intermingling of the philosophical root with the "vulgar" root of political economy. With Adam Smith, "the political philosopher could retire in favour of the business man – for the latter could attain the philosopher's *summum bonum* by just pursuing his own private profit".[41]

Regarding the universality of classical economists' thinking, it should be framed within the general Enlightenment perspective. Smith's discourse is clearly an expression of that perspective. He sees in a certain organizational structure of the economic system, the embodiment of a principle of individual freedom: perfect in its essential features, and therefore not in need of any change. The propositions of classical economists are valid, as Ricardo stresses later, "in all countries and all times"[42]: this is the "cosmopolitanism" and a-temporality of the economic science. In fact, the harmony of a natural equilibrium was the Enlightenment's inspiring concept in any branch of thought, not only in economics. Its universal validity makes classical economic theory as essentially detached from actual historical experience and modes of productive organization (a point that will be strongly challenged by the German Historical School as well as by Marx, see Sects. 1.10 and 1.11). In fact, with the exception of many, specific samples taken from the past—instrumentally mentioned by Smith, to give evidence and more emphasis to his own theses, of universal validity,[43]—his historical analysis is limited to few pages in Book V of the *Wealth*, where he makes a stylised, tentative and conjectural description of the evolution of man's economic development by succinctly listing successive, different states of society, from hunters to shepherds to peasants, up to the man devoted to manufacturing and commerce.[44]

If we turn our attention to international aspects and foreign trade, it is evident the classical economists' "cosmopolitanism" (we would say "globalism"), and therefore their attack on protectionism and mercantilist policies, in favour of free trade. Let's consider the following passage from Hume's essay on the balance of trade: "Our jealousy and hatred of France are without bounds, and the former sentiment, at least, must be acknowledged very reasonable and well grounded. These passions have occasioned innumerable barriers and obstructions upon commerce…But what have we gained by the bargain? We lost the French market for our woollen manufacture, and transferred the commerce of wine to Spain and Portugal, where we buy much worse liquor at a higher price…Each new acre of vineyard planted in France, in order to supply England with wine, would make it requisite for the French to take the product of an English acre, sown in wheat and barley, in order to subsist themselves; and it is evident, we have thereby got command of the better commodity".[45]

Fifty years later, Ricardo resumes this topic and creates a "model": his well-known case study of Anglo-Portuguese trade (formalized in the "theory of comparative advantage") shows a situation of equilibrium that, once reached, is the most economically efficient and stable for both countries[46]: if cloth production in England requires the labour of 100 men for one year, against 120 men necessary to produce wine, and if wine growing in Portugal requires just 80 men's work, while for cloth production 90 men are needed, it will be in Portugal's interest to produce only wine (even though the production of cloth costs less than in England) and import cloth from England: with the labour of 160 men, all devoted to wine growing, Portugal will have obtained both wine and cloth, against 170 needed in order to produce both in its domestic market.[47] This situation, which transposes on the international level what Smith had written about the pin factory, is—as mentioned—efficient and well balanced, nor in need of any change (unless—it has to be added—we are concerned by the fact that Portugal will remain an enormous vineyard and England will remain suffocated by the smoke of its cloth factories). Classical economist praises free trade because it permits every nation to maximize its own product, given certain resources and productive capabilities. The German Friedrich List will object to this model by observing that this equilibrium prevents the less advanced economy from changing its productive structure, and therefore increasing its income in the long run.

A stable monetary system, removed from the vagaries of the sovereign, is a precondition for making the self-regulating, free-market work smoothly. The theoretical foundations of stable money are provided by David Hume, in his essay on money.[48] It is a masterly, concise enunciation of the "quantity theory of money": "the prices of every thing depend on the proportion between commodities and money, and…any considerable alteration on either of these has the same effect either of heightening or lowering the prices...It is only the overplus [of a commodity], compared to the demand, that determines the value".[49]

If the money stock is made not only of gold, but also of paper credit, and if the growth of the paper component is excessive, monetary stability is compromised. To limit the increase of paper credit (paper circulation), caused by the search for profit of the banking system, convertibility of paper into gold has to be made mandatory.[50] The convertibility requirement deprives the sovereign of the power to modify at his discretion the money stock, and perfectly fits with the working of a self-regulating market.[51] The quantity theory of money was thus integrated into the mainstream of orthodox monetary conduct, forming the central core of nineteenth-century classical monetary analysis and policy.

Institutionally, some pieces of legislation provided the necessary steps to make Britain a free trade and gold standard country, thus implementing liberalism in the most advanced form: the Act for Resumption of Cash Payments of 1819 (following the Napoleonic wars that had obliged the United Kingdom to suspend gold convertibility) and the Bank Charter Act of 1844, for a full enactment of the gold standard; and the Bill of Repeal (Importation Act) of 1846, which opened the British market, by abolishing the protection assured by the Corn Laws.

In the classical economy of Smith, Ricardo, or the French J.B. Say, product maximization cannot be hindered by a lack of demand, because any economic activity generates incomes, in the form of wages, rents, profits, which are equal to the product's value. Economic downturns are not due to a fall in demand, but to factors that are exogenous to the economic system, to "externalities", as wars or interferences (from government, for instance) that unsettle the free working of market forces. This is a statement which will be denied by economists as diverse as Marx and Keynes.

Any good is in demand because of its utility. But how is its price assessed on the market? Value has two different meanings, sometimes expressed by utility of that good, and sometimes by the power of purchasing other goods which the possession of that particular good conveys: therefore, of any good the value in use has to be distinguished from the value of exchange.[52]

The value in use of a good is connected with the utility that a person derives from using that good; while the value in exchange is linked to its price. The first type of value, the goods' utility, explains the economic drivers of society; the second, the exchangeable value, explains that any society can only work thanks to the system of prices.

Smith and Ricardo are, with different accents, in agreement on how the value of exchange of a commodity is determined. Smith writes: "[Its value] is equal to the quantity of labour which it enables [a person] to purchase...Labour, therefore, is the real measure of the exchangeable value of all commodities...What every thing is really worth to the man who has acquired it, and who wants to dispose of it or exchange it for something else, is the toil and trouble which it can save to himself, and which it can impose on other people". "Labour, it appears evidently, is the only universal, as well as the only accurate, measure of value".[53] And Ricardo: "If the quantity of labour realized in commodities, regulates its exchange value, every increase in the quantity of labour must augment the value of the commodity, as every diminution must lower it".[54] This "labour theory of value" will be the starting point of Marx's reflection and criticism, and—for opposite reasons—will be criticized as "unscientific" by the "marginalists" (or neo-classical) economists of the second half of the nineteenth century. If the exchange value of a commodity is explained in terms of a cost theory, as the value of labour-power employed in the production process, how to explain the origin of rent and profit?

Indeed, the proportionality between the variation in the quantity of work and that of the value of a commodity would exist in the absence of machinery employed in its production.[55] Therefore, the exchange value of a commodity depends not only on the labour employed, but also on the capital employed in the production and on the land upon which the capital insists. Capital and land must be included in the process of determination of a commodity's exchange value.[56] In this regard, Smith says that this exchange value is inclusive of the "natural" prices of the three factors of production—land, labour and capital, which means rents, wages and profits,—which make up for the cost of production of a commodity. The "natural" price may differ from the "market" price, but only for the reason that the market price takes into account accidental and temporary deviations from the first.[57] But classical economists did not adopt a criterion to determine the natural price of capital and land.[58] With reference to the agricultural sector, to the land rent, Ricardo, who maintains a vision of the social classes (factors of production) which is antagonistic, as distinct from the complementary vision of Smith, observes that the land has diminished returns (as demand increases, less fertile lands are cultivated), so that capitalists and rentiers compete in order to take from the labourers an increasing share of the commodity's value. This fundamental contrast between capital and labour opens the way to Marxist radical criticism: the historical tendency of the profit rate to decrease, unless labour is more intensely exploited (see Sect. 1.11 below, and Chapter 3).

However, with reference to profits, if we abandon the concept of a natural price of the factors of production, it remains undetermined how the value of a commodity can be divided between them, and in particular between profits and wages. We cannot go beyond the general statement that the price of a commodity is higher when more labour is needed to produce it. "This was the problem that flummoxed Ricardo".[59] This issue will receive further attention from Karl Marx and later from Piero Sraffa. Sraffa is considered as the economist who could reconcile Marx and Ricardo, the Marxian and the classical views (see Chapter 3).

1.3 Positivism and John Stuart Mill

In this and the following Sects. (1.3–1.5) we shall deal with the trend to consider the economic discipline as a "science", disconnected from any "philosophical" basis or background. We relate this trend to the widespread assertion of positivism: itself—it should be stressed—a well defined philosophical stream of thought. The affirmation of this trend is coherent with some broad developments that characterized the nineteenth century: an extended period of international peace after the Napoleonic wars (wars were few and circumscribed), monetary stability, great advancements in natural and physical sciences, strong technological progress. In sum, a relatively tranquil age which gave to economic activity some features of constancy and consistency similar to those observed in the natural world, and therefore susceptible to be formalised in scientific "laws".[60] A science of economics emerged, which affirmed to be totally disconnected from ethical, political, social issues and rather put on the same level of natural sciences.

A different reading leads to consider this scientific approach as consistent with the existing social structures, well consolidated in that "tranquil" age. These structures were those of an individualistic society, and the scientific criterion meant the affirmation of the bourgeois values of economic liberalism.

According to Hobsbawm's definition, positivism is a "belated child of the eighteenth-century Enlightenment".[61] It remains to be seen what of the Enlightenment is kept by positivists, and what is left aside. They certainly maintained the massive intellectual break with the past that had been the focus of Enlightened thinkers. However, the relation of cause–effect in human behaviour was seen by positivists with the same approach followed by the scientist in natural sciences. In natural sciences, any hermetic vision of a spiritual universe had been "finally superseded by models of Nature viewed as matter in motion, governed by laws capable of mathematical expression. This enthronement of the mathematical philosophy in turn sanctioned the new assertion of man's right over Nature so salient to enlightened thought". "The conviction grew that social no less than natural events were fundamentally governed by natural laws – and hence in principle amenable to scientific enumeration, explanation and control".[62] This is a vision that assumed an interpretative paradigm based on testability of any hypothesis. Positivism introduced concepts and methods proper of the natural sciences into social investigation.

But Enlightenment had also another side, based on hypotheses and theories that do not have the noncontroversial status of verifiable or falsifiable facts or mathematical-logical propositions: the "ideological" side. There was the conviction "that there existed certain objectively recognized human goals which all men…sought after, namely happiness, knowledge, justice, liberty, and what was somewhat vaguely described but well understood as virtue; that these goals were common to all men…-Moreover, human nature was fundamentally the same in all times and places; local and historical variations were unimportant".[63] As we have seen, this was the essence of the Moderate Enlightenment at the basis of nineteenth-century liberalism.

The economic man—*homo oeconomicus*—guided by a strict, scientifically measured, utilitarian view—the *homo* which is investigated by positivist, neo-classical economists—does not seem to fit fully into the broader vision of the social man, as envisaged by Adam Smith. Paradoxically, positivism seems to deprive social sciences, in particular the economic discipline, of any philosophical background. But, as we shall see, the social philosophy's inferences that can be drawn from it are far from negligible.

So, it is legitimate to ask how the philosophy of positivism came to influence economics, and up to which extent was this influence relevant. The discipline that opened a link between this new philosophy and economics was sociology, and the man who started sociology was Auguste Comte. The philosopher and political economist who—so to speak—took the bull by the horns was John Stuart Mill. Comte's *Cours de Philosophie*

Positive was published in 1835, his *Système de politique positive* in 1851–1854, and *Auguste Comte and Positivism*—the John Stuart Mill's reply to positivism—followed in 1865.[64]

Mill is actually attracted by Comte's approach to philosophy, but remains a disciple of the Enlightenment, and this creates a considerable uneasiness to accept his conclusions. Let's look at Mill's clear explanation of positivism's main points, and at the reasons of his partial but decisive dissent. According to positive philosophy, we are unable to know the essence of any fact, our only knowledge is limited to phenomena, to what appears to us as "fact", and this knowledge is relative, in the sense that of any fact we know only its relation to other facts, in a way of succession or similitude. These relations, if constant, by either sequence or similitude, reveal the cause of facts and are termed "laws". Theory is formulated after facts have been observed; a theory should not be created in order to observe facts. This means a prevalence of inductive reasoning from experience over deduction from paradigms, or even more from postulates. An interesting example of proto-positivist investigation is given by the classical economist Robert Malthus in *Principles of Population*: he starts actually from postulates (regarding the essentials of human life), but his purpose is to explain how much the societal sphere is embedded in biophysical and environmental systems.[65]

We might add that in classical economics, as described in the previous Section, the concept of "laws" was not connected to any "naturalism". The adjectives "natural" or "normal" were actually used, but just to mean something defined under the simplest possible conditions, or simply "self-evident", or "usual", anyway without any reference to natural science. Comte, instead, wanted to use the term in its "proper" meaning: also humanities have natural laws defined in terms of natural causation.

Sciences—as investigation of constant relations between facts, that is of "laws" upon which all phenomena must depend—are classified by Comte in an ascending order, in which each science represents an advance in speciality or an increase in complexity in respect to the preceding science in the series. They are six, starting with mathematics,[66] and arising up to sociology, or social science, which is defined as the science, the phenomena of which depend on, and cannot be understood without, the principal truths of all the other sciences.

Each science moves, in turn, in three stages—theological, metaphysical, and positive. According to Comte, only in the positive state, the human mind, recognizing the impossibility of attaining to absolute concepts, gives up the search for the inner causes of phenomena, and confines itself to the discovery, through reason and observation combined, of actual laws that govern the succession and similarity of phenomena.

In fact, theology and metaphysics are by Comte considered as non-scientific, because they do not look at the causes, that is to relations between facts themselves, but rather see facts as ascribed to "celestial" causes, or "divine ordnances" (as in theology), or to "realized abstractions" (as in metaphysics). The positive stage, according to Comte, has been occasionally reached in sociology sometimes in the past (by authors as diverse as Montesquieu, Machiavelli, Adam Smith, Bentham), but this positive stage in sociology has yet to be fully developed. The social science has been so far developed up to the metaphysical stage only, and it has to be "upgraded" to the positive stage, according to him.

It should be observed that those "realized abstractions" seem to be reluctant to be pushed aside. In other words, the positive stage of sociology leads to a strong commingling of science and philosophy. Herbert Spencer coined the term of "survival of the fittest".[67] By using the language of biology, he mixed the Benthamite utilitarian happiness, human progress and the need that government adapts itself to man's self-interest in a sort of science that equates "right" with "natural". This means liberalism mistaken for biology".[68] "The *pontifices* of positivism, Comte and Spencer, wallow in the metaphysics, thinking to be out of it".[69]

Differently from the a-historical character of the works of classical economists, Comte attributes decisive importance to the historical method. "The historical comparison of various consecutive states of humanity is not only the principal scientific tool of the new political philosophy: developed, it will prove to be the very basis of the science. It is here that the sociological science distinguishes itself sharply from the biological science". This call to history may appear pretty odd, when we think of the very different approach followed by the almost contemporary German Historical School of Economics (see Sect. 1.10). Later in the same text, however, Comte seems to step back from this passage when he writes that the historical method is "equivalent to that of zoological comparison in the study of individual life". "The necessary sequence of various social states corresponds exactly, from the scientific point of view, to the graded coordination of various organisms, having regard to the differences of the two sciences: the social series…cannot be either less real or less useful than the animal series".[70] Again, there is a *sequitur* from natural to social science.

At this point, Mill enters the scene, and observes that we must explain the philosophy of science, as distinguished from the science itself: a task that Comte—Mill says—has not fulfilled. By philosophy we mean the scientific knowledge of Man as an intellectual, moral and social being, that is the science itself considered not as to its results, but as to the processes by which the mind attains them: the logic of the science.[71] Man cannot be seen as a "piece of machinery" and studied as we study the production of physical phenomena. It is true—Mill admits—that, for Man, the rule of duty has been for long dictated by a divine authority (theological stage) or, more recently, considered as a corollary of some Natural Rights, as in Rousseau, whom Mill disregards (metaphysical stage).[72] But "Comte resolutely denies the moral right of every human being…to erect himself as a judge of the most intricate questions that can occupy the human intellect". "Whatever goes by the different names of the revolutionary, the radical, the democratic, the liberal, the free-thinking, the sceptical…all passes with him [Comte] under the designation of metaphysical…with no permanent validity as social truth". According to Mill, "there is a positive doctrine…which claims the direct participation of the governed in their own government, not as a natural right, but as a means to important ends, under the conditions and the limitations which those ends impose".[73]

To stress this point, Mill gives an example: "Take for instance the doctrine which denies to government any initiative in social progress, restricting them to the function of preserving order…an opinion which, so far as grounded on so-called rights of the individual, he [Comte] justly regards as purely metaphysical; but does not recognize that it is also widely held as an inference from the laws of human nature and human affairs, and therefore, whether true or false, as a positive doctrine". In other words, Mill identifies—*horribile dictu* to the ears of a positivist—metaphysical and positive doctrine. The same issue will be faced by Walras and Pareto, with an opposite, "positive" view (see Sect. 1.5).

How does Mill, at the same time a great political economist and a champion of liberalism, approach the utilitarian concept? "I regard utility as the ultimate appeal on all ethical questions; but it must be utility in the largest sense, grounded on the permanent interests of man as a progressive being".[74] He supports free trade, but—he adds—"free trade is a social act…it rests on ground different from the principle of individual liberty". As limits to free trade he cites: "what amount of public control is admissible for the prevention of fraud by adulteration; how far sanitary precautions, or arrangement to protect workpeople employed in dangerous occupations, should be enforced on employers. Such questions involve considerations of liberty, only in so far as leaving people to themselves is always better, *ceteris paribus*, than controlling them: but that they may be legitimately controlled for these ends, is in principle undeniable".[75]

These comments of Mill sound incompatible with Comte's conclusion regarding the positive stage of sociology: "there is no liberty of conscience…in astronomy, in physics, in chemistry, even in physiology", that is in other sciences; and why should there be such a liberty in sociology? When politics will reach a positive stage, and new doctrines will be found, there will be an "established opinion" and no liberty will be needed. "The incompetent tribunal of common opinion is radically irrational, and will and ought to cease when once mankind have again made up their mind to a system of doctrine". A different philosophy is "not only incapable of aiding the necessary reorganization of the society, but a serious impediment thereto".[76]

Comte's reasoning ends up being a sort of negation of liberalism. He finally admits that no liberty is needed when a well established, scientific opinion prevails (when a positive stage in social science is reached), so that free-thinking will be just an unnecessary obstacle to the reorganization of society. This sort of conclusion may not have had a large number of followers in the field of economic discipline, but that "scientific" approach became, and from a certain viewpoint is still today, "a part of the stock in trade of economics".[77]

Positivist philosophy is a wedge between two stages of evolution of the economic discipline in the second half of the nineteenth century. It prepares the ground upon which the incoming Neo-classical School will flourish at the turn of the nineteenth century, by focussing on the individual and considering his social and economic activity as governed by "laws", to be scientifically discovered, similarly to the methodologies of natural sciences. In this process, the "political economy" of the Classical School gives way to the new science of "economics" of the Neo-classical School. Was the process consistent with the idea of liberalism? And did it imply a different ideology, specifically an implicit political and social conservatism? How was this change of tack evaluated by observers of different backgrounds?

Maurice Dobb, the Marxist economist, wrote that a class component is necessary to explain the sudden, almost unopposed affirmation of neo-classical thinking: "it was not many years after the publication of '*Das Kapital*' before a rival value-theory was to rise and with remarkably little resistance to conquer the field. This was the [neo-classical, marginal] utility-theory, which seems to have germinated simultaneously in several minds".[78] The new theory was framed directly to provide a substitute answer to the questions which Karl Marx had posed in his *Capital*. "If only by the effect of negation, the influence of Marx on the economic theory of the late nineteenth century would appear to have been much more profound than it is fashionable to admit".[79] The individually-centred neo-classical theory would have been—according to this interpretation—an attempt to give a "scientific" answer to the Marxian social class contradictions, Marx's "scientific socialism".

A severe criticism of Comte came—on the opposite side—from a libertarian as Hayek, who rated Comte even more anti-liberal than the prototype exponent of the ethical State: "There are in Hegel no such fulminations against the unlimited liberty of conscience as we find through the works of Comte, and Hegel's attempt to use the machinery of the Prussian State to impose an official doctrine appears very tame compared with Comte's plan for a new 'religion of humanity' and all his other thoroughly anti-liberal schemes for regimentation that even his old admirer J. S. Mill ultimately branded as liberticide".[80]

It has been argued that in his usage of the term "law", Comte confuses description with prescription[81]: a "confusion" that seems frequent with social scientists and particularly with the economists.

Robert Heilbroner thought that this intellectual development, from political economy to economics, had to do with the evolution of the capitalistic system: a system characterized by "well-demarcated classes [as a] natural and necessary condition for any stable social order" (what he calls "the aristocratic political view") was displaced by a system that reflects an increasingly democratic outlook and downplays, or even denies, the presence of social classes.[82]

The neo-classical scheme, based on the marginal utility-theory, disembodied from the structure of society, made this structure theoretically irrelevant. The class division, essential to comprehend both the Classical School and Marxism, disappeared into a microscopic configuration of the economic society; that very configuration which, later, Keynes would attack through his macroeconomic vision.

It might be argued that positivism, by assuming a mechanistic approach to the functioning of the social and economic system, where single agents pursue their optimal utility by interacting with others, without any solidarity or communality of interests, ends up by favouring the class of the individualistic bourgeoisie (this will be very evident with Walras and Pareto). Positivism favours the conservation and strengthening of the current social positions. Inside liberalism, we should wait for the convulsions of the twentieth century to see challenges to the pre-existent societal structures, and different philosophical approaches by "liberal" thinkers. By this, we don't want to downplay the fact that the economic system as explained by neo-classical economists, and put in practice by policies consistent with this intellectual framework, provided an excellent opportunity for clever and resourceful people, of any social class, to contribute to unprecedented rates of output growth and to climb the social and economic ladder to levels of wellness that the previous "aristocratic"[83] structure of society wouldn't have allowed.

1.4 Marginal Utility: Jevons and Marshall—Are We in the Field of Liberalism?

The shift from classical to neo-classical theory can therefore be seen as a change of vision of the social order; the former order characterized by a society structured on three classes—labourers, landlords, capitalists—and the latter considered as a place of interaction of single economic agents, persons and businesses, atomistically considered as rational machines: an interaction that determines reciprocal transactions aimed to maximize their individual utility.

Utility is analysed and measured, while other motivations of Man's behaviour are irrelevant, from an economic point of view. While classical economists had considered value as an objective characteristic of commodities, neo-classical economists shift their attention to commodities' subjective properties, which concern consumption and demand. The measure of utility is made with the method of "small increments", that is observing the "marginal principle": the demand of a certain good will increases up to the point where a small further increment of that good brings to the purchaser more loss than gain of satisfaction. Individuals freely making their choices should logically bring to the conclusion that free competition leads to maximization of utility for both parties involved in the exchange. The maximization of utility reached in a free exchange is extended through mathematical processes to maximum welfare for the whole economy, in a situation of equilibrium. "The theory of marginal utility... places the main emphasis on a complex of problems which the classical economists passed over too lightly, namely, the foundation for determination of value and price".[84]

Another assumption is in fact necessary to complete the utility-based theory: the market where goods and services are bought and sold must operate in perfect competition. If market is open to any entrant, the number of firms operating on the marketplace is such that no one firm by any change of output within its capacity can affect the market price of a commodity.

The neo-classical model is therefore based on two main concepts: maximization of utility in any free transaction, and a market structure based on perfect competition. What is outside this model is not of interest to the economist, it's a problem of "distributive" justice that negatively affects the theoretical perfection of a market of "commutative" justice, that is a market that assures the maximisation of utility for the parties involved in the transaction.

We can continue attributing to the economists of the turn of the century, the general label of "liberals", but it appears that ethical concerns are confined to the backstage; political and institutional aspects are given for granted, as not deserving particular mention. As mentioned earlier, this approach is consistent with an implicit social conservatism. The Enlightenment vision centred on the rational individual remains, but Man is more a calculating machine than a person with moral as well as utilitarian concerns. The question of whether there can be a fair chance to free the world from the pains of poverty cannot be answered by economic science, even though the answer depends upon facts and inferences which are hard to neglect by the moral economist.

William S. Jevons starts by criticizing the previous theory of political economy, as systematized by Ricardo, and completed in its details by J. S. Mill: "there was nothing in the Laws of Value which remained [for Mill] or any other future writer to clear up".[85] This sort of exhaustion arises from "the exclusive importance attributed in England to the Ricardian School", and has brought to "the present chaotic state of Economics",[86] so that "Many would be glad if the supposed science collapsed, and became a matter of history, like astrology, alchemy and occult sciences generally".[87]

Jevons' change of tack derives from his view that while "prevailing opinions make labour rather than utility the origin, or the cause, of value..., repeated reflection and inquiry have led me...to the somewhat novel opinion that value depends entirely upon utility".[88] Utility can be measured in quantitative terms, and "as [economics] deals throughout in quantities, it must be a mathematical science in matter if not in language".[89] Economics is close to Statistical Mechanics (see above the same terminology used by Comte).

In fact, utilitarianism is not so novel as Jevons asserts, since he himself quotes Bentham as its most assertive supporter: "I have no hesitation in accepting the Utilitarian theory of morals...happiness of mankind as the criterion of what is right or wrong".[90] The relevant novelty of Jevons thinking is that, given the quantitative character of the matter observed, he thinks, as other neo-classical economists, that utility has just a physical meaning (pleasure to be acquired, and pain to be avoided), so that it can be expressed in quantitative forms, most appropriately in mathematical forms. Strictly connected to "utility" is the concept of "happiness". Let's leave the word to Jevons himself: "the objective of Economics is to maximize happiness by purchasing pleasure...at the lowest cost of pain...I have attempted to treat Economy as a Calculus of Pleasure and Pain".[91] It was later observed, derisively, with reference to Maffeo Pantaleoni's economics,[92] that in his work "the hedonistic principle is discussed as more appropriate to a cookery-book or to a Kama Sutra than to political economy".[93] Jevons admits that there are issues of the greatest importance, as the safety of a nation, or the welfare of great populations, but that "is not my purpose to inquire here".[94]

If we think of Alfred Marshall as the prototype of this new vision, the presence of Comte's positivism is well visible. Similarly to Keynes, who, as we shall see later on, draws his "notes of social philosophy" at the end of his *General Theory*, Marshall devotes the Appendix C of his magnum opus, *Principles of Economics*,[95] to the "Scope and Method of Economics", and starts by quoting Auguste Comte. While taking a distance from him in stressing that economics has to maintain a "distinctive role" from sociology ("the whole range of man's action in society is too wide and too various to be analysed and explained by a single intellectual effort"), Marshall remains in a positive mode by stressing that economic forces combine mechanically, and that economics is a branch of biology broadly interpreted. And he concludes: "There is a large and debatable ground in which economic considerations are of considerable but not dominant importance...[in this case the economist] will be able to speak with less and less confidence...the more he concerns himself with conditions of life and with motives of action which cannot be brought to some extent at least within the grasp of scientific method".[96]

Alfred Marshall focusses on "demand" as the main determinant of exchange value. Demand of a commodity is related to its utility for the individual who purchases it, and utility marginally decreases as the availability of the commodity increases. Marshall, on the other end, does not see the "supply" side, that is the cost of production, in particular the labour costs, as the yardstick of value. While the classics observed that there is just one "natural" price of a commodity, essentially derived from its cost, so that any "market" price cannot be other than a temporary divergence from the natural one, with Marshall any distinction between natural and market price disappears; the price—the exchange value—of a commodity is determined by the crossing of the curves of its demand and supply on the marketplace. "Until recently - he writes - the subject of demand or consumption has been somewhat neglected... The first [cause of this new attention] is the growing belief that harm was done by Ricardo's habit of laying disproportionate stress on the side of the cost of production, when analysing the causes that determine exchange value".[97] Marshall observes that the conditions of demand have bigger importance in the determination of a good's price particularly in the short period, when the conditions of its supply cannot be changed; while only in the long run, when more or less investments can be realized, the conditions of supply have greater relevance, because they can be adjusted to changes in demand: "the influence of cost of production on value does not show itself clearly except in relatively long periods".[98]

As we have stress earlier, the neo-classical economic system can work only on the basis of perfect competition, where the formation of prices is unhindered by obstacles that limit a good's supply and demand. Marshall appears to touch the ethical side when he devotes some space to "competition". He admits that it can be seen under different perspectives: as a result of selfishness, so gathering an "evil savour"; or as a result of deliberateness, which is so essential to the maintenance of energy and spontaneity. He wants to consider the term as not implying any moral qualities, but just as putting in evidence the undisputed fact that modern business and industry are characterized by self-reliant habits, forethought, deliberate and free choice; he does not rule out that a certain departure from individual freedom may occur when cooperation seems to offer the best route to the desired end.[99]

It will be incidentally observed that it was in the far-away United States that the first law of discipline of competition was introduced with the Sherman Antitrust Act of 1890, the year of publication of Marshall's *Principles.*

The transition to—or acceptance of—positivism by neo-classical economists was suffered, to a certain extent: on the one hand, their very refusal of the term "political economy" in favour of "economics", almost to imply that the former term would indicate a subordination of economics to politics, means trying to set the discipline as a positive science freed from judgements of any other kind; on the other end, particularly with Alfred Marshall, ethical aspects, expelled through the door, re-enter from the window through the conviction that the primary goal of man is the drive to a constant improvement of one's own character and of intra-personal relations.[100]

1.5 Economics as Pure Science: Léon Walras and Vilfredo Pareto

Léon Walras, investigating the problem of the roots of "value", attacks frontally the classical economists' view (as Smith's, Ricardo's, Mc Culloch's) according to which labour is the origin of value, because this theory fails to attribute value to things which, in fact, do have value; but he also is dissatisfied with the identification of value with utility, which is too broad a definition. The value of a good, and therefore its price, is given not only by its utility but also by its scarcity (*rareté*).[101]

His pure theory of economics studies value—defined as above—in exchange relationships, and he approaches the problem of "value in exchange" as a natural phenomenon, subject to the "laws" of exchange. The method of natural sciences is therefore useful to economics. In addition, these phenomena are measurable, and pure economics should be a branch of mathematics. The science of economics—which anyway must be kept separate from the social science (in agreement with Marshall)—has no moral connotation, no true interest in ethics.[102]

Marginalism is perfected by Walras to the level of a general equilibrium of the economic system, mathematically expressed as a synoptic view of the interdependent operations of the system in a hypothetical regime of totally free competition. His complex set of equations is at the same time a description of the system and a prescription of how it should be organized: as we have seen, a not uncommon approach of positivism.

Walras' definition of exchange is fully coherent with the utilitarian perspective: "The exchange of two commodities for each other in a perfectly competitive market is an operation by which all holders of either one, or of both of the two commodities, can obtain the greatest possible satisfaction of their wants consistent with the condition that the two commodities are bought and sold at one and the same rate of exchange throughout the market".[103] In this way, a relative social maximum of utility is achieved, under the condition that the market where the exchange is enacted is a perfectly competitive market, with a single price for the commodity concerned, and organized in such a way that no impediment exists to the free flow of buyers and sellers.

Despite all this, it has been observed that the static multi-equational equilibrium of the Walras model appears "profoundly moralistic, at least in terms of the individualistic, bourgeois moral outlook characteristic of nineteen-century European culture". Walras's equilibrium is "not only an analytical idea, but an ethical idea as well, constituting an indispensable pillar of social justice".[104] If justice in exchange (a "commutative justice") is the only form of justice that an economist can envisage, and any correction to the distribution of wealth is outside his boundaries, the free process of single price determination is the most efficient way to attain justice. One can see how the concept of ethics can be stretched.

If Walras's approach is considered as correct, few corollaries follow: prices and quantities of goods produced under free competition, and uniform prices, are the best obtainable; any chance for a trader to profit by the exchange at the expense of his counterpart is ruled out.[105]

Of course it would be possible for the buyer to obtain greater utility through a more favourable, lower, price, and for the seller to similarly obtain greater utility through a higher price, but this outcome would of course require multiple prices. According to Walras, an effective increase in social utility might in this way be realized, but we must assume that the rich sellers will have to renounce some luxuries, while the poor buyers will be able to afford necessities: a problem that falls outside pure economics, since it has to do with the distribution of wealth and social ethics.

The issue of wealth distribution is therefore relevant, but it belongs to disciplines that do not coincide with economics. Of the two fundamental problems that any economic doctrine has to face—production of wealth and its distribution—the latter has difficulty to work its way through neoclassical thinking. It will be necessary to wait for the evolution of the economic discipline, and the metamorphoses of liberalism, later in the twentieth century when new social instances will bring again to the fore the "distribution issue".

Pareto is an outstanding example of applied positivism to economics. Similarly to Jevons, his criticism of the Classical School—nothing more than a "genre of literature"—is without appeal: "These literary economists, even though have composed works of great value, have so far been unable to persuade most of their readers and, far from gaining ground, they lose ground by the day. With the exception of England, the reign of free trade mainly because it is in the interest of certain entrepreneurs, the rest of civilized countries tilts more and more towards protectionism. State socialism and socialism in general make progress day by day. Maybe the economic science is practically as useless as the literary political economy: actually it cannot be more useless than that, and deserves, at least, the merit to understand the true causes of phenomena".[106]

His positivism rests on three pillars: analogy between social sciences and natural sciences; definition of "value" only in relative terms, which means that the value of something can only be defined in relation to other things, a point already stressed by Comte when he speaks of the essence of "facts" (see above); absence of meta-economic considerations—or, to use his words, ideologies—in his *Weltanshauung*. This absence notwithstanding, what emerges from his reflections is an implicit—almost Panglossian—determinism, which ends up as a form of conservatism: adopting a "scientific" approach, far from meaning neutrality in economic philosophy, hides strong political implications.

Pareto's positivism is clearly defined in his *Corso di economia politica*, where he states that the reciprocal dependence of economic phenomena and the general equilibrium of an economic system present surprising analogies with the equilibrium of a mechanical system.[107] As rational mechanics is devoted to the study, in abstract, of the equilibrium of forces and their movement (while applied mechanics, moving closer to reality, studies the same object but in certain concrete conditions: hence physical-chemical sciences), pure political economy is devoted to the study, in abstract, of the *homo oeconomicus*, an entity that acts only on utilitarian motivations: on an ophelimity basis, as Pareto says (while applied political economy is devoted to beings who approximate the real man, acting under different motivations). But, importantly, it would be an error to suppose that the real man can escape the laws of pure economics.

Regarding utility, as the basis upon which the *homo oeconomicus* acts, Pareto is a positivist when he goes even beyond other neo-classical thinkers, by attacking the neo-classical concept of marginal utility. Walras tilted towards the concept of *rarité* (see above); Pareto relies on the "ordinal" concept of ophelimity: coherently with Comte's philosophy, any object can be valued not *per se*, by attributing it an absolute, cardinal number (this pen's value is, to me, 3; and this chair value is, to me, 5), but only in relation to others, that is in an ordinal way (this chair is to me more valuable than this pen, and nothing else can be added).[108] Following this reasoning, and through ordinal indices of ophelimity, he builds "curves of indifference" that lead to the general economic equilibrium.

While other neo-classical economists preferred to avoid the issue of wealth distribution, as "non-scientific", and while Walras identified the general, static equilibrium of his system as itself insuring the "commutative justice", if not the "distributive justice", Pareto tackles more overtly the issue of distribution, which will gain increasing weight in economic thinking, during the 20th century, in respect to wealth production.[109] His "scientific approach" starts from an inductive, statistical observation: wealth distribution does not change substantially, independently from different regions, time periods, organizations, even taking into account unknown factors (hazard) that may influence wealth distribution in both ways. In mathematical terms, if on a system of Cartesian axes we report on the abscissae levels of income, and on the ordinates the number of persons whose income exceeds a certain level (Pareto uses logarithmic scales), and if a curve is drawn, it is a straight line, and this line has, for all the countries concerned, the same inclination towards the abscissae, of around 56 degrees. The inference from this observation is that, any hazard notwithstanding, this constant wealth distribution depends on the nature of man. Income distribution is not the effect of hazard.[110] This drastic statement is perfectly in line with the scientific (positivist) approach: social sciences at the top of natural sciences.

Pareto's inference from this "law" is that "in the long run—as a norm and on average—[a decrease in incomes inequality] is impossible...In order to obtain, on average, a decrease in income inequality in a general, permanent way, it is absolutely necessary an increase in total incomes, in relation to the population".[111]

A few years later, however, Pareto would become less rigid: "these conclusions cannot be extended beyond those limits [based on data of the 19th century, regarding civilized [sic] populations]. It's only a more or less probable inference that, in other times and populations, we may perhaps observe shapes more or less similar to the one we have found".[112]

The inevitability of such an income distribution—with the determinism that it implies—has been criticized from several quarters. Pigou observes: (1) That even small difference in the angle inclination may have important consequences in terms of income distribution; and (2) That over time the curve's slope has declined (as in Prussia), with a greater equality in income distribution. "To build upon [Pareto's comparisons] any precise quantitative law of distribution is plainly unjustifiable".[113]

Einaudi, around half a century later, will write that the "constant norm of wealth distribution is only valid within societies where there is a lack of institutions knowingly willing to change that distribution".[114]

And Schumpeter twice returned to this "law": in *Ten Great Economists*, he observed that "Granted that up to quite recent times the distribution of incomes according to brackets has remained remarkably stable, what are we to infer from this? This problem has never been attacked successfully".[115] And later, with a good deal of common sense, he wrote: "Whatever may be thought of the statistical measures devised for [income distribution], this much is certain: that the structure of the pyramid of incomes, expressed in terms of money, has not greatly changed during the period covered [UK in the 19th century, in his case], and that the relative share of wages plus salaries has also been substantially constant over time...The measure of income distribution (or of inequality of incomes) devised by Vilfredo Pareto is open to objection. But the fact itself is independent of its shortcomings he took to be".[116]

More recently, Picketty writes that "Pareto's judgement was clearly influenced by political prejudices: he was above all wary of socialists and what he took to be their redistributive illusions...Pareto's case is interesting because it illustrates the powerful illusion of eternal stability, to which the uncritical use of mathematics to social sciences sometimes leads".[117]

We may add that it would be simpler to mention the unchanging income distribution as a historical evidence, a specific case, and not to call it a "law".[118]

Beyond any determinism in income distribution, as so far described, Pareto adds that any attempt to reach a different distribution would be inefficient in terms of total welfare. The collective welfare is increased, according to Pareto, only if you can make someone better off without making anyone else worse off.

Pareto's "optimality" is of no help in choosing among different Pareto optimum allocations in which income distributions are different. To make this choice, we need some principles that are value judgements, which cannot be deducted from objective knowledge about the "nature" of the world.

"Pareto's efficiency" or "optimality" represents, in fact, the extension to the societal economic welfare of the concept of ophelimity. If total income remains unchanged, the loss that high earners suffer from a redistribution of income is higher than the gain obtained by lower earners. Pareto gives the example of Prussia: "If incomes above 4,800 marks were reduced to that amount, and the difference were distributed to those who receive an income lower than 4,800 marks, each of them wouldn't receive anything more than around hundred marks". No public policy action can be a Pareto improvement. "The aim of achieving a Pareto optimum is intrinsically very conservative...[It] directs attention away from the question of whether the existing distribution of wealth is so unequal that it should be changed".[119]

His political philosophy conclusion is: "State socialism is mostly useful to politicians, but its economic consequences consist in a waste of wealth and, in such a way, they worsen, rather than improve, people's conditions".[120] The more income is concentrated, the more the loss to high earners is higher than the gain of the low earners. Pareto's optimality ends up being a deeply illiberal view.[121]

From Pareto's point of view, this conclusion would be not only acceptable, but the sole correct: it would be the "scientific" conclusion. Indeed, in a science that has reached its positive stage, a theory can be formulated only on the basis of what can be logically and experimentally demonstrated. If we consider as true what is in agreement with one's sentiment, we are outside science and enter the field of false theory, or ideology. Ideology is as an ethical–political programme disguised as scientific–philosophical theory, as a value judgement transformed into a factual statement. Ideology can be effective, if respondent to one's purposes; or useful, if respondent to certain social needs. But truth, effectiveness and usefulness cannot be mixed up, or reciprocally intertwined, because only the first is based on logic and experiment, while the other two are based either on religious or metaphysical opinions. A "true" theory defies any judgement of efficacy and usefulness.[122]

We have mentioned above the ambiguous allure of the labour theory of value on Karl Marx. But as we have done in connecting classical, and—to an extent—neo-classical, economics to the Enlightenment, we cannot move to Marx without starting from Historicism, from the centrality of the State and from the economic ideas that, more or less explicitly, derive from this *Weltanschauung*.

1.6 Historicism: Economic Nationalism and Marxist Socialism

We can now go back to the first Section of this chapter, and move from the stream of thought that sees the rational individual at the centre of the economist's attention, to the other philosophical strand that sees the society—and, for it, the State—as embodying the rational order.

The perspective of economic reasoning is, in fact, very different if its philosophy is rooted in the assumption of the rationality of the State. The most comprehensive theoretical view of the idea of the State as the utmost expression of rationality can be found in Georg Hegel. The idea of State is rooted in history. Through its historical evolution, the State embodies progressively the idea of liberty. According to Hegel, Liberty is realized objectively and positively only by the State: it is through the State that the individual enjoys his freedom. The arbitrary, subjective will of the single is not, in fact, Liberty. All what man is, he owns that to the State: only in the State the single individual finds the reason of his existence. The rationality of the historical process—which develops in a dialectic form of thesis, antithesis and synthesis—is teleologically aimed at the full enactment of the concept of Liberty. There is a sort of astuteness of reason, which progressively, providentially, works throughout History: we should not look at actions and events simply as they appeared to those who were their protagonists, and—as such—linked to their particular interests and passions: personal motivations are degraded by Hegel to mere accidents of an essential and necessary process.[123]

Hegel helped to establish the modern State as a privileged object of enquiry and reflection. It is not just the site of sovereignty and power; it is the engine that makes history, or even the embodiment of history itself. This sort of "statist idealism" would have been well in the mind of German policymakers as well as historians and economists:

Bismarck wrote in 1882: "The turnover of individuals is irrelevant...The State and its institutions are only possible if they are imagined as permanent-identical personalities".[124]

The Hegelian vision is therefore deterministic, because it does not admit deviations from a path that will bring, finally, to political and administrative arrangements that will realize fully that liberty. "The History of the World, with all the changing scenes which its annals present, is this process of development and the realization of the Spirit – this is the true Theodicaea, the justification of God in History".

Remarkable is the distance between the Enlightenment vision which puts at its centre the individual's rationality, and Historicism which sees the State in its evolution as the embodiment of rationality. This deterministic systematization of the idea of State sets aside the apparent chaos of the individual's democratic rights, and favours the overwhelming principle according to which liberty cannot exist without the State's organization. In the State all the components of the body politic are connected, and only within the State the freedom enjoyed by the individual makes sense. The State is the completion of the individual as a finished entity. The abstract, a-historical idea of the free man is a product of the Enlightenment, which emerged well after the State.

It has been debated whether Hegel can be considered as a political economist and if an economic doctrine can be inferred from his writings.[125] It is not our intention to deal with this issue, but it would be difficult to deny that the centrality of the role of the State through its historical evolution had a considerable weight on those who felt the influence of Hegel's thought, also in the field of political economy. Within the economic discipline, to follow a Hegelian approach meant the adoption of a perspective rather far from the one followed by classical economists. Moreover, the adoption of a historicist perspective ends up by considering the classical doctrine of economics, paradoxically, as itself historicist, "under the appearance of its abstractions and mathematical language".[126] From this point of view, the "market", a constant point of reference for classical economists, far from responding to a logical-deductive scheme (typical of the Enlightenment), is the result of a long historical process, that is of the laws of a capitalistic society, as they emerged historically. Considering the market as an entity detached from the historical process can be due to the fact that—to use Marx's word—the "vulgar" economist is not always aware of the philosophical view which is behind his own thinking. For instance, "Ricardo never reflected historically on his own thinking…He never takes a historical perspective…and sees as natural and unchangeable, the laws of the society where he actually lives…Ricardo was not a utilitarian, not because he had another philosophy, but because he had none".[127]

We can see how the Hegelian systematization is at the origin of both economic nationalism and Marxist socialism. Both are focussed on the centrality of the State, and on the role of historical enquiry as necessary to understand its economic, as well as social and political, structures (an enquiry that often takes in the Hegelians a deterministic twist); both despise (no other word is appropriate) the "cosmopolitanism" (globalism, in modern parlance) of the Enlightenment and the classical economic theories. Both share history's teleological character, which heads—as a final goal—towards the harmony of all nations, trade freedom among equals and universal peace (in the nationalists' view), and towards man's emancipation (in the socialists' view). And both—a circumstance that is not theoretically relevant, but politically meaningful—look critically at Germany's conditions in the nineteenth century, and give Germany a primary role in their analysis.

To be sure, we should avoid any confusion of philosophical premises and economic reasoning. Economic nationalism and Marxist socialism cannot be flattened on Hegelian philosophical thinking, in the same way as the Classical School of economics cannot be identified *in toto* with Enlightenment philosophy. The economic problem that the three streams of thought have to face is, in the first case, the explanation of the working of a free market (and, as a sub-product, the emergence of England as the hegemonic power); in the second case, the historical analysis of economic growth (having particularly in mind Germany's backward conditions); in the third case, the investigation about the subordinate condition of the working class, only removable by overturning the existent social order.

The German Historical School is deeply steeped in economic nationalism; and of particular interest—being frequently quoted in current debates on the resurgence of nationalism, or if we prefer "sovereignism"—is the figure of Friedrich List. Nations' economic history, from their growth to their decadence, which is substantially absent in classical economists' work, occupies the central stage in List's analysis. It is not difficult to see a Hegel's imprint (even though List never quotes Hegel, at least in his *National System of Political Economy*) in various aspects of his work: in the central role of the State, which is the main reason of opposition to the British economists; in the historical analysis which permeates his research; in the recognition that the ultimate objective of all the nations is their union, the perpetual peace and the universal freedom of trade.[128]

"Friedrich List – wrote the Italian economist and historian Marcello De Cecco – is the intellectual opposite of Smith and Ricardo. The latter try to establish political economy as an exercise in logic, a study of the internal consistency of abstractly formulated logical systems; the former attempts to immerse himself in the reality of economic history, and to derive the most important lessons from it. His work, much more than Smith's, is an inquiry into the real causes of the wealth of nations. For him, economics is one of the arts of statesmanship...[List] is a scholar who understands that free trade is not a revealed truth, but only a form of economic policy...If [other] countries wanted to modernise their economies, to become as politically powerful as Britain, he thought they should blend protectionism and corporativism, skip the bourgeois revolution, and base their growth on state intervention...The great majority of economists who in the last 150 years have had at their disposal both approaches, the classical and the Listian, have without hesitation opted for the former".[129]

Here again we notice two polarities in economic thought; as Lunghini observes: "Walras [the neo-classical economist] shows a theoretical framework that, for the first time in the history of economic science, encompasses the whole logical structure of the interdependence of economic quantities. The whole conception and the technique are rigorously statistical [but] are valid for a stationary state only. [The other polarity is] the theory of economic development, which rejects the idea that only externalities can explain the shift of an economic system from one equilibrium to another".[130]

One may wonder whether De Cecco's assessment, of a substantial irrelevance of List's ideas in the discipline of economics, is correct, or should be somewhat qualified. In this regard, it seems opportune to distinguish the role of List in the evolution of mainstream economics, and his role in influencing economic and trade policies of important countries, and first of all of Germany. From the first point of view, we find in the work of List—and other economists', particularly of German nationality, who came after List—that aspect so acutely observed by Schumpeter: the difficulty of reconciling a vision centred on the State and on the historical analysis with the construction of theoretical models based on the rationality of individual behaviour. The German Historical School never could—or would—aim at that abstract theoretical perfection that combines, in an apparently rigorous logic, all the factors that influence any economic transaction in a certain society. This School lacked a coherent comprehensive theory, and this was an obstacle for those who want to find a rational explanation of everything. It was therefore at a disadvantage in respect to classical economics or even Marxist economics. The opposite view, the classical, or—better—neo-classical view of the free market, clearly prevailed, became mainstream, leaving small room to those who wanted to pursue alternative routes of research. From this perspective, De Cecco's comment is absolutely appropriate.

Later on, we shall mention the influence of List and the Historical School on the economic policies of diverse countries, and our conclusions will be somewhat different. But in order to look at the importance of List, and of Marxist socialism, in the political and economic discourse of the nineteenth century and beyond, it is necessary to mention the sociopolitical situation of Germany towards the middle of that century.

1.7 Germany and Britain in the Nineteenth Century

Germany has a primary role in the analyses of both the socialist doctrine of Engels and Marx, and List's and the Historical School's theories. And a great relevance has also the role of Great Britain, the hegemonic power of the nineteenth century, to which Germany is emphatically compared.

The main difference between Germany and Britain—a difference often stressed in List's writings, particularly when he is critical of Adam Smith and his "school", which he calls "cosmopolitan (*Kosmopolitische*) school"—can be found in the fact that Germany was still in search of her own national identity, even though Prussia appeared as the main driving force toward unity, while Britain, by then well consolidated as a single political entity, had been able to create an environment propitious to an individualistic and resourceful bourgeoisie, and to the incoming industrial revolution.

It is worthwhile to remember how the British bourgeoisie looked at the German people towards the middle of the nineteenth century: "Britain was used to looking at Germany as a sort of poor, backward and rather comic relation…Henry Mayhew, the co-founder of Punch, could only hope to make the poverty and backwardness of Germany in general imaginable to his readers by comparing it with the most irredeemably wretched of countries, Ireland…Karl Marx, himself a London German asylum-seeker, [wrote about the import of German workers]: the purpose of this importation is the same as that of the importation of Indian coolies to Jamaica, namely perpetuation of slavery...no one would suffer more than the German workers themselves, who constitute in Great Britain a larger number than the workers of all the other Continental nations. And the newly imported workers, being completely helpless in a strange land, would soon sink at the level of pariah".[131]

Beyond specific observations, statistical evidence seems to indicate that, in 1820, the national product of Britain was 38% higher than Germany's (even being difficult to compare the two countries, Germany being still fragmented into more independent states, of very different size, population and economy). Even more so, on a per-capita basis, Britain's product was over 60% bigger than Germany's.[132] But the scientific and technical education provided by far-sighted German governments led, in Britain, to anxiety and interest in that country, which until 1870—the year of the German victory in the war with France—had been largely ignored.[133] When the First World War broke out, the German GDP had already caught up and overcome the British. This dynamic speaks loudly of the German ambition to be first in Europe, and one may wonder whether List had well understood in advance the terms of the issue at stake and suggested the appropriate economic policy.

It is therefore useful to compare the theoretical approaches of List and Smith, which are influenced by very diverse social conditions. Smith looks at a society well consolidated in its existing network of economic and social relations. He explains to his readers how this society works; and if the single components of this society can exploit their potential without being hindered by obstacles of any kind, important changes to the social and economic structure and the body politic are not needed.

State is confined, in the work of Adam Smith, to a pretty secondary role, is almost absent other than in particular circumstances; but its presence is not needed. There is, in Smith, a fundamental optimism which is certainly of an Enlightenment nature, but is at the same time different from the French one. *Egalitè* is not a topic worthy of overwhelming attention, and perhaps the great critic of the French revolution, the conservative Edmund Burke,[134] would have been in agreement with Smith's view of what Enlightenment should be.

List's work leads us towards the introduction of full historicism in the economist's research, and it is necessary to put his approach into the political and social context at the basis of his more important book: *The*

National System of Political Economy.[135] It seems appropriate to devote the following two Sections to a synopsis of the main concepts of the book, having in mind how far they are from the current mainstream economics and at the same time how close to the widespread economic and political debates of today.

1.8 The Political Economy as a System of "National Economy"

It is useful to start by saying that List was intellectually born as a liberal, and that his nationalistic approach takes origin from his observation of the economic policies of the country of which he was a temporary guest: the United States.[136] There, Alexander Hamilton, the first Treasury Secretary of the Confederation, pursued an interventionist and protective policy, in order to get rid of the former home country, Britain. Hence, List's attention to the small German states belonging to the *Zollverein* (customs union), whose completion was strongly advocated by him; and, hence, his hope that protective duties were introduced to stimulate both growth and the free market inside the Zollverein.[137]

List is critical of Smith, because he does not recognize that other "systems of political economy", based on the concept of "nation", may replace the efficiency of a globalized economy. According to Smith—he writes—most of government regulations to promote well-being are unnecessary. Smith's vision means that the nation is nothing more than a lexical invention that only exists in politicians' mind. The "national economy" is instead—according to List—the science which, by correctly understanding interests and circumstances which concretely engage specific nations at a certain moment of time, teaches how a single nation can be brought to that state of industrial development that, once reached, will also allow the union with other nations on an equal basis, while trade freedom will become possible and useful as a consequence.

The British national interest is that, having Britain reached—as a well distinct and independent nation—a high degree of industrial development, trade freedom is for them an opportunity. The surplus of capital they have available propels them to export their laws and economic activities in far-away countries. The whole England is becoming an immense manufacturing city. Asia, Africa and Australia are being civilized by Britain, and new states are created on the British model. The French, Spanish, Portuguese are "unproductive races" and end up by furnishing their best wines to the British, keeping the worst for themselves [the Ricardian theory of comparative advantage comes to the mind]. In the optimal sort of arrangement, according to the British, France would keep some factories, Germany would export to Britain toys, cuckoo clocks, philosophical writings and perhaps some troops to be killed in the deserts of Asia or Africa. It is then necessary that the less developed nations arise "artificially" [that is, by their own efforts, to be protected adequately], to the level that Britain has already reached.[138]

Smith's doctrine—List writes—sinks into materialism, particularism, individualism. The Smithian idea of a commodity's "exchange value" must be replaced by the concept of "productive capacity". In a broad sense, expenditure for education, promotion of justice, defence of the nation, contributes to that "capacity", by forming the "mental capital of the human race". The Smithian "popular school" makes us believe that the State, the body public, must not be taken into consideration by the political economy. According to that school, man who breeds pigs is a productive member of the community, but he who educates men is a mere non-productive.[139] Nation must sacrifice part of its material wealth in order to make gains in culture, professional ability and organizational skills. But a new industrial power cannot emerge if unprotected. If a loss of value derives from protective duties, this loss will be compensated by a stronger productive capacity that will then provide for plenty of material goods, and independence in case of war.[140]

The example, given by Smith, of the pin factory as a model of division of labour, has—according to List—the opposite meaning: it is not a division, but a union of energies, intelligences and capabilities for a shared objective of production. The reason for working together in that factory is not the division of labour, but its cooperation and unity. And this is true not only for the single factory, but for the whole manufacturing and agricultural power and the whole economy of the nation. Industry and agriculture must join in a single confederation, under the aegis of the State.[141] [This mention of shared interests of all those who participate in the production process (of capital and labour), an interest made subject to the superior interest of the nation, seems anticipation of the corporative doctrine, which is attractive to authoritarian regimes and also present, not by chance, in some current debates: a point on which we will come back later on].

If the individual interest must be subject to the interest of the nation, there is no room for policies of laissez-faire, laissez-passer (an expression—List observes—which sounds no less agreeable to robbers, cheats and thieves than to the merchant, and on that account it's dubious that can be adopted as a maxim),[142] and for the idea that politics must stay away from the economic realm.[143]

The national interest stays between the interests of individual and of the entire humanity, and the nation exists in opposition to other nations having the same degree of liberty. However, the nation cannot be small, must be created through alliances, as has been the case for Britain or the United States, or the German *Zollverein*, the customs union. Protectionism—more or less intense according to diverse industries—is rightly adopted if a country's economic development is hindered by competitive pressures coming from more advanced countries. Regarding Germany, List observes that she will protect her own industry, and this protection will only be lowered when the country will have reached a level of growth that will enable her to face external competition, however to be carefully contained. List adds contemptuously that the theory of trade freedom is correct only for those countries—as Portugal, [The Kingdom of] Naples, Turkey and other "barbarous and half-civilized" [!]—which are "foolish" enough not to pursue industrial development through an adequate level of protection.

The economy of a certain people becomes coincident with that of a nation when the State embraces the whole nation, and the degree of independence of a nation can be measured on the basis of the size of her population, territory, wealth and power, the relevance of her institutions, and the level of her civilization. Only in this way a stable and politically influential nation can be established.

1.9 List: Protectionists, Mercantilists, Physiocrats and the Idea of Europe

If we set aside List's sometimes intemperate language (typical, however, of his own political *élan*), his "system of political economy" is based on a well-crafted historical analysis of policies and economic doctrines, which appears in harmony with the much later approach followed by Schumpeter, mentioned at the start of this essay.

List thinks protectionism is a necessity, but it is also conditional on specific, historically determined circumstances. And here we notice a "liberal" List. Protection is only justified in order to increase the manufacturing activity of a nation, and only up to the point when the nation—thanks to an extended territory, a large population, important natural resources, advanced agriculture and well developed political institutions—can compete at the same level with other developed countries. Protectionism is therefore instrumental. It can consist of import quotas or duties.[144]

The whole Listian system is connected with the mercantilist doctrine, and is in obvious contrast with the physiocratic one, which, in turn, had a remarkable influence on Adam Smith. The growth of the big European monarchies stimulated domestic production and trade, thanks to duties on imported goods, and this development of a national industry was accompanied by consolidation of national liberty. Political institutions were reinforced, tax receipts increased, and so also the population and the military power. List says that this model of growth—the "industrial system"—was theorized for England by James Steuart and for Venice by Antonio Serra, but found its more complete enactment in France, with J. B. Colbert, the finance minister of Louis XIV. List complains however that mercantilism ignored the international side, by persuading governments to prohibit rather than moderately protect, and by ignoring that the ultimate end of international relations should be the future union of all nations, the establishment of [Hegelian?] perpetual peace and of universal freedom of trade.[145]

The final chapters of *The National System* are devoted to the European question. What people call "the maintenance of the European balance of power [an implicit reference to Britain] has nothing to do with the attempts, by the less powerful nations, to impose a check on the encroachment of the more powerful". If we consider the overwhelming interest that Continental nations have in common, that of opposing the maritime supremacy of the British, we shall be convinced that nothing is so necessary to these nations as a union, and nothing more ruinous as Continental wars.

Napoleon's Continental system was too Franco-centric; pursued the humiliation of other European nations for the benefit of France, rather than looking for their elevation and equalization; destroyed trade between European manufacturers and tropical countries, obliging the first to the use of substitute articles. In the meantime, however, it is possible to look ahead at a tighter union—both commercial and political—of Germany, Holland, Belgium and Switzerland. This mighty national body could merge institutions and dynasties, with Germany as the "central point" of a durable Continental alliance, and guarantor of lasting peace. Again, we are pretty close to current debates.[146]

Worthwhile observing that even free market economists could not easily dismiss List's argument in favour of protectionism. List found sympathetic ears in Alfred Marshall. Marshall, critical, as we have seen, of the Classical School, wrote that German economists were right in criticizing the "insular narrowness and self-confidence of the Ricardian School. In particular they resented the way in which the English advocates of free trade tacitly assumed that a proposition which had been established with regard to a manufacturing country, such as England was, could be carried over without modifications to agricultural countries. The brilliant genius and national enthusiasm of List overthrew this presumption; and showed that the Ricardians had taken but little account of the indirect effects of free trade"[147]: an implicit admission, by Marshall, that classical economics cannot be valid at all times and places.

1.10 German Economic Historicism

There are several features that make List's work eccentric in respect to the German Historical School of economics. Schumpeter, who puts List in the classical system and not in the Historical School, seems on the one side to belittle List's contribution, complaining about a lack of rigorous analysis and his journalistic language; on the other side to stress the innovative aspect of his work, more rooted in economic sociology than in economics proper. With List, " the group of facts of national growth, so neglected by the 'classics', emerges in a most apt formulation and was for the first time applied in a concrete way which even the modern businessmen, who had no use for romantic mysticism, could grasp, especially in the fields of tariffs policy...In this context List's contribution to economic sociology is of first importance: he made accessible to the wider public his conception of the national economy in the setting of its historical causes as the embodiment of historically unique circumstances".[148]

If we recall De Cecco's observation that List's influence on students of economics was as weak as Smith's and Ricardo's was strong, this should be qualified because the robust theoretical movement that developed in Germany in the second half of the nineteenth century took strength from List's ideas; but it's also true that this movement had languished from the start of the new century and can be considered practically extinguished in the aftermath of the First World War. In this period, the prevailing academic opinion in Germany adopted doctrines and methods of neo-classical economic thinking, giving life to new developments with the Austrian School and then with the German ordoliberalism (Chapter 2).

The German Historical School of economics grew stronger in parallel with the birth of the German unitary State and the establishment of the Reich. As mentioned earlier, List remained an eccentric figure, because his work preceded the School at least by a couple of decades, and also for his specific insistence on protection of the national economy as a necessary instrument to make it internationally competitive. But it was the major representative of the German School, Gustav von Schmoller, who devoted to List his attention and praise: "Friedrich List was the first economist to put together, in great style, economic developments in Europe and America, historical research with empirical observation, extracting from his findings an important theory of the socio-economic evolution...Although he basically remained a great agitator, his work marks the beginning of a new period for our science...he was able to bury the wrong ideas of economic institutions and of natural ideals that could be put into practice everywhere".[149]

Later, Schumpeter spent some pages on the Historical School; and, more recently, the vicissitudes of the School have been reassessed by a historian of modern Germany, Erik Grimmer-Solem. Both share the idea of a relative vagueness of its scope and heterogeneity of the writers who are considered as belonging to the School, so that the School itself is still seen as an "enigma". Its birth can be explained by the high level reached by historiography in Germany's intellectual life; there, historiography's importance was even greater in comparison with other social sciences, while, on the other side, theoretical economics, as expressed by the Classical School, had never taken roots. A line of demarcation between the two schools—within the limits in which such lines can be traced—is found in their methodology: inductive, and based on the observation, collection and analysis of facts as historically determined, in the case of the Historical School; and deductive, based on general premises of universal validity, in the other case. The German School considers instead these premises of a dubious character, fundamentally prescientific and destined to be replaced by a serious investigation of facts; to be more specific, they are premises that, even though reflecting historically determined situations, receive from classical economics a general, a-temporal validation.

If we recall the basic distinction, mentioned at the start of this essay, between assuming either the individual or the State as the rational prime mover of social and economic life, the following words of Schmoller leave no doubt about where the Historical School posits itself: "The idea that economic life has ever been a process mainly dependent on individual action – an idea based on the impression that it is concerned merely with methods of satisfying individual needs – is mistaken with regard to all stages of human civilization".[150]

The two schools hated each other (we have mentioned earlier the frontal attacks launched by List on the "cosmopolitan school"). Schmoller was prone to caricature the other School as a selfish doctrine masquerading as economic science; on the opposite side, in the opinion of the neo-classical economist Carl Menger, the Historical School was "an amorphous object of derision" (Grimmer-Solem).

Rejection of classical economics is, however, accompanied by a meaningful opposition to socialist theories, in particular Marx's and Lassalle's. "Marx considers man as an automaton of techno-economic conditions; in reality, it is man who determines these conditions according to ideas and superior purposes. Any mode of production, any class relation, any form of ownership, even if they depend on technique, cannot be explained other than by reference to causes which are spiritual and moral".[151] Loathing Marxism is apparently surprising, given their dismissal of classical economics and the strong social component of their ideas. "Though they sympathized with socialists' description of injustice, they were early on struck by the lack of empirical grounding of their theories and the impracticability of their political programmes. Countering Lassalle… was especially urgent in that he prophesized the demise of the *Mittelstand* [middle enterprises and middle bourgeoisie, whose role these economists saw as central in German politics and economics]. A commitment to empiricism, moral philosophy, and liberal reformism was clearly visible in the writings of historical economists in the 1860s and early 1870s".[152]

The research criteria followed by the German School are listed by Schumpeter.

Relativity, according to which it is untenable the idea that there are generally valid practical rules in the field of economic policy.

Unity of social life, for which there is an inseparable correlation between all its elements: consequently, the School has a contempt for the economists who never lean towards the next field, remaining insulated into their own domain.

Anti-rationalism, which sees a multiplicity of motivations in human behaviour, and attributes relatively minor importance to a merely logical insight where this behaviour is concerned [is this the "irrational behaviour" of more recent theories?].

Evolution, a criterion—notes Schumpeter—not unknown to Marx: according to this approach it is not rewarding to isolate phenomena and reconstruct effective conditions on a merely intellectual basis, it is rather necessary to look at individual correlations, that is: not at general causes of social events but at concrete causations of the specific events in which we are interested.

Organic point of view: economy cannot be split up into an agglomeration of independent economic individuals, the economic events are not merely the resultant of individual components.[153]

The younger writers of the School—among them, not only Gustav Schmoller, but also Lujo Brentano, Adolf Held and Georg Knapp, to name a few—were in fact more influenced by the statistical method than by the ideas of the Romantic movement and the Hegelian philosophy. In this regard, while the beginners of the School (the so-called "old" Historical School) were still imbued with the "philosophy of history" (Giambattista Vico's, for instance), the abovementioned economists were more detached from the Hegelian influence, looking more directly to factual developments as the rapid urbanization, the wave of industrialization (in which Germany was a powerful second, after the first wave led by England), the growth of trade unions and socialism. Unsatisfied by the answers given by the economic doctrines of the classical orthodoxy, they submitted these doctrines to empirical verifications, by combining the historical and the statistical instruments. "There is little doubt that the centrality of the 'social question' in German public affairs meant that economics in Germany continued to be political economy encompassing a broad range of social phenomena and political questions. But this too was not particularly novel to the alleged 'Historical School'. After all, classical, Marxian, and nationalist economics were tied to discrete political programmes – Smith, Ricardo, Marx, and List's economics were analytical foundations upon which their respective programmes for political change were built".[154]

With the Historical School, two main ideas emerge, which are unified by the relevance given to the historical analysis and the centrality of the State: the urgency of a social reform, however far from Marxist revolutionary ideas, and a revaluation of mercantilist policies, including protectionism.

Regarding social reform, differently from classical economists, whose political programme was minimalist (the "invisible hand", the phasing out of trade barriers), social ethics asked for a visible hand, founded on man's natural sociability and constructive moral action. "The main question of the day was, in Schmoller's view, a question of justice: how to overcome growing inequalities, strengthen the middle and create greater mobility between classes, a question which was not solely economic but also moral and cultural".[155] He emphasized the common interest of workers and capitalists; well-paid labourers would have been more reliable; he also fought for an official recognition of trade unions; and believed in the small enterprise, which more easily would have realized that communion of purposes.[156] It is notable that there is, in List, the same relevance of a shared interest of social classes, hinting to corporativism (see above, Sect. 1.6).

Policies of social reform can be, at least partly, explained by the pressure of the vigorously rising socialist movement. On the one hand, the authoritarianism of the German Crown and of the (mostly Bismarck's) government brought to the Anti-Socialist Act of 1878, under which the Socialist Party had to cease any activity and socialist associations had to be dissolved and their funds seized. On the other hand, between 1883 and 1889 a series of laws created a complex system of social insurance including a health-insurance law and a workmen's compensation scheme; in case of disability, or after having reached a certain age, pension was provided (the related costs had to be covered, in different cases, by employers, or employees, or the State). In 1891, a protecting law for workers was enacted, providing for a different maximum of hours per working day for men, women, children and a mandatory rest.[157] Social reform was extended to the industrial middle classes, which were entitled to some protection (to confirm the government's attention to *Mittelstand*). As we shall see later on, it is understandable why Marx looked at this apparent collusion between the Crown and the working classes as a mine against social revolution: a reactionary form of "feudal socialism", in his own words.

With reference to mercantilism, as noted earlier List had praised mercantilist policies, mentioning in particular the French minister Colbert, as a strong affirmation of central State over localisms, and against the "cosmopolitanism" of Smith's doctrine. With List, in the German context this view implied the adoption of protectionist policies, at least in so far they are necessary to put countries on the same footing and allow a fair competition between them. Schmoller, as List, praises Colbert because "his administration was, primarily, a struggle against the municipal and provincial authorities", but his view on protectionism is more nuanced than List's. Essentially, in his work *The Mercantile System*, he identifies mercantilism with the national State: mercantilism is "State making and national economy making at the same time...The essence of the system lies not in some doctrine of money, or of the balance of trade; not in tariff barriers, protective duties, or navigation laws; but in something far greater: - namely, in the total transformation of society and its organization". Mercantilism's essence consists of "casting the weight of the power of the State into the scales of the balance in the way demanded in each case by national interests". Therefore, according to Schmoller, the terms of the relation between free trade and protectionism must be put in context: "Free trade has a favourable bias especially towards consumers' interests, protectionism towards producers' interest; export industries prefer the first, the second is preferred by enterprises that still have market share to exploit. The part of agriculture, which is able to export, is for free trade; the other part, overwhelmed by agricultural imports, is protectionist. Merchants are in prevalence for free trade, they are cosmopolitan; craftsmen are rather protectionists. The abstractly liberal mind is inclined towards optimism, the protectionist towards pessimism. Free-trade attitudes always tend to prevail in phases of growth, protectionist attitudes in periods of economic stagnation and decay. The free trader is confident on the international division of labour, the protectionist on development of national forces; the first wants to abandon the weaker branches of production, being certain that some healthier national productions will replace the others, while the protectionist is diffident, wants to act immediately and defend the status quo. Free trade and protectionism are antithetic trends that exist in every developing national economy".[158]

These sentences, however they can be valued, sound extremely actual, today.

The influence of the above mentioned theories is visible in German economic policies, first with the creation of the *Zollverein* of the small German pre-unification States, and after with the birth of the Reich. The *Zollverein* was initially created by an accord between some States, including Bayern, Würtemberg, Baden, in 1820, and completed under the hegemony of Prussia in 1832.[159] When the second industrial revolution began about 1870, centred on Germany (and the United States), its fulcrum was represented by new technology and heavy industry—as steel, chemicals, electricity and electrical products—, and Germany protected these infant industries behind high tariff walls. In general, after the victorious war on France in 1870 and the birth of the Reich in 1871, under Bismarck a strong interventionist State gave rise to the creation of a system of "organized capitalism". We have mentioned social insurance and a nucleus of welfare state, but collective bargain in labour contracts, the cartelization of industry and the nationalization of the railways should also be mentioned. Regarding protectionism, some historians give also weight to the cessation of huge war reparations payments by France, which put an end to the expansion of the German economy and reduced State revenues as a consequence: the tariffs wall was erected also to face this fall.[160]

But it should be reminded that, following the victorious war, the Reich unified the currency and immediately adopted the gold standard: a step of the greatest importance for the birth of an international monetary system, when only one country, Britain, had formally introduced it. This decision meant a sort of consecration of Germany as a world power. Credit for this move is attributed to a liberal statesman and economist, Ludwig Bamberg: a recognition that a liberal disposition was also existent in the statist Germany, reflecting a western liberal orientation that had never fully disappeared (Pierenkemper-Tilly).

1.11 Marxist Socialism

Marx himself wants to clarify his rapport with Hegel. "I therefore openly avowed myself the pupil of that mighty thinker, and even here and there, in the chapter on the theory of value, coquetted with the modes of expression peculiar to him. The mystification which dialectic suffers in Hegel's hands, by no means prevents him from being the first to present its general mode of working in a comprehensive and conscious manner. With him it stands on its head. It must be turned side up again, if you would discover the rational kernel within the mystical shell".[161] Hence, Marx's materialistic idea that history is the denial, the antithesis of the Hegelian, idealist conception of history: this means that ideas are born as a reflection of material conditions, and not the opposite. What remains, in Marx's work, of Hegel's thinking? Just a little, Schumpeter observes: the dialectic method, which explains any real development with the conceptual development; the historical method [which approximates Marx to the

Historical School]; the way of expressing his concepts with that obscurity which is typical of some phrases of his master.[162]

The influence on Marx of the Hegelian philosophy of history, of the German Historical School of economics and the Classical School was well recognized by Maurice Dobb: "His analysis of capitalist society was approached from the standpoint of a general philosophy of history, by which it can be said that the descriptive and classificatory emphasis of the historical school and the analytical and quantitative emphasis of abstract Political Economy were combined".[163]

But the economic interpretation of history belongs to Marx, not to Hegel; the only latent Hegelism of Marx can be found in his dialectic historicism, in the centrality of the State, and in the teleological character of history, towards man's emancipation. Marx and Engels, "had both been enchanted by the Hegelian dialectic",[164] but Marx's political economy has with evidence a Ricardian imprint, in its references to the labour theory of value, and the fundamental division of society into different social classes. Marx does not recognize the contribution of capital to the product creation, which he defines as "surplus-value", because the only value of a product is given by the labour employed to create it.

Therefore, the explanation of profit, according to Marx, lays not in any cost of productive activity contributed by the capitalist, but in the class structure of the society. The relation between owner of means of production and labourer depends on that structure, as historically determined. In a society admitting slavery, the master takes the whole product, over the mere subsistence of the slave: an issue of surplus-value does not exist. In a capitalistic society, instead, the labourer is formally free, no law or custom obliges him to work for a master. However, since the proletarian is devoid of means of production, he must sell on the market his labour, which is for him necessary to produce his subsistence: labour-power is sold by the labourer on the market to the capitalist as if it were a commodity, acquiring a value. The product is sold by the capitalist at a value which is greater than the value of the labour-power. As a consequence, the profit of the capitalist is the result of the capitalistic society's class structure, based on the fundamental distinction between capitalist and worker.[165]

As mentioned earlier, according to Marxist economists the Neoclassical School and the marginal utility-theory came out as a reaction to the socialist doctrine. One of the first criticisms of Marx comes from Alfred Marshall: "It is not true that the spinning of yarn in a factory...is the product of the labour of the operatives. It is the product of their labour, together with that of the employer and subordinate managers, and of the capital employed; and that capital itself is the product of labour and waiting: and therefore the spinning is the product of labour of many kinds, and of waiting. If we admit that it is the product of labour alone, and not of labour and waiting, we can no doubt be compelled by inexorable logic to admit that there is no justification for Interest, the reward of waiting[166]; for the conclusion is implied in the premiss,...Marx do[es] indeed boldly claims the authority of Ricardo for [his] premiss; but it is really as opposed to his explicit statement and the general tenor of his theory of value, as it is to common sense".[167]

The materialistic conception of history does not mean that every human action is the result of economic motivations, or that the emergence of the socialist society is inevitable. In their *Manifesto of the Communist Party*, Marx and Engels detach themselves from the Hegelian Left, to which even they had previously belonged, and from a determinism that gives the socialist State's advent for certain; without proletariat's self-consciousness, nothing could prevent the exploitation of wage-earners from their masters.[168] "Marx himself spent much of his time trying to organize a revolutionary political movement, instead of sitting back and wait until the presumably iron laws of history delivered to mankind a socialist society".[169]

In the *Capital*,[170] Marx is inclined to believe that—independently from the awareness of the working class of its social condition as a prerequisite for a successful revolution—"a law of the tendency of the rate of profit to fall" can be formulated as a prediction of the historical necessity of a collapse of capitalism. This "law" can be explained by dividing a capitalistic investment into two categories:

- Means of production—raw materials, machines and other devices—which Marx calls "constant capital";
- Labour, which is in turn divided into two components: wage—the amount of work that is done for production of workers' remuneration—which Marx calls "variable capital"[171]; and surplus-value, the amount of work appropriated by the capitalist. In the words of Marx, "the surplus-labour of labour-power is the gratuitous labour performed for capital and thus forms surplus-value for the capitalist, a value which costs him no equivalent return".[172]

The rate of surplus-value is the ratio of surplus-value to the variable capital, and gives a measure of the intensity of exploitation of labour by the capitalist.

The rate of profit rate is instead the ratio of the surplus-value to the total capital, constant and variable. Competition urges the capitalist to make his factory more efficient with new technology, which requires more capital investment, and this drives the inflexible, or constant, amount of capital higher in relation to the flexible, or variable, amount (labour). This means that, even if the level of labour exploitation—the surplus-value—remains the same, the profit rate has a tendency to fall.

Marx gives an example: suppose that the labourer works as many hours for himself as he does for the capitalist, that is, the ratio of the surplus-value to the wage is 100%. The rate of profit, however, depends on the amount of total capital employed in the production. If wages—variable capital—are equal to 100, and the surplus-value is equally 100, and the constant capital employed is 50, the profit rate is $100/150 = 66.6\%$. But, as just mentioned, competition urges the capitalist to increase the amount of constant capital, say, to 100. Even if the rate of labour exploitation—that is, the rate of surplus-value—remains the same (100%), the profit rate decreases: $100/200 = 50\%$, and this decrease continues as additional amount of constant capital has to be invested.[173]

The law of the tendency of the profit rate to fall can be contrasted through a decrease in wages, that is a more intense exploitation of the labourer: an increase in the surplus-value. In other words, that "law" would be faulty if the capitalist had the capacity to reduce wages by the amount necessary to keep constant his profit ratio, i.e. to increase his surplus-value.

Which of the two tendencies would prevail, it's logically impossible to argue. Marx, in Vol III of the *Capital*, may himself have left the issue unsolved: his historical method may have induced him to think that any solution would depend on the interaction between technological progress and the configuration of social classes relations at any given time and stage.[174] But, if wages are already at a subsistence level, any further decrease would be made impracticable. Anyway, that "law", or "tendency", is evidence of a Hegelian determinism, and at the same time a reminder of Ricardo's influence on Marx.[175]

Marx and Engels observe the close link between the forces of production (technology, machines, human capabilities), which are continuously evolving, and the legal framework that encapsulates them (property rights, labour relations, division of labour). The causality goes from the first to the second, not vice versa (that is, modes of production are not conditioned by institutions). The bourgeoisie, which legally owns the instruments of production, uses the powers of the State—of its State—to validate the distribution of the product which it approves, being functional to its interest, and denies the working class the entire product to which this class is entitled. The bourgeoisie relies on the authority of its State so that the product distribution it approves is accepted as a general rule, and creates a system of values—political, juridical, ethical, religious, philosophical (the superstructure created over the material economic structure[176])–whose general observance guarantees the distribution of product imposed by the capitalists on the working class.

But, "the bourgeoisie cannot exist without constantly revolutionising the instruments of production, and thereby the relations of production and with them the whole relations of society".[177] A gap therefore emerges between modes of production and society's institutional framework. This framework, made up of those values as defined by the capitalistic class, becomes obsolete. With the birth of socialism, that gap is filled, and a new organization of the production forces is defined; within this new organization, the proletarian class, which has mostly suffered from that obsolescence, puts things at their right place, by destroying the capitalistic institutional framework, fully inadequate. The new set of institutions is in fact the one that introduces public ownership, in a classless society.

The constant revolution of the instruments of production and thereby of the relations of production, the constant expansion and the exploitation of world markets that are related to the "cosmopolitan" character of production and consumption, are the source of recurrent situations of "epidemic" overproduction—an insufficient demand, in Keynes' terminology—("like the sorcerer who is no longer able to control the powers of neither world whom he has called up by his spells"—*Manifesto*). The bourgeoisie gets over those crises by enforced destruction of a mass of productive forces and by the conquest of new markets (*Manifesto*). Paradoxically, the ruling class is induced "to restrict further the cost of production of a workman, almost entirely, to the means of subsistence that he requires for his maintenance and for the propagation of his race", while the lower strata of the middle class—small tradespeople, shopkeepers, handicraftsmen and peasants—gradually sink into the proletariat.[178]

The shift of ownership of the means of production from the bourgeoisie to the State, that is to the proletariat organized as the ruling class, will occur in different ways according to different countries. In the *Manifesto*, Marx and Engels see a gradual transition in the most advanced countries, which at the beginning will consist of the following measures[179]:

- Abolition of property in land, whose rent is applied to public purposes;
- A heavy progressive income tax;
- Abolition of rights on inheritance;
- Confiscation of property of all emigrants [affluent people who move abroad];
- Centralization and nationalization of credit;
- Same for communication and transport;
- Extension of factories and instruments of production that are State-owned;
- Obligation to work;
- Combination of agriculture and industry, and harmonization of work conditions between towns and country;
- Free education and abolition of children's factory labour; technical education for industrial purposes.

A programme that sounds not so far from some socialist or communist parties' in the Western world, in particular after the Second World War (The British Labour Party wrote, in 1948: "Our own ideas have been different from those of continental socialism which stemmed more directly from Marx, but we, too, have been influenced in a hundred ways by European thinkers and fighters, and, above all, by the authors of the Manifesto").

In Marxist socialism, the State disappearance is only to be meant as abolition of a bourgeois institution. The State becomes a proletarian institution, devoid of any hierarchical, vertical structure. Marx accepts Smith's and Ricardo's vision of a society divided into classes. But, while according to the two classical economists maintenance of different classes is the prerequisite of creation of new wealth, Marx thinks that only its abolition can disenfranchise the working class from the subordination imposed by the bourgeoisie. In the proletarian State, "the proletariat organised as the ruling class",[180] its organs must be democratic, not aimed at maintaining capitalism as a mode of production. In the bourgeois society the State is the ultimate protector of the social structure: "It is only under the shelter of the civil magistrate – Smith writes, and the *Manifesto* repeats, with an obviously opposite meaning - that the owner of that valuable property…can sleep a single night in security".[181]

The "dictatorship of the proletariat" is not, in dialectical terms, the antithesis of democracy; its antithesis is the "dictatorship of the bourgeoisie", so long as the ownership of the means of production remains in the hands of the middle-class. Its meaning is that "in the proletarian dictatorship the society is organized so that the State power is in the hands of the working class, which uses all the force necessary to prevent it being seized from them by the class which formerly exercised its authority".[182]

Marxist socialism distances itself from both the reactionary socialism and bourgeois socialism. Within the first, a further distinction is made between feudal and petty bourgeois socialism: both are reactionary, because they look at the past.

Regarding feudal socialism, Marx and Engels argue against the Hegelian Left, to which, as mentioned, both had formerly belonged. It should be recognized—they say—that labourers' emancipation cannot happen in every country in the same way. Capitalism is a stage of man's development. Marxism affirms the historical nature of the economic problem. The Hegelian Left, which qualified itself as the "true" German socialism, is unable to grasp the diverse historical conditions of different countries: while, in France, socialism can well have as an objective the attack to the bourgeoisie already in power, because France is already beyond the feudal and aristocratic society, in Germany (which both Marx and Engels look at with passionate attention as their own country) the working class is still immature for revolution, because the German capitalism is not yet developed to the point to make that class a "proletariat". The German government looks at an alliance between the Crown and the working class through measures of welfare (see Sect. 1.10), apparently at the expense of the bourgeoisie, but substantially at the expense of the proletariat.[183] In Germany, the bourgeoisie has just started struggling against feudal aristocracy and absolute monarchy. To fight for socialism in these conditions means to delay the success of the bourgeois liberal revolution, by scaring them with the menace of a proletarian attack, whose preconditions are still immature.[184] In nineteenth century Germany, only an accomplished liberal revolution against a feudal system can be the prelude to an immediate and subsequent proletarian revolution.[185] The "true" socialism of the Leftish Hegelians is utopian and abstractly philosophical: it is indeed infected, according to Marx, by the German romanticism and therefore by a nationalism deriving from Hegel and Fichte, who saw the Prussian monarchy as coinciding with the ultimate purpose of the absolute, the end of history.

Also reactionary is the petty-bourgeois socialism. At this sort of socialism looks a social class that is already disappearing under the push of the bourgeois revolution, that is the class of small merchants, hurled down into the proletariat by the action of competition; they see the moment—the *Manifesto* stresses—when they will completely disappear as an independent section of modern society; the same view is held by the class of small peasant proprietors, who suffer from the concentration of land in a few hands. The "last words" of both are: corporate guilds for manufacture, patriarchal relations in agriculture. These two classes, as far as they still exist, remain a fraction of the middle class, they are conservative, not revolutionary, they want to differentiate from the proletariat and are therefore potentially reactionary.[186]

At the same time, Marxist socialism rejects the ideas of the conservative or bourgeois socialists,[187] as Owenites in England and Fourierists in France, who aim at a bourgeoisie without proletariat, that is at maintaining all the advantages of the bourgeois mode of production and society, without the dangers and struggles that result from them. It is crazy any doctrine of socialism that is based on bourgeois goodwill as a source of change. The economist who is a conservative socialist works for a betterment of technical education, for profit-sharing, for subsidies to unemployment caused by technological developments. He wants to mitigate the harshest conditions of capitalism, without interfering with the organization and ownership structure of capitalism. This kind of socialism believes that the advancement of the working class means a change in material living conditions without revolution; but this change is nothing more than some administrative reforms that leave the relation between labour and capital unchanged.

The issue of protectionism is seen from the same perspective: it is apparently a form of defence of national industry and therefore of labour; in reality, it is based on a fictitious harmony of interest between them: a harmony shown already by Smith and Mill to be fallacious; but exalted by List and still used to discourage and repress the growth of trade unions.[188]

In this chapter we have shown that the neo-classical economics of the turn of the nineteenth century, in the name of "science", had lost the ethical value that had supported Adam Smith's vision, according to which—as recently observed—"purposive human activity of all kinds was seen as embedded in ethics: as conduct, that is, not merely as behaviour".[189] Smith had advocated a society that would exalt the freedom of the individual—convinced that his action would benefit his own and in the end the general well-being,—at the same time maintaining a social framework where different classes might coexist in their different roles. This was, essentially, the liberal kind of society according to the economists of the Classical School.

The Neo-classical School, and its marginal utility theories that reacted to the Classical School, and came then to prevail, wanted to go beyond the classical economics of Adam Smith, David Ricardo or John Stuart Mill. Neo-classical economists emphasized competitive free markets as a prerequisite for attaining a position of equilibrium. But we have distinguished two approaches. The first approach was based on the "discovery" of the correct market price through new relevance given to the "demand" for goods (Marshall). The second on the construction of a general equilibrium of the economic system, mathematically formulated (Walras).[190] In any case, the "value of things" would move from an objective criterion (the production costs, and the labour component in particular) to a subjective one (the individual rational preference, expressed by a marginal utility function).

Being influenced by the new positive philosophy, both approaches—the Walrasian and the Marshallian—defined themselves as "scientific", implicitly or explicitly distinguishing "truth" (statements empirically verifiable and possibly systemized in "laws") from "ideology" (implying values beyond empirical verification as ethics, conscience, trust…). According to the father of positivism, Comte, if certain "laws" are scientifically identified as explaining an economic system governed by the principle of utility, no freedom of thought would be any more necessary to address societal economic issues.

The titles of the main marginalist works included often the adjective "pure", and the prefaces of these books hastened to stress their "purely scientific" purpose, just to define their contents as devoid of any component having to do with concepts exogenous to utilitarianism. In particular, ethics was expelled from the field of research in economics, unless seen as a sort of embellishment or quantitatively minor component of utility, numerically measured. At best, commutative justice supplants any sort of distributive justice. According to different writers, either moral concerns should be out of sight of the economist's theory, or morality has to be identified with personal utility, or the pursuit of material happiness.

But an implicit social philosophy could not be eliminated, and positive ideology sounded as an intellectual support of the conservation of existing social and economic structures. Marx wrote: "[t]he vulgar economy...seeks plausible explanations of the most obtrusive phenomena, for bourgeois daily use, but for the rest, confines itself to systematizing, in a pedantic way, and proclaiming for everlasting truths, the trite ideas held by self-complacent bourgeoisie with regard to their own world, to them the best of all possible worlds".[191]

If we take the observation point of a scholar, or a policymaker, towards the end of the nineteenth century, concerned as he might have been with the overwhelming themes of the economic growth, production and distribution of wealth, independence and strength of a nation, widespread social unrest in an increasingly industrialized world, three great strands of thought—an individualistic liberalism, nationalism, socialism—would be present in his mind. They had matured and fought each other for a large part of the century. Even though they did not come from scratch, and had rather reflected the development of new economic and social conditions, these three streams had marked a decisive cut in respect to the past. The main works of Adam Smith and Marshall—standard-bearers of classical and neo-classical schools—came out respectively in 1776 and 1890, Walras's model of general equilibrium, well coherent with the bourgeois, *fin-de-siécle* environment, was out in 1900, List's and Schmoller's main books were published in 1846 and 1890, Marx's Capital appeared in 1867.

The influence of those philosophies on economic thought in the twentieth century is the object of the following two chapters, while the forth will bring us to issues that are of immediate relevance today. The fifth and final chapter will try to respond whether, and to what extent, liberalism, nationalism and socialism—as economic ideologies—can still provide a guide to scholars' and policymakers' reflections and decisions.

Notes

1. Schumpeter (1954, Chapter I).
2. This new vision "shake[s] off the joke of authority, accustom[s] men to think for themselves, give[s] new hints, which men of genius may carry further, and by the very opposition, illustrate[s] points, wherein no one before suspected any difficulty": Hume (1740). The text was reprinted and prefaced by John Maynard Keynes and Piero Sraffa, Cambridge University Press, 1938, See p. 4 of this edition.
3. Schumpeter (1954, p. 23).
4. Marx gives this definition of the *vulgar economy*: "[It] deals with appearances only, ruminates without ceasing on the material long since provided by scientific economy, and then seeks plausible explanations of the most obtrusive phenomena, for bourgeois daily use, but for the rest confines itself to systematizing in a pedantic way, and proclaiming for everlasting truths, the trite idea held by self-complacent bourgeoisie with regard to their own world, to them the best of all possible worlds". Marx's reference was mainly to the nascent Neo-classical School. See Marx (n.d. [1867], vol. I, p. 58).
5. Schumpeter (1954, p. 26). A bullionist economic policy looks at the accumulation of precious metal reserves. Bullionism can be seen as an early mercantilism. In today's terms, it translates into a policy aimed at a strong surplus in the trade balance.
6. Schumpeter (1954, p. 35).
7. Plumpe (2016, p. 43).
8. Schumpeter (1954, p. 33).
9. Heilbroner (1988).
10. The same partition—between "Western" economics, or "Ricardism" on the one hand, and the "nation, State, economy" stream of thought, on the other hand—is made by the Italian philosopher Benedetto Croce (1951, pp. 275–277) (originally published in *La Critica*, 36, 1938).
11. I am adopting this convincing partition from Fawcett (2014, pp. 120–124).
12. Israel (2010, p. 106).
13. pp. 106–107.
14. As we shall see, a society structured in different classes is a central point in Smith's thought.
15. Israel (2006, p. 604).
16. Locke (1690, Chapter 7, 85).
17. Israel (2010, p. 179).
18. A political group during the French revolution.
19. Israel (2014, pp. 285 and 368).
20. Israel (2010, pp. 63–65).

21. Rousseau (1913, pp. 83 and 22).
22. p. 83.
23. p. 83.
24. de Voltaire (1770).
25. Rousseau (1913, pp. 255, 260, 269, 273, 280).
26. Israel (2014, pp. 644–645). See also Gioja (1831, p. 27).
27. Israel (2010, p. 181).
28. Smith (1811, vol. 2, p. 50). It is fair to add that this wording is an interpretation of Smith's thought by his editor, William Playfair.
29. Burke (1800, p. 14).
30. Smith (1853, Part VI, Sect. II).
31. Bentham (1823, pp. 2, 9, 24 25).
32. A theme well emphasized by Hayek, more than a century later (see Chapter 2).
33. Bentham (1823, pp. 310, 313, 323).
34. The contrast between the British Enlightenment, driven by wealth, and the French one, driven by equality, is perhaps the same we find in the drivers of the English Glorious Revolution of 1688, and the French Revolution of 1789.
35. Porter (2000, p. 261).
36. Porter (2000, p. 202).
37. Smith (1811, vol. 2, pp. 19–20).
38. Israel (2010, p. 107).
39. Smith (1811, p. 11). This phrase is perfectly in line with what David Ricardo writes: "[the] pursuit of individual advantage is admirably connected with the universal good of the whole" (2004, p. 81).
40. Stein (1994).
41. Keynes (1926, p. 11).
42. Ricardo (2004, p. 76).
43. See, for instance, the case of metayers (*coloni partiarii*) in France, vol. 1, p. 276.
44. Smith (1811, vol. 2, pp. 152–155).
45. Hume (n.d. [1770]) Discourse V.
46. Ricardo (2004, pp. 82–87).
47. Ricardo (2004, p. 82).
48. Hume (n.d. [1770]) Discourse III.
49. Hume (n.d. [1770], p. 35). This emphasis on the demand in the price determination will be neglected by the classical economists and, later in the 19th century, will be on the contrary reaffirmed by neo-classical economists (see below).
50. Hume had invoked a "*public bank*" that might destroy the excess of paper credit (Discourse III).
51. Ricardo (1810).

52. Ricardo (2004, p. 5).
53. Smith (1811, vol. 2, Book I, Chapter V, pp. 21 and 25).
54. Ricardo (2004, p. 7).
55. Ricardo (2004, p. 19).
56. Ricardo (2004, p. 48).
57. Ricardo (2004, pp. 48, 52–53); Smith (1811, Book I, Chapter 5).
58. "Abstinence – that is, non consuming – was suggested by John Stuart Mill and a number of other writers, as the 'contribution' of capital [to production]":Heilbroner (1988, p. 117).
59. Robinson (1961, p. 55).
60. Shackle (1980). The essay is reproduced in Ford, J. L.: *Time, Expectations and Uncertainty in Economics*, Edward Elgar, 1990.
61. Hobsbawm (1997, p. 144).
62. Porter (2000, pp. 138–139 and 149).
63. Berlin (2000, p. 277).
64. Mill (2018). The quotations reported in the text are from pp. 5–9, 19–20, 22–25, 30–37.
65. Malthus (1926). His postulates are: "that food is necessary to the existence of man", and "that the passion between the sexes is necessary, and will remain nearly in the present state". His inference from these "postulates" is that "the power of population is indefinitely greater than the power in the earth to produce subsistence for man", and that, consequently, "this implies a strong and constantly operating *check on population* from the difficulty of subsistence" (pp. 11, 13–14).
66. Mathematics, astronomy, physics, chemistry, biology, sociology or the social science.
67. Spencer (1992).
68. Fawcett (2014, p. 79).
69. Bobbio (1977, p. 82).
70. Andresky (1974, pp. 192 and 197). Pareto, a convinced positivist, seems to take distance from this extreme assimilation, when he makes a distinction between *residues* and *derivations* in man's ideologies. The former are expressions of sentiments, of instinct, the latter are expressions of the human need to use reason. Ideology is a mixture of logical and non-logical impulses. This is the basic difference from the animals, they do not (cannot) have derivations, just instinct. See Bobbio, p. 101.
71. Mill (2018, p. 25).
72. pp. 30–31.
73. pp. 33–35.
74. Mill (2010, p. 18).
75. pp. 138–139.
76. Mill (2018, pp. 33–35).
77. Heilbroner (1988, p. 12).

78. Marginal utility "is notoriously an invention of bourgeois economists, post-marxist and anti-marxist": Sraffa (2017, p. 3).
79. Dobb (1937a, pp. 24–25).
80. Hayek (1955, p. 203).
81. Andresky (1974, p. 17).
82. Heilbroner, Milberg (1995, pp. 22–23).
83. Heilbroner, Milberg, p. 23.
84. Schumpeter (1954, p. 188).
85. Jevons (1965).
86. p. XVI.
87. p. XVI.
88. p. 1.
89. p. VII.
90. p. 23.
91. pp. 23 and VI.
92. The Italian Maffeo Pantaleoni was an important exponent of the Neoclassical School.
93. Naldi (2000, p. 92).
94. Jevons (1965, pp. 25–26).
95. Marshall (1966).
96. pp. 636 and 643.
97. pp. 70–71.
98. p. 301.
99. pp. 4–8.
100. Dzionek-Kozlowska (2015).
101. Walras (1954, p. 201).
102. Walras makes a distinction between pure economics (as mentioned above); applied economics (which deals with the policy implications of the pure theory); and social economics (which regards the wealth distribution). See Tarascio (1967).
103. Walras (1954, p. 142). The discussion that follows is based on Jaffé (1977).
104. Jaffé, p. 375.
105. A logical inconsistency is found here by Maurice Dobb: "[T]here seems to be an Hegelian contradiction in 'perfect competition' as a concept, since, if competition worked perfectly and without friction, it would never be in the interest of a seller to cut his price, knowing as he would that all competitors would immediately follow suit and deprive him of all gains in so doing" (1937b, p. 203).
106. Pareto (1971).
107. Libro II, Sezione 592.
108. On ophelimity, see Libro II, Sezione 642–653.
109. Libro III, Sezione 958.

110. Sezione 962.
111. Sezione 965. Pareto adds: "I am once again in need to resort to mathematics to explain this proposition". He seems to cloth in a mathematical formula arguments that are insufficiently explained in ordinary language.
112. Pareto (1919, p. 370). See also Findlay Shirras (1935).
113. Pigou (2013, p. 649).
114. Einaudi (1967, pp. 244–245).
115. Schumpeter (1997, p. 120).
116. Schumpeter (1942, pp. 65–66).
117. Picketty (2014, p. 367).
118. The same sense of futility of attempts to redistribute wealth through State intervention is shown, one century before Pareto and without using a single mathematical formula, by Robert Malthus. He aims to demonstrate that "the immense sum collected in England for the poor [the so-called Poor Laws] does not better their condition", it's a waste (1926, p. 71).
119. Christ (1990, p. 39).
120. Pareto (1971) Sezione 967. Observes Jaffé, in his already quoted article on Walras: "[Walras's maximization of social satisfaction is] essentially definitional… is nothing more and nothing less than an anticipation of Pareto's optimality, with the same virtues and the same defects…Walras's aim, even in his 'pure economics', was prescriptive or normative rather than positive or descriptive" (p. 379). The same aim is applicable to Pareto's optimality.
121. Sen (1970).
122. See Bobbio (1977, Chapter III, Section 6).
123. Hegel (1899, pp. 105 and 15).
124. Clark (2019, pp. 163 and 156).
125. Spirito (1939).
126. Lunghini (2001).
127. According to Sraffa, quoted by Lunghini (2001, p. 265).
128. List (1885, Chapter XXIX).
129. De Cecco (1971, pp. 20 and 25).
130. Lunghini (2003, p. 186).
131. Hawes (2014, pp. 12–15).
132. Maddison (2001).
133. Trevelyan (1944, p. 557).
134. "I must think such a government [the French government] well deserved to have its excellencies heightened, its faults corrected; and its capacities improved into a British constitution": Burke (1790, p. 195).
135. The original German version of the book was published in 1844, and is based on works written by List in the two previous decades. See Tribe (1995, p. 33).

136. List became an American citizen, and then US consul when he went back to his home country.
137. For an effective unification of the domestic market, List promoted the development of railway network and technology (steam locomotive). On List as "American": Tribe, pp. 32–65.
138. List, Chapter XI.
139. G. M. Trevelyan (1944) properly observed: "The Prussian State was educating the whole Prussian people. The paternal rulers of Germany in the early Nineteen Century educated their subjects, but gave them little political freedom and no share in government. The English State gave the common people great political freedom and some share in government, but left them to be educated by private religious charity" (p. 518).
140. List, Chapter XII.
141. Chapter XIII.
142. Chapter XXI.
143. Chapter XIV.
144. Chapter XXVII.
145. Chapter XXIX.
146. Chapter XXXV.
147. Marshall (1966).
148. Schumpeter (1954, p. 100).
149. Schmoller (1904, vol. I, p. 178).
150. Schmoller (1967, pp. 3–4).
151. Schmoller (1904, vol. II, p. 1096).
152. Grimmer-Solem (2003, p. 136).
153. Schumpeter (1954, p. 179).
154. Grimmer-Solem p. 33. More in general, see pp. 19–34.
155. Grimmer-Solem, p. 139.
156. Schmoller (1904, vol. II, pp. 606–661).
157. Stolper (1967, pp. 44–46).
158. Schmoller (1904, vol. II, p. 1017).
159. Pierenkemper, Tilly (2004, pp. 8–9).
160. Pierenkemper, Tilly, pp. 136–141. According to these authors, the German economy in the 19th century was more oriented to the free market than what is commonly thought. The different view would be biased by the prevailing, but incorrect, opinion, of German economists, concerning State's pervasive role in the economy as the driving factor of industrialization: an hostility towards the 19th century liberalism. See Zussman (2002); Stolper (1967, pp. 35–37).
161. Marx (n.d. [1867], vol. I, Book One). Afterword to the second German edition of January 24, 1873, pp. 14–15 (www.marxists.org).

162. "If Marx in fact had borrowed elements of thought or even merely his method from metaphysical speculations he would be a poor devil, not worth taking seriously": Schumpeter (1954, p. 119).
163. Dobb (1937a, p. 23).
164. Lasky (1948, p. 14).
165. Dobb (1937c, pp. 56–64).
166. The identification of capital with "waiting", according to neo-classical economists, is well explained by Joan Robinson:"[Capital] produces extra output that a longer gestation of period makes possible. Since capital is productive, the capitalist has a right to his proportion" (1974, p. 58).
167. Marshall (1966, pp. 487–488).
168. Lasky (1948, p. 15).
169. Streek (2017, p. 230).
170. Marx (n.d. [1894]), edited by F. Engels, vol. III, Part III.
171. Because labour's employment and remuneration can be adjusted.
172. Marx (1956 [1885]), edited by F. Engels, vol. II, Part 1, p. 22.
173. Marx (n.d. [1894], vol. III, Chapter 13, pp. 153–154).
174. Dobb (1937d, pp. 109–110).
175. Piero Sraffa writes in 1947: "Marx's available text is not clear (we have fragments published by Engels), and is open to different interpretations. My opinion is that Marx's law is methodological and not historical, therefore not statistically verifiable. As far as we know, it seems that in every specific capitalistic society the ratio of surplus-value and the rate of profit are extraordinarily stable over time. This is not in contradiction with Marx's law if that 'trend' is meant as a particular abstraction, that is as the result of a group of forces (accumulation), while other forces (technological progress, new inventions and discoveries) do not operate. The result is that this trend fall obliges capitalists to unending technical revolutions, in order to avoid the fall of the profit rate". See Sraffa (2017, pp. 7–8). On Sraffa and the labour theory of value, see this essay, Chapter III.
176. Marx (n.d. [1867], vol. I, p. 58).
177. Marx (n.d. [1867], vol I, p. 354); Marx, K., Engels, F.: *Manifesto of the Communist Party*, 1872, in Lasky (1948, p. 126).
178. Lasky (1948, pp. 132–135).
179. Marx, Engels, *Manifesto*, in Lasky, pp. 151–153.
180. Marx, Engels, *Manifesto*, in Lasky, p. 152.
181. Smith (1811, Book V, Chapter I, Part II, p. 164).
182. Lasky (1948, pp. 67–71).
183. *Manifesto*, III.I, Reactionary Socialism: Feudal Socialism; Petty-Bourgeois Socialism, pp. 153–161.
184. Lasky (1948, p. 51).
185. Lasky, pp. 53–54 and 58.

186. *Manifesto*, p. 139.
187. *Manifesto*, III. II Conservative or Bourgeois Socialism (161–166).
188. Lasky (1948, pp. 54–55).
189. Norman (2018, p. 183).
190. Heilbroner, Milberg (1995, p. 25).
191. Marx (n.d. [1867], p. 58).

References

Andresky, S. (1974). *The Essential Comte, Selected from Cours de Philosophie Positive (1830–42)*. Abington, NY: Routledge.

Bentham, J. (1823 [1789]). *Principles of Morals and Legislation*. Oxford: Clarendon Press.

Berlin, I. (2000). *Three Critics of the Enlightenment*. Princeton, Oxford: Princeton University Press.

Bobbio, N. (1977). *Saggi Sulla Scienza Politica in Italia*. Bari: Laterza.

Burke, E. (1790). *Reflections on the Revolution in France*. London: Dodsley.

Burke, E. (1800). *Thoughts and Details on Scarcity*. London: Rivington & Hatchard.

Christ, C. (1990). A Philosophy of Life. *The American Economist, XXXIV*.

Clark, C. (2019). *Time and Power: Visions of History in German Politics, from the Thirty Years' War to the Third Reich*. Princeton, Oxford: Princeton University Press.

Croce, B. (1951 [1939]). *Conversazioni Critiche*. Bari: Laterza.

De Cecco, M. (1971). *Economia e finanza internazionale dal 1890 al 1914*. Bari: Laterza.

de Voltaire. (1770). *Letters Concerning the English Nation*. Glasgow: Robert Urie.

Dobb, M. (1937a). The Requirements of a Theory of Value. In *Political Economy and Capitalism: Some Essays in Economic Tradition*. London: Routledge.

Dobb, M. (1937b). Concerning Frictions and Expectations: Certain Recent Trends in Economic Theory. In *Political Economy and Capitalism: Some Essays in Economic Tradition*. London: Routledge.

Dobb. M. (1937c). Classical Political Economy and Marx. In *Political Economy and Capitalism: Some Essays in Economic Tradition*. London: Routledge.

Dobb, M. (1937d). Economic Crises. In *Political Economy and Capitalism: Some Essays in Economic Tradition*. London: Routledge.

Dzionek-Kozlowska, J. (2015). Alfred Marshall's Puzzles: Between Economics as a Positive Science and Economic Chivalry. *Lodz Economic Working Papers*, 5.

Einaudi, L. (1967 [1944]). *Lezioni di politica sociale*. Torino: Einaudi.

Fawcett, E. (2014). *Liberalism: The Life of an Idea*. Princeton, Oxford: Princeton University Press.
Findlay Shirras, G. (1935). The Pareto Law and the Distribution of Income. *The Economic Journal,* 45(180), 663–681.
Gioja, M. (1831 [1797]). *Dissertazione sul problema quale dei governi liberi meglio convenga alla felicità dell'Italia*. G. Ruggia.
Grimmer-Solem, E. (2003). *The Rise of Historical Economics and Social Reform in Germany 1864–1894.* Oxford: Clarendon Press.
Hawes, J. (2014). *Englanders and Huns*. London, NY: Simon & Schuster.
Hayek, F. (1955). *The Counter-Revolution of Science: Studies on the Abuse of Reason*. New York: The Free Press.
Hegel, G. F. (1899 [1837]). *The Philosophy of History*. New York: The colonial Press.
Heilbroner, R. (1988). *Behind the Veil of Economics: Essays in the Worldly Philosophy*. London, NY: W.W. Norton.
Heilbroner, R., & Milberg, W. (1995). *The Crisis of Vision in Modern Economic Thought*. Cambridge: Cambridge University Press.
Hobsbawm, E. (1997). *On History*. London: Weidenfeld and Nicolson.
Hume, D. (1938 [1740]). *An Abstract of a Treatise of Human Nature*. Cambridge: Cambridge University Press.
Hume, D. (n.d. [1770]). *Political Discourses*. London, NY: The Walter Scott Publishing.
Israel, J. (2006). *Enlightenment Contested: Philosophy, Modernity and the Emancipation of Man, 1670–1752.* Oxford, NY: Oxford University Press.
Israel, J. (2010). *A Revolution of the Mind: Radical Enlightenment and the Intellectual Origin of Modern Democracy*. Princeton, Oxford: Princeton University Press.
Israel, J. (2014). *Revolutionary Idea: An Intellectual History of the French Revolution from the Rights of Man to Robespierre*. Princeton: Princeton University Press.
Jaffé, W. (1977). The Normative Bias of the Walrasian Model: Walras Versus Gossen. *The Quarterly Journal of Economics, 91*(3), 371–387.
Jevons, W. S. (1965 [1871–1888]). *The Theory of Political Economy*. New York: A. Kelley.
Keynes, J. M. (1926). *The End of Laissez-Faire*. London: Hogarth Press.
Lasky, H. (1948). *Communist Manifesto, Socialist Landmark: A New Appreciation*. London: George Allen & Unwin.
List, F. (1885 [1844]). *The National System of Political Economy*. London: Longman, Green & Co.
Locke, J. (1690). *Second Treatise of Government* (www.gutemberg.org).
Lunghini, G. (2001). David Ricardo: La storia come ordine naturale. *Rivista di storia economica, 17*(2), 259–269.

Lunghini, G. (2003). Benedetto Croce e l'economia politica. *Economia politica, 2,* 185–200.

Maddison, A. (2001). *The World Economy: A Millennial Perspective.* Paris: OECD.

Malthus, T. R. (1926 [1798]). *First Essay on Population.* London: Macmillan.

Marshall, A. (1966 [1890]). *Principles of Economics.* London: Macmillan.

Marx, K. (n.d. [1867]). *Capital: A Critique of Political Economy* (Vol. I). Moscow: Progress Publishers (Marxist.org).

Marx, K. (1956 [1885]). *Capital: A Critique of Political Economy* (Vol. II). Moscow: Progress Publishers (libcom.org).

Marx, K. (n.d. [1894]). *Capital: A Critique of Political Economy* (Vol. III). New York: International Publishers (marxists.org).

Marx, K., & Engels, F. (1948 [1848]). Manifesto of the Communist Party. In H. Lasky (Eds.), *Communist Manifesto, Socialist Landmark, a New Appreciation.* London: Allen and Unwin.

Mill, J. S. (2010 [1859]). *On Liberty.* Harmondsworth: Penguin.

Mill, J. S. (2018 [1865]). *Auguste Comte and Positivism.* Amazon Fulfilment.

Naldi, N. (2000, October). The Friendship Between Piero Sraffa and Antonio Gramsci in the Years 1919–1927. *European Journal of the History of Economic Thought, 7,* 2.

Norman, J. (2018). *Adam Smith: What He Thought, and Why It Matters.* London: Allen Lane.

Pareto, V. (1919). *Manuale di economia politica, con un'introduzione alla scienza sociale.* Milano: Societa' Editrice Libraria.

Pareto, V. (1971). *Corso di economia politica,* Libro III, Sezione 964. Torino: UTET (*Cours d'Économie Politique,* Rouge, Pichon, 1897).

Picketty, T. (2014). *Capital in the Twenty-First Century.* Cambridge: The Belknap Press of Harvard University Press.

Pierenkemper, T., & Tilly, R. (2004). *The German Economy During the Nineteenth Century.* New York: Berghahn Books.

Pigou, A. C. (2013 [1920]). *The Economics of Welfare.* Edited by N. Aslanbeigui & G Oakes. London: Palgrave Macmillan.

Plumpe, W. (2016). *German Economic and Business History in the 19th and 20th Century.* London: Palgrave Macmillan.

Porter, R. (2000). *Enlightenment: Britain and the Creation of the Modern World.* London: Allen Lane.

Ricardo, D. (1810). *The High Price of Bullion: A Proof of the Depreciation of Bank Notes.* London: John Murray.

Ricardo, D. (2004 [1817]). *The Principles of Political Economy and Taxation.* Mineola: Dover.

Robinson, J. (1961). Prelude to a Critique of Economic Theory. *Oxford Economic Papers, 13*(1), 53–58.

Robinson, J. (1974 [1962]). *Economic Philosophy*. New York: Penguin.
Rousseau, J. J. (1913 [1762]). *The Social Contract and Discourses*. London: J.M. Dent.
Schmoller, G. (1904 [1890]). *Lineamenti di economia nazionale generale*. Torino: UTET.
Schmoller, G. (1967 [1884]). *The Mercantile System and its Historical Significance*. New York: August Kelley.
Schumpeter, J. A. (1942). *Capitalism, Socialism, Democracy*. New York: Harper & Brothers.
Schumpeter, J. A. (1954 [1912]). *Economic Doctrine and Method: An Historical Sketch*. New York: Oxford University Press.
Schumpeter, J. A. (1997 [1952]). *Ten Great Economist: From Marx to Keynes*. London: Routledge.
Sen, A. (1970). The Impossibility of a Paretian Liberal. *Journal of Political Economy, 78*(1), 152–157.
Shackle, G. L. S. (1980). Evolution of Thought in Economics. *Banca Nazionale del Lavoro Quarterly Review*, 132.
Smith, A. (1811 [1775]). *An Inquiry Into the Nature and Causes of the Wealth of Nations* (the Playfair edition). Hartford: Oliver D. Cooke.
Smith, A. (1853 [1759]). *The Theory of Moral Sentiments*. London: Henry Bohn.
Spencer, H. (1992 [1889]). *The Man Versus the State*. Carmel: Liberty Classics.
Spirito, U. (1939). Economia ed etica nel pensiero di Hegel. In *Dall'economia liberale al corporativismo. Critica dell'economia liberale*. Milano: Principato.
Sraffa, P. (2017). *Lettere editoriali (1947–1975)*. Torino: Einaudi.
Stein, H. (1994, March 7). Remembering Adam Smith. *Wall Street Journal*.
Stolper, G. (1967). *The German Economy 1870 to the Present*. London: Weidenfeld and Nicolson.
Streek, W. (2017). *How Will Capitalism End*? London, NY: Verso.
Tarascio, V. J. (1967). Léon Walras: On the Occasion of the Publication of His Correspondence and Related Papers. *Southern Economic Journal, 34*, 1.
Trevelyan, G. M. (1944). *English Social History: A Survey of Six Centuries, Chaucer to Victoria*. London: Longmans, Green and Co.
Tribe, K. (1995). *Strategies of Economic Order: German Economic Discourse 1750–1950*. Cambridge: Cambridge University Press.
Walras, L. (1954 [1900]). *Elements of Pure Economics, or the Theory of Social Wealth*. London: Allen & Unwin.
Zussman, A. (2002). *The Rise of German Protectionism in the 1870s: A Macroeconomic Perspective*. Stanford Institute for Economic Policy Research, discussion paper 01-19.

CHAPTER 2

Metamorphoses of Liberalism in the Twentieth Century

2.1 Causes of New Thinking on Liberalism

If we distinguish two overwhelming themes of any economic doctrine—the production of wealth, and its distribution—the second theme strongly emerges in the twentieth century, and liberalism undergoes ample and profound metamorphoses.

The past century saw "always more widespread professions of liberalism",[1] but declaring oneself a "liberal" might hint at rather diverse visions. The issue of wealth distribution, and the connected theme of a wider role of the State in the economy, meant on one side moving towards ideas closer to statism and socialism—as in the case of liberal socialism, social market economy, even ordoliberalism[2]—ideas sometimes seen as a "third way", as an alternative between liberalism and socialism. On the other side, it meant a retrenching from the "cosmopolitanism" of classical thinkers—which had been a landmark of the nineteenth-century liberalism—towards a new relevance of the national interest.

The original version of this chapter was revised: An incorrect name in Chapter 2 has been updated. The correction to this chapter is available at https://doi.org/10.1007/978-3-030-53317-5_6

A. Roselli, *Economic Philosophies*,
Palgrave Studies in Classical Liberalism,
https://doi.org//10.1007/978-3-030-53317-5_2

These tendencies, however, did not exhaust the wide field of professions of liberalism, because, at the same time, a strong ideological component was also present in libertarian theories which affirmed the ethical value of reinstating the central position of the individual as economic agent.

The relations between different strands of thought became blurred. They made often hard to discover the underlying philosophy of an economic theory, and to assess to what extent liberalist, socialist and nationalistic views might converge in the same person; in addition, a writer's economic philosophy might change, and his economic theory might well be affected as a result.[3]

How can we summarize the attitude of a liberal mind in early twentieth century, as shaped by the classical and then neo-classical economic doctrines of the nineteenth century? Was there a common wisdom, or at least a prevailing opinion, of the liberal man at the turn of the century, as embodied in social, or even religious, conventions, and in economic theories focussed on the concept of man's individual utility? Keynes gives a good, and in a way humorous, *résumé* of this consensus, by observing, in 1926: "I trace the peculiar unity of the everyday political philosophy of the nineteenth century to the success with which it harmonised diversified and warring schools and united all good things to a single hand. Hume and Paley, Burke and Rousseau, Goodwin and Malthus, Cobbet and Huskisson, Bentham and Coleridge, Darwin and the Bishop of Oxford, were all, it was discovered, reaching practically the same thing – Individualism and laissez-faire…the company of the economists were there to prove that the least deviation into impiety [meaning a detachment from that consolidated wisdom] involved financial ruin. These reasons and this atmosphere are the explanations…why we feel such a strong bias in favour of laissez-faire and why State action to regulate the value of money, or the course of investment, or the population, provoke[s] such passionate suspicions in many upright breasts".[4]

Can we see that common wisdom, as exposed by Keynes, as a really liberal view? Or should liberalism have a wider conceptual space (ethical, political) and not be necessarily identified with the utility-driven economic liberalism that emerged from that approach? As we shall see, Keynes would explicitly affirm that economics is a moral science.[5] He found "repellent" the "mixture of Hegelian and biological language",[6] thus rejecting both any statist vision and the positivist attitude of neo-classical economists. The question came out from the discontent of several thinkers, and various factors contributed to a re-examination of the relation between liberalism and that individualistic view, as follows.

Political, Economic and Social Factors

Until Britain maintained its hegemonic position, a global or "cosmopolitan" vision prevailed, an essential part of the classical and neo-classical analysis. For a long while, the growth of nationalism, with the establishment and consolidation of often powerful states, and of socialism's international attractiveness, were not enough to challenge that pre-eminent intellectual and political position. Freedom of enterprise and freedom of exchange in competitive markets, and a set of institutions functional to that economic system, were the corollary of this vision.

But an increasing weight of Germany was emerging, defying Britain's supremacy. Germany positioned itself, at the same time, as the main political antagonist of Britain and the expression of economic philosophies, and economic policies, rather far from that liberal perspective prevailing in Britain. In the final decades of the nineteenth century, British intellectuals were warning their own country that national education and national discipline "in the Teutonic hearth of Europe" were creating a new power jealously defying the "ill-distributed wealth" of Britain.[7] As mentioned in the previous chapter, according to today's estimates, in the early years of the new century German GDP per capita climbed above the British. This sort of statistics was not available to the contemporaries, but they could see the success of German intellectual and political approaches, its growing weight in international economy, and Germany's reliance on a State centred vision over the cosmopolitan, individually focussed perspective. The Entente Cordiale between Britain and France (1904) can be seen in this light.

At the same time, a changing productive structure of the industrial countries, rather far from that existing in Adam Smith's Britain, made it difficult to put into practice a really free market, the pre-condition assumed by neo-classical economics for an unhindered competition. This evolving structure was indeed made of large industrial complexes and raised new issues affecting the concentration of economic power and the alteration of the price system. Hence, the need to put barriers to industrial cartels and monopolies. Competition could not be given for granted. As we have seen above (Chapter 1, Marshall in particular), the competition issue surfaces in the literature of neo-classical economists, but still in a cautious attitude, in the uncertainty that the freedom of the entrepreneur might be negatively affected.

"The system in which [the American people] had confidence—Herbert Stein writes with reference to his country's capitalism of the 1920s – was not the free-market system of atomistic competition, of the Invisible Hand. It was the business system, which is a different thing. It was a system, in which the benefits flowed from the character and wisdom of identifiable businessmen".[8]

In these new modes of production workers would become increasingly aware of their conditions, regarding not only their remuneration, but also their health and retirement needs, and try to attain social equality. Under the same roof of huge factories, workers lived in close proximity and were thus able to organize themselves into unions. Workers' unions increased their voices against "the capital". A more equal distribution of the industrial product would be reclaimed. The socialist vision was gaining ground, both in the Marxist version and in other not so extreme strands of thought. This was, for instance, the case of Britain, where shortly before the First World War, numerically significant groups of socialists gathered under the banner of the Fabian society.[9]

The War

The Great War gives a further, heavy blow to the liberal economic vision: we see interventions by the State in the economic life in order to finance the war effort and organize the whole society along with schemes functional to war purposes; obstacles to international trade are introduced; everywhere, an abnormal expansion of the money supply and inflation are registered and, as a consequence, gold standard—the monetary system as an emblem of the liberal society—is suspended in every country involved in the war, with the exception of the United States. But, not by chance, "suspension" was the word, because all governments had in mind, once the parenthesis of war would be closed, to restore the economic and monetary conditions that had previously prevailed, the freedom of exchange, the lost globalization.

Vain are however both winners' and losers' attempts, to go back to pre-war economic and social conditions. We shall not dwell on the political evolution of these post-war years. Enough is to remind few relevant developments. Not only the Russian Empire had totally disappeared from the concert of the great powers, but the Soviet State was proposing itself as a radical alternative to the liberal State and as a system of government that looked for a full enactment of that socialist philosophy we have described in the previous chapter, by turning upside down the pre-existing social arrangements, erecting itself as an antithesis to the liberal capitalistic order and finally establishing a proletarian order on a worldly basis.

Elsewhere, important changes were underway: the difficult industrial reconversion from war to peace, the lasting inflation, social unrest, partly related to the veterans' discontent and delusion, and also fuelled by socialist propaganda and by the observation of what was going on in Russia, war reparations hitting defeated Germany, the burden of inter-Allied debt weighting on public finances. All these factors made extremely hard any effort to go back to pre-war societal structures and economic and monetary arrangements. There was, in fact, a return to pre-war institutions, inclusive of a gold standard re-enactment, but this happened on the basis of exchange rates that did not reflect the economic and financial conditions of the respective countries, and however in a context of difficult social conditions which made hard any "playing by the rules", first of all the price and wage deflation necessary to make countries internationally competitive. During the 1920s, pre-war globalism leaned on fragile foundations.

International movements of merchandise and capital, encouraged by the precarious restoration of fixed exchange rates, favoured those economies which had exited the war in a better shape (the United States), or had been astute enough to go back to the gold standard with competitive exchange rates (France). To the economies more disadvantaged by the return of their currencies to the gold parity at unrealistic rates, sometimes encouraged by reasons of political prestige (see Mussolini's "quota 90"[10]), sticking to that parity meant a futile and costly exercise, not only in terms of output, but also in terms of domestic deflation and social unrest. What went under the name of "money war" represented a much deeper disturbance, it was evidence of disintegration of the international order, attested by the substantial failure of the League of Nations. Anti-globalism, in shapes strongly nationalistic and corporative, and socialism, took the upper hand.

All these factors created a favourable environment to the success of different economic theories, both relying on the overwhelming figure of the State: the ethical State at the root of nationalism, and the historical materialism of Marxist socialism leading to the proletarian State.

The Great Depression

The financial crash and the ensuing Great Depression were a further reason to rethink previous schemes of economic thought. Neo-classical economists, focussed on Walrasian theories of general equilibrium, had no key to put these events into their logical schemes, and their mostly monetary explanations of the crisis suffered irrelevance. The American economist Irving Fisher famously wrote on The New York Times, shortly before the crash, that the stock market had reached what looked like a "permanently high plateau"; and after the crash, he added that the slide was only temporary. The intellectual and political bewilderment that accompanied the crash, the output collapse and social suffering in several major economies, have been described at length elsewhere and here there is no need to spend further words on that.

The sense of crisis that the new century had brought, the economic and social turmoil connected with the First World War, had already made the previous century appear a long phase of tranquillity, economic and social stability, by then definitively lost. In this environment, the Great Depression was all the more noticed with a sense of unwelcome surprise because, as a matter of fact, it had followed almost a decade of economic growth and financial euphoria. It strengthened the search of new ways of dealing with these new challenges. Liberal thought needed a reassessment.

The Depression reinforced the attractiveness of ideologies well far from the liberal idea. On the one side, nationalistic countries found in these developments a confirmation of the necessity of a large role of the State in the economy, made politically easier by the very authoritarianism of their rulers. On the other side, the Soviet Union, and Marxian economists everywhere, could look with complacency at an apparently uninterrupted growth of its economy until the Second World War, blind to the horrors of its regime (see Chapter 3).

The awareness of these new conditions is well expressed by Basil Blackett, a director of the Bank of England and, at full title, a member of the British establishment, who observed, in 1931: "The spread of the technique of trade-union organization and side by side with it the increase of humanitarian and social conscience regarding problems of housing, health, sanitation, and working conditions generally, have rendered impossible or inadmissible many of those brutal economic adjustments which our grandfathers were able to regard as due to the intervention of a wise providence, which used enlightened self-interest and unregulated human competitiveness as its mysterious means to perform wonders in the cause of moral and material progress".[11]

Philosophical Developments: Ideal Historicism

In the first decades of the century, different visions of liberalism, till then focussed on economic factors, emerged: after Enlightenment, Historicism, Marxism and Positivism, new lines of liberal thought looked at the relation between Economics and Morality, as the "ideal historicism" of the Italian philosopher Benedetto Croce and his followers, as Robin G. Collingwood in Britain.

Regarding Economics and Morality, the problem of the relation between the Philosophy of economics and the Science of economics was put in radical, displacing terms by Croce in several works, the main one being published in 1908.[12] His approach to this issue should be put into the framework of his own philosophical system, which classifies both economics and morals within the same field of the "Philosophy of the Practical".[13]

In order to explain his system and how it is connected to economics, Croce goes back to the origin of the political economy in terms quite similar to Schumpeter's (see above, Chapter 1): it is in the eighteenth century that Scottish philosophers, as Hutcheson and Hume, wanted to "put their mouth" (*mettere bocca*) on economics and, in turn, economists didn't want to neglect issues related to ethics. Adam Smith, at the same time a philosopher and an economist, is the expression of this trend. However, over time, economists introduced the concept of utility as a matter of individual's "speculation", devoid of ethical content. The core of the disagreement, which we have mentioned above, was on the concept of "value": an objective concept, inspired by moral instances, with the former; and a subjective one, inspired by purely economic, to the extreme hedonistic, considerations, with the latter: a difference between "value as it is, and value as, in a certain way, it should be".[14]

With remarkable similarity of accents between him and twentieth-century Marxists (whose ideas on political economy will be dealt with in Chapter 3), Croce: (a) attacks the banalization of the concept of utility of neo-classical economists, (b) reduces the science of economics to their abstract schemes, and (c) believes that this specific—abstract and individually utilitarian—science of economics has nothing to do with any philosophical idea of utility.

To be clear on this point, it is to be stressed that Croce identifies economics with the neo-classical theories, and totally neglects other, alternative directions that were taken by the economic discipline, Keynesian economics, for instance. As a matter of fact, I have not found any evidence of Croce's reaction to Keynesian thought, in particular to Keynes' firm view that economics is "a moral science". It is a matter of speculation that Croce's reaction would have been very sympathetic.[15] This explains why many economists, even respectful of Croce as a philosopher and historian, have regretfully complained that Croce did not understand economics.

Only by confining economics into the boundaries of an individually utilitarian science it is possible to accept Croce's idea that economic and moral actions must be kept distinct: the first having to do with the egoistic pursuit of utility, as explained by neo-classical economists; and the second, with the pursuit of a superior level of "universal thought" ("utility", in philosophical terms).

What this "universal thought" means, Croce himself stresses that it does have no specific content[16]; for certain, it is not simply resolved in altruism, religious observance, or other similar concepts, neither is it confined to a generic "to do good", in the common sense of the word. It means, rather, to go beyond the egoistic purpose, and to behave in conformity with the general interest of the whole humanity, as emerging from the actual, historical circumstances of time and place under which the individual has to act (this is the "ideal historicism" of Croce's philosophy).

Abstract as this idea can be, it is better grasped if translated into concrete—Practical, if we like—terminology. Croce's approach, in that specific historical moment (that is, at the time of his writing, early twentieth century), can be seen as "political pedagogy, an attempt to educate the Italian ruling class to be up to the scratch with its duties", an invitation to look at a wider European context and abandon the then widespread nationalistic and colonial dreams. At the same time, Croce—an uncompromising anti-Marxist—looks at maintaining a balance between the contrasting interests of different social classes, not giving room to social revolutionary impulses.[17]

This is the core of liberalism in Croce's thought: historically determined intellectual schemes—also in the field of economics—must not be mistaken for insights of a universal, a-temporal validity. Here, any sympathy for the British economists of the Enlightenment—of the Classical School—ceases. He cannot accept the Ricardian scheme of ideas having validity "in all places and all times" (see above, Chapter 1).[18]

That is why Croce brings an attack on all the economic theories developed in the course of the previous century:

About the Classical School: "the empirical concepts of liberismo (liberism, as economic liberalism[19]) were raised to the level of natural laws. However, they were not of an absolute value, but just empirical, that is based on historical and contingent facts. The economists who formulated and supported those 'laws' defended, in the name of science, particular interests of certain social classes[20] (this looks like Marx)".

Regarding the German Historical School: "it was dreamed, especially by the German economists,...of an economic science founded on ethics", but the School makes a confusion of economic and ethical values, and in practice favours the interests of certain nations.[21]

And about neo-classical economists: "the application of mathematics to the economic science has been made similar to the application of mathematics to mechanics; and the *homo oeconomicus* has appeared totally similar to the 'material point' in mechanics"...The limit of this approach is in the fact that economics based on the concept of utility neglects qualitative distinctions, and cannot give any relevance to moral facts [meant in the Crocean sense as above explained]. The two orders of acts are, in the neo-classical scheme of "pure economics", undistinguished. Pure economics, working through mathematical language, has a sound foundation, if we put aside the fact that it does not consider even the smallest vestige of the concept of human action.[22] Croce adds: "[On the whole] the nature of economic discipline as a quantitative discipline...where the atomism of postulates and definitions cannot be overcome, does not allow its organic development from a superior principle, which only belongs to philosophy".[23]

Between the philosophy of economics and the economic science there cannot be disagreement, because they are heterogeneous concepts. Philosophy would commit an abuse if it invaded the field of economics. To mix the two—Croce thinks—gives origin to at least three errors: (1) to see economic calculus as the only able to give man all the truths which he needs: "to those most pure and mathematical economists – Croce writes ironically - I would like to say: please deliver yourself from the pains of philosophising: do calculate, do not think!"; (2) nationalism and economic liberalism are historical facts, not "laws", and economists who sustain the first or the second are not scientists, but politicians; (3) *homo oeconomicus*, builder of diagrams and calculator of levels of utility and curves of indifference, is believed to be a really existent animal, but the balance sheet of human life cannot be built as a profit/loss account, measured according to their intensity or duration. This generates "the fallacious belief that mathematical constructions and economic calculus are identified with [man's] real psyche or the Spirit".[24]

Croce, by identifying economics with the then prevailing neo-classical thinking, is led to a sceptical attitude towards the economic discipline in general: he observes the philosophical weakness of the principles adopted by these economists as foundation of their theories, and shows an attitude of superiority, cordially reciprocated by the economists with whom he had long and harsh debates, in particular with Pareto[25] and Einaudi, notwithstanding Einaudi's deferential and generous attitude towards the philosopher (see also Chapter 5).

If the economic act is dismissed simply as the result of individual egoism, and the economic discipline abstains from considering its wider and deeper social implications, the presence of any "vision" in setting the terms of the economic analysis is denied. This may explain the relatively minor role played by economic events in Croce's major historical works.

This long digression on the difficult, almost painful rapport between Croce and the economic discipline should help to define an approach to our theme of "economic philosophies" along few concepts:

1. any economic theory that aspires to climb above the level of "vulgar economics" needs to rest on postulates that are mostly of a non-economic character.
2. there is not a single, exclusive, correct vision underpinning economic theory, and there cannot be a single, superior economic theory as a consequence. Only a vision that responds to the advancement of the human spirit in a certain time and place is entitled to be defined as "liberal";
3. as a consequence, liberalism may comprehend diverse social and economic organizations, bodies of institutions, modes of productions, which are not necessarily valid "at all times and places" (to use, again, Ricardo's terminology, see Chapter 1), but related to the specific historical circumstances in which they arise and develop

(ready, so to speak, to be superseded by others when time is ripe for them).

4. the connection between ethical liberalism and economic liberalism has therefore only a historical character. The difficulty arises when economic liberalism claims for itself the value of supreme law of social life and insists on standing close by ethical liberalism, which, in turn, considers itself as supreme law of social life. "Two laws of equal standing and on the same matter are too many, one is redundant". Since ethical liberalism rejects any authoritarian regulation of the economic activity as a mortification of human inventiveness, it moves along the same line of economic liberalism. It is possible—Croce writes—that liberalism approves many economic liberalism's precepts, which have brought so many benefits to modern civilization; but this approval is given on ethical, not on economic ground. The issue before the liberal ideology—under certain times and places and in specific circumstances—is not to ascertain whether a certain economic measure is "liberistic",[26] but rather whether it is "liberal"; not whether it is quantitatively productive, but qualitatively valuable.[27]

The true liberal man, if we follow Croce's reasoning, has in mind a superior—"universal"—ethical value that, according to diverse historical circumstances, may subsume any economic theory that is the most appropriate to deal with the contingent situation that he has to face and resolve.[28]

Croce's intellectual approach is far from the economist's, but the philosophical questions that he raises respond to needs that are also relevant to the economic discipline.[29]

The affirmation of totalitarian States in the decades following the First World War, led Croce to new reflections on liberalism, its ethical foundation and its relation with the economic discipline. He gave evidence of what to be a liberal means in the specific political and economic circumstances of those years. In 1925, Croce observed: "It is with particular insistence that we hear in these days that the idea of liberalism is by now extinct, and that today's and tomorrow's world belongs to the opposition and fight between two fundamental trends, socialism and communism on one side, and reaction or fascism on the other".[30] Croce did not enter the domain of economics, but recognized that the superiority of the liberal idea was exactly in the "necessity to maintain, as far as possible, a free playing field to the spontaneous and inventive forces of individuals and social groups, because only from these forces one can expect any mental, moral and economic progress". And he added, to confirm liberalism as an ethical idea that is above any political, economic or institutional arrangement: "To a truly conscious liberal it sounds impossible to adhere to authoritarian and reactionary, or communist ideals, because liberalism includes all of them, within their acceptable limits".[31]

Worthwhile stressing again that, according to him, liberalism, as an ethical idea, is to be identified with the dialectic evolution of human history itself: dialectic, because capable to include the diverse organizations of the economy, politics, law. Liberalism can well accept different and changeable organizations of ownership and production. Liberalism tout court and economic liberalism, or "liberism", can well coexist, but their connection is of a relative, historical nature. Economic liberalism cannot be seen as a supreme rule of life; on the contrary, we can speak of a "liberal socialism", when measures which the economic doctrine qualifies as "socialist" are coherent with the liberal vision, defined as above. This is the meaning of the sentence of Croce—who was however severely anti-Marxist—according to which "Marx is correct when he strongly brings to our attention the social conditionality of profit: ' how much blood, how many tears yet drip from it'"[32] ["*di che lacrime grondi e di che sangue*"].[33]

Sections 2–5 of this chapter deal with shapes of liberalism that emphasize the ethical content of the idea, and take a critical stand against laissez-faire. Sections 6 and 7 focus on the explicitly libertarian aspect of liberalism; taking however a distance from the positivist, natural-science related doctrine of the neo-classical economists, these thinkers stress the moral value of economic individualism. Section 8 is devoted to that peculiar form of liberalism that is the—mostly German—ordoliberalism.

2.2 Rathenau's Statism Versus Einaudi's "Liberism"

With war still going on, a singular industrialist, statesman and intellectual from Germany, Walther Rathenau, observed that "Of the largest world economic catastrophe in history we cannot get rid through the stained financial arrangements and the old atonement devices as loans, duties and monopolies".[34] Therefore we should not step back from "interfering into industrial freedom and personal rights, from State's collaboration and social equality, even from social and geographical upheavals". Rathenau was critical of the liberal economic system, and relied on the experience of the planned war economy, that is on "the system of State's economic discipline". He noted critically that the liberals wanted to abolish that "economic discipline" once the war would be over so that "the economic liberty and super-liberty might be restored, sometimes relying on private enterprise's needs to find directions for our collective life".[35] He was instead looking for specialization and productive coordination, which could abolish duplications and waste in the production of the same merchandise, phase out unrestrained competition, harbinger of useless expenses "to attract customers".[36] "It is not true – Rathenau wrote – that a desperate anxiety for being competitive makes us stronger... [S]ince, in the following year, the defeated will anxiously try to beat the winner, it would be better for them to reach an agreement, rather than fight each other on our shoulders the struggle for supremacy in being capable and inventive".[37] He also believed in protectionism in commodities trade, and in import quotas. His programme should have been enacted through unions of professions and industrial unions, which must be corporations recognized and supervised by the State with extensive powers of intervention.[38] "Somebody will say – Rathenau added – that these are the old guilds and the old corporations of arts and crafts!" Not at all, he replied. Unions are a "collective" of production, "where all members are organically bound together...linked in a living unit...not a confederation but an organism".[39] And yet "The new economy will not be a State economy, but a private economy subject to the judgement of the public authorities, a private economy...that will need State's collaboration".[40] What we have here with Rathenau is a pro-State, protectionist and corporativist vision, which is the antithesis of liberal thought. As will be easily observed, his philosophy is similar to List's (see Chapter 1), and to the nascent Italian corporativism (see Chapter 3).

It is not therefore by chance that a ferocious criticism of Rathenau's book can be found in the review written soon after its publication by the liberal economist Luigi Einaudi. Referring to Rathenau's book, he rejected the idea that the ongoing war was "the bonfire of the old economic world", observing that Rathenau's thought was "unclear, vague, indefinite". "The current war – Einaudi writes – is not different from so many other wars, barring the adoption of new techniques,...and its consequences shall be similar...Rathenau's culture is not really deep, he needs to believe in a word regeneration...and he thinks to be the prophet of this new economic order". Einaudi's liberalism cannot accept the creation, under State's guidance, of professional and industrial unions, or cartels. "The will to operate according to one's own duty, to act wisely, to acquire wealth and not simply to consume, cannot be taught by unions of industrialists and enterprises, consortia and other similar devices".[41]

The main points of Einaudi's economic vision can be summarized as follows:

an economic system based on the free struggle of economic agents;
the moral component of this struggle;
the role of the State in allowing that this struggle develops in fairness, through absence of interference but insuring equality of opportunities for all the players;
a public finance designed to make the State as a factor of production.

As we shall see, Einaudi's liberalism is rather close to Hayek's, in his insistence on the ethical value of the individual freedom, and to ordoliberals', in stressing the strong role of the State.

We may consider separately the points of his economic philosophy.

Regarding the first point, Einaudi can be seen as belonging to the stream of economists adhering to the neo-classical marginalist revolution and, actually, he does not bring relevant theoretical contributions to that logical scheme, but his interest is not so much in the level of equilibrium reached by an economy operating in a regime of free competition, as in the way the economic equilibrium is reached.[42] He observes that the Walrasian general equilibrium of the economic system cannot be the result of the spontaneous working of economic agents, whose interaction has a mechanical explanation, mathematically expressed, but is reached through an unending struggle of those economic agents, individuals and firms.

The second point means that this struggle has a moral meaning, is seen as expression of freedom. To give examples, with reference to the conflicting forces of workers and entrepreneurs, Einaudi writes: "An industrialist is liberal if he believes in his own spirit of initiative...he is socialist when he asks protective duties by the State. A worker is liberal if he joins his fellow workers to create a common instrument of cooperation or defence; he is socialist if he invokes from the State an exclusive privilege to protect his organization, or calls for a law or court judgement to prohibit strike-breakers to works...Liberal is he who believes in material or moral improvement achieved through voluntary effort, sacrifice and willingness to work in harmony with others; socialist is he who desires to impose improvement through force".[43] Therefore, he favours freely created unions as an instrument of that struggle, but strongly rejects subsidies or protection accorded by the State to one or the other side of the struggle. This ethical aspect of free competition approaches Einaudi's thinking to Adam Smith's Classical School; his *Weltanshauung* cannot be flattened on the "scientific" approach that keeps ethics out of economics.

Third point: Einaudi is aware of the central, if quantitatively limited, role of the State in the economy. To this purpose, the State itself has to be attuned to the free economic system: it cannot be an authoritarian entity. We have here a reversal of Croce's scheme: according to Croce, a liberal State can be compatible with economic systems not necessarily to be identified with economic liberalism. According to Einaudi, the liberal idea is surely ethical, but one single idea, because a distinction between ethical and economic liberalism cannot be done, they are exactly the same concept: this is the main point of contrast with Croce.

State's role is not only of non-interference in the struggle, but also to preserve and enhance fair competition. Regarding the market, State intervention will firstly consist of fighting private monopolies, and transforming natural monopolies into public utilities. Regarding the economic agents, the State has a pro-active role, which is another aspect of the vision of liberalism as a struggle: as a liberal, Einaudi cannot accept the concept of agents' absolute equality (it is clear that he is closer to Adam Smith's Moderate vision, than to the egalitarian vision of the French Radical Enlightenment); but he thinks that a State's priority is to insure equality at the start, that is in terms of opportunities which any person should be provided with. Only this sort of equality may allow a struggle to be fought along fair terms. It means "lowering the peaks" by progressive taxation, and "raising the lows" by social legislation, concerning minimum wage, limits to working times, prohibition of children's work, protection extended to non-unionized workers, insurance against accidents at work, disability and retirement pensions. This social legislation, far from being in contradiction with the liberal State, is the precondition to be closer to that abstract hypothesis of free competition which is the main focus of liberal economic thinking.[44]

Einaudi's approach seems here to be close to the ordoliberal thinking, maturing exactly in that period in Germany. Ordoliberals thought that, in order to attain that abstract scheme of free competition, effective market competition, far from being identified with laissez-faire, requires a set of rules aimed at placing individuals and firms on the same level in terms of opportunities to compete.

The fourth point is the stress put by Einaudi on the State's role as an economic entity itself, whose activity is examined as both a productive agent, a producer of collective goods, as well as an optimizing agent, aimed at revenue maximization.[45] His assumption is that public finance theories should use the analytical tools familiar in the study of the working of the private sector.[46] He is one of the main exponents of a group that created an "Italian Fiscalist School" on public finance. Their research contributed to the growth of this discipline as a branch of economics, far from a pure accountancy approach, Public finance took since different roads. On the one hand, Keynesian economists looked at the problem from a different perspective, and with different outcomes, being based on a strong pro-active intervention of the State in shaping the economy (the "functional" public finance, quite far from Einaudi's "liberist" view (see Sect. 5 in this chapter). On the other hand, also Buchanan's libertarian theory of "public choice", based on a very limited role of the State, has been seen as closely connected to the Italian School (see Chapter 4).

2.3 Pigou's Doubts

The adoption of an ethical concept of liberalism is, indeed, necessary in order to bring under its widespread wings the theories of economists which give the State a further, central role in shaping the economic system. This role may have different accents and dimensions: it can be related to an alignment of private and social costs in the production of goods and services through taxation (as in Pigou), to macroeconomic management (Keynes), to an ample provision of services through public expenditure (Beveridge), Essentially, the State puts a remedy to market failures, without its necessary involvement in the ownership of means of production, the essence of socialism. It is preferable the experience of central planning in what remains a capitalistic society, as in 1930s Britain, to real socialism of Soviet Russia (Pigou); demand management does not imply nationalizations (Keynes); the necessity of socialism—as government ownership of capital—has yet to be demonstrated (Beveridge). These three thinkers are remarkable examples of the metamorphosis of an idea that remains, essentially, a liberal idea.

There can be a certain reluctance to include Arthur C. Pigou in the list of liberal thinkers of the twentieth century. On the one side, he is alien to any speculation of social philosophy and stresses that his research is essentially practical: his impulse is not a philosophical impulse, "the knowledge for the sake of knowledge... On what philosophical basis generalisations of this sort [the laws of economic science] rest, we are not here concerned to inquire". The reason of the economist's investigation is "the study of men's social behaviour [as leading to] practical results of social improvement", under certain economic circumstances. One is almost tempted to set aside Pigou when dealing with "economic philosophies". In addition, he "sets out the argument of his *Economics of Welfare* in terms of exceptions to the rule that laissez-faire ensures maximum satisfaction; he did not question the rule".[47]

On the other side, however, he is fully immersed in that stream of thought which is dissatisfied with resting on the orthodox neo-classical schemes that prevail in his research environment. His practical realism makes him diffident of any abstract, pure, "scientific" mathematical scheme.

From this perspective, Pigou "help[ed] economists turn nettlesome political controversies into technical problems". He—and Keynes—"established economists as a toolkit to be used by policymakers and pioneered the role of government economic advisers".[48]

At Cambridge, where he takes the chair of political economy that belonged to Alfred Marshall—in an apparent continuity of men and doctrines—his realistic approach leads him to look at an "economic welfare" with different eyes from the utilitarianism of those schemes. As Keynes, in fact Pigou distances himself from the economy of laissez-faire. In *The Economics of Welfare* of 1920—his magnum opus—he shows some scepticism in the optimistic assumption according to which "if only Government refrains from interference, will automatically cause the land, capital and labour of any country to be so distributed as to yield a larger output and, therefore, more economic welfare than could be attained by any arrangement other than that which comes 'naturally'"[49]. Even if Smith himself qualified this natural freedom by admitting State action to limited extents, he stopped short from realizing that—Pigou writes[50]—"the working of the self-interest is generally beneficent, not because of some natural coincidence between the self-interest of each and the good of all, but because human institutions are arranged so as to compel self-interest to work in directions in which it will be beneficent".[51]

The editors of the 2013 Palgrave edition of *The Economics of Welfare*[52] point out that it is incorrect to assume this book as the intellectual inspiration for the British Welfare State, as it was established after the Second World War.[53] In this regard, there is no question that Beveridge should be seen as its main begetter. But that reference to "human institutions" acting beneficially is an opening to the relevance that should be given to the public interest, which corrects the individual's self-interest. What these institutions do (or should do)?

The economic welfare is related by Pigou to the concept of "national dividend", by which he means the total of "objective services, some of which are provided in form of commodities, others in direct form", made available to the public. It is the volume of current net output: the net addition to the resources of the community available for consumption or for retention of capital stock, after allowing for the wastage of the stock of real capital existing at the beginning of each period.[54]

The provision of these services is, however, altered by costs (or benefits) that are not reflected in their price. The specific demand and supply curves of any commodity or service—on which the neo-classical economists' attention was focussed—cannot reflect those costs (or benefits). Here is his detachment from his master, Marshall, and the lasting contribution of his "practical" approach: what is now seen as Pigou's extraordinary actuality is his theory of external costs and benefits caused by economic activity.[55] These "externalities" alter the cost/profit relation, seen in a private perspective only.[56] The total value of a merchandise or a service must be broken down into two components: private value and social value.[57] In this way, we abandon the concept of value as related to a specific good and to a single economic agent, the social value must be related to an entire community. The social value measures the cost/benefit generated by the enterprise outside itself [the typical example in today's discourse is the pollution from factories or, if we so prefer, industry's induced climate change. On the other side, new digital goods, as search engines on internet, have a huge and unmeasured benefits to consumers, a consumer surplus[58]]. If the externality is a cost, the enterprise's production is higher than what it would be if that external cost were internalized; the contrary happens if the externality is a benefit (the production is less than otherwise). This internalization, in both cases, would align the private and social values of the production. In the presence of externalities, the best way to mitigate differences between private and social values, is for the State to use "coercive legal devices for directing self-interest into social channels": to give incentives to reduce/to increase the interested activities, and the most obvious form is that of taxation/subsidies.[59] As we shall see (Chapter 4), James Buchanan will face the same problem in a different, individualistic perspective: for example, the choice between pollution and economic growth on the one hand, and a cleaner environment on the other, should be demanded exclusively to the individual consensus, not to the State.

If we think of the overwhelming importance of environment-related issues in today's world, Pigou's contribution cannot be underestimated.

Importantly, even if economic welfare (which is "economic" because it can be measured by a money rod) does not coincide with the more general welfare, which is made also of non-economic components, it is conducive—on a judgement of probability—to enhance the latter. Notwithstanding the reluctance of Pigou to enter the philosophical/institutional side, the inference that can be made out of this connection is that political and economic institutions coherent with the general welfare should also be coherent with the economic welfare (even though Pigou writes that his realistic approach is a positive science of what is and tends to be, not a normative one, of what ought to be.[60] The economist does not "stand advocate for or against any political programme". One could add that Pigou's standpoint is an evidence of the reluctance of some economists to see themselves as "normative economists" rather than "positive scientists").

The veil of economics is therefore particularly thick in Pigou's economics. But his philosophy openly emerges in *Socialism versus Capitalism*.[61] Which of these two political systems is more conducive to the equalization of products' social and private values? He starts with his usual caveat: "It is not the business of an academic economist, nor it is within his competence, to stand advocate for or against any political programme. But it is his business, and it should be within his competence, to set out in an orderly way the dominant considerations, so far as they are economic, which are relevant to the argument".[62] The reader will not find anything doctrinaire in his book: Marxist dialectic materialism or unavoidability of social classes' conflict. There are only practical questions: of wealth and income distribution, particularly in presence of "a class that lives by owning, who not only need do no work, but who in fact do none…the spectacle of this class is repulsive to persons of public spirit"[63]; and of the efficient allocation of resources between different sectors of production. Is socialism necessary to reduce inequalities and inefficiencies?

He put the issue in the context of British politics. On distribution, he notes that if socialism were introduced by confiscation of the means of production, the State could secure a great part of income largely flowing now to the rich, and retain or redistribute it among the poor, and inequality would be reduced. But if the British Labour party decided to purchase those means at a fair value, socialism would have no effect whatsoever; simply, shareholders would become rentiers.[64] Taxation—mainly through inheritance wealth tax and highly progressive income tax—would then be the instrument of redistribution; it would however be hampered by the fear to damage capital accumulation. Only a confiscatory socialism would be the only effective remedy to redress income and wealth.

On the efficient allocation of resources, Pigou uses his concept of externalities: he notes that, under capitalism, cost externalities, whereby employers throw part of their costs upon outsiders, allow them to produce more than they would if these costs were internalized: the social cost is not a burden to the employer. But, in practice, the assessment of this cost and of the consequent taxation is difficult, and a central planning authority wouldn't have a comparative advantage in this regard.

In conclusion—Pigou says—a vague concept of socialism is to be preferred to capitalism; but again in a pragmatic way, if we take as socialism the system of today's Russia, and as capitalism the British system, where capitalism coexists with socialist central planning, the latter is preferable, however—he adds—with an extensive use of taxation and a nationalization of large sectors of the British industry (the Bank of England included, as it was, in 1946).

2.4 Keynes' Liberalism

The small book *Economic Philosophy*, by Joan Robinson,[65] is an excellent summary of the ideological premises of economic liberalism in the nineteenth century, thus setting the stage for the new "rules of the game" as envisaged by the "Keynesian revolution". "The General Theory brought out into the open the problem of choice and judgement that the neoclassical economists had managed to smother. The ideology to end all ideologies broke down. Economics once more became Political Economy"[66]... "Keynes brought back the moral problem into economics by destroying the neo-classical reconciliation of private egoism and public service".[67]

As a matter of fact, it is clear that, for Keynes, the ethical aspect is central to the economic discipline, and this is sufficient to keep it separate from natural sciences. In a letter to Roy Harrod, he points out that "In chemistry and physics and other natural sciences the object of experiment is to fill in the actual values of the various quantities and factors appearing in an equation or a formula; and the work when done is once and for all. In economics this is not the case and to convert a model into a quantitative formula is to destroy its usefulness as an instrument of thought…the pseudo-analogy with the physical sciences leads directly counter to the habit of mind which is most important for an economist proper to acquire …it deals with introspection and with values…with motives, expectations, psychological uncertainty". And the example of the falling apple follows: "It is as though the fall of the apple to the ground depends on the apple's motives, on whether it is worth while falling to the ground, and whether the ground wanted the apple to fall, and on mistaken calculations on the part of the apple as to how far it was from the centre of the earth".[68]

It is interesting to observe that Keynes' "early beliefs", back to his university years, already show an "escape from the Benthamite tradition…it was this escape from Bentham, joined with the unsurpassable individualism of our philosophy, which has served to protect the whole lot of us from the final reduction ad absurdum of Benthamism known as Marxism"[69]): a gradual detachment from the dominant economic thought that would lead him to ask, well before his *General Theory*, whether he himself could be qualified as a "liberal".[70]

In a not often quoted article of 1933,[71] Keynes writes: "I was brought up, like most Englishmen, to respect free trade not only as an economic doctrine which a rational and instructed person could not doubt, but almost as a part of the moral law…Yet the orientation of my mind is changed [and] my background of economic theory is modified". So—he writes—protectionism of the nineteenth century is not to be seen as a blot upon the efficiency and good sense (looks like List). Many countries (Russia, Italy, Germany and in part the United States and Great Britain) are embarking on a variety of politico-economic experiments that go beyond profit's maximization as a guide to investment decisions. National self-sufficiency is revalued and, with it, tariff protection to lift unemployment and capital controls in order to avoid that a too high interest rate to attract foreign investments goes to the detriment of domestic policies. Old liberals thought to serve not only the survival of the fittest, but also "the great cause of peace, the glorious fertility of the untrammelled mind against the forces of privilege and monopoly and obsolescence". Keynes looks rather with some sympathy to the new economic experiments, to economic nationalism, to self-sufficiency, even though he sees three dangers: the Silliness of the doctrinaire ("Mussolini perhaps is acquiring wisdom teeth"), Haste, Intolerance. There is a clear danger, or almost certainty, that these economies cannot connect to the liberal idea, that is the difficulty to accept their policies without a conversion to authoritarianism.

Regarding competition, Keynes' critical view had already been expressed in *The End of Laissez-Faire*: Competition as "a state of affairs where the ideal distribution of productive resources can be brought about through individuals acting independently by the method of trial and error in such a way that those individuals who move in the right direction will destroy by competition those who move in the wrong direction...It is a method of bringing the most successful profit-makers to the top by a ruthless struggle of survival, which selects the most efficient by the bankruptcy of the less efficient"[72] (This sounds like Rathenau, or Schumpeter.[73])

Those new ideas not only took root in countries that were moving to openly authoritarian regimes, but also—as Keynes noted in his article—had an influence in countries of well established liberal tradition. Regarding trade, United States' protectionism was not new, however. The country had grown very fast between the end of the Civil War and 1917 with the help of stringent tariffs. The attraction of isolationism, after the First World War, was strong. The introduction of the Smoot Hawley Tariff in 1930 erected important barriers to imports, a strong trade surplus notwithstanding. Regarding money, a very tight monetary stance by the Federal Reserve encouraged huge capital inflows, however sterilized by the central bank with a policy of "managed money" that was in contrast with the "rule of the game" that the gold standard required for large surplus countries. The abandonment of its gold parity by the British pound in 1931, and then by the US dollar in 1933, marked the prevalence of nationalistic interests and the critical point of the gold standard collapse. The United Kingdom adopted the Imperial Preference in 1932.

In front of massive economic disruptions and unemployment, and of heavy attacks to the liberal economic philosophy, the reactions of the economic discipline were twofold: on the one side, the primary cause was seen in an insufficient demand for goods and services that the economic system is able to produce, and therefore in a "market failure"; on the opposite side, externalities, price rigidities were blamed as an impediment to an otherwise efficient market to work properly. The former causation is the substance of the macroeconomic, Keynesian "revolution"; the latter stays behind a number of explanations that, beyond the neo-classical theories, explore new ways of a strict economic liberalism.

Keynes has nothing to object to the classical theory, within its own limits: "Regarded as the theory of individual firm and of the distribution of product of a given quantity of resources, the classical theory has made a contribution to economic thinking which cannot be impugned".[74] But Keynes wants to go beyond those limits, and his General Theory (1936) is important, first and foremost, for the qualitative jump it makes in respect to the then prevailing economic theories, in particular to the neo-classical theory.

We have mentioned earlier the two main neo-classical approaches (Walrasian and Marshallian) to the definition of an economic equilibrium, the former focussed on the overall economic system, the latter on many individual markets. Both show that total output results from the interaction of individual agents, moved by their marginal utilities and costs. Keynes shifts from an individually centred analysis to the aggregate behaviour of groups of economic agents (consumers, investors, rentiers...), whose demand is unrelated to individual utility functions. "It is the replacement of price determination as the essential task of economics, by the previously non-existent task of determining the level of aggregate demand".[75] Keynes' aggregate approach takes the place of a summative approach, to define the new object of economics. The "sciencelike", "pure", economics (based on marginal utility, mathematically measured) is lost. It will be reminded that, according to Ysidro Edgeworth, the neo-classical economist, "the Utilitarian principle that policy should be directed to the greatest good for the greatest number requires the summation of the happiness of separate individuals".[76]

Macroeconomic theory is the branch of the economic discipline that analyses the whole economic system, as an entity which is different from the total sum of its single components. The invention of macroeconomics requires inserting society and its structure into the study of economics: a conviction shared by both Marx and Keynes.[77]

Ours is not a history of economic thought, our interest is focussed on which social philosophy Keynes' thinking rests. On this issue, Keynes was not explicit, and this can explain why he is still regarded, according to a view, as a reluctant collectivist, or as a socialist liberal according to others, or yet in other ways.[78] It is from his analysis as an economist that Keynes derives elements of his social philosophy, and this happens only in the final chapter of his *General Theory*.[79] It is therefore necessary to spend some words on the main features of his theory.[80]

The main problems of the society we live in are—according to Keynes—the inability to assure full employment and the inequality in wealth and income distribution.[81] Keynes therefore impinges upon the two fundamental issues of the economic discipline in the twentieth century: the production and distribution of a given output, with a new emphasis on the second. Regarding employment, Keynes writes that it depends on the proceeds which the entrepreneur expects to receive from the production output, which he seeks to maximize in respect to his costs. He therefore increases production and employment only up to the extent that the costs increase is more than balanced by a higher consumer demand. Classical economists think that the consumer demand is necessarily equal to the income received by the factors of production employed by the entrepreneur, so that production and employment can expand *pari passu* up to reaching a situation of full employment. But—Keynes observes—not all the output is consumed (the propensity to consume is lower than "one"). A growth in employment can occur only when the amount of investments can absorb the excess of what is produced over what the community decides to consume.

The demand for investments by the entrepreneur is not added to consumer demand in such a way that full employment is automatically assured. The demand for investment depends: (1) On the yield expected from the investment; (2) On its cost, that is on the rate of interest. The lower is the expected yield, and the higher the interest rate, the smaller will be the demand for investments. This can well stabilize at a level that is lower than what is coherent with full employment. The aggregate demand, for consumption and investment, associated with full employment is therefore "a special case, only realized when the propensity to consume and the inducement to invest stand in a particular relation to one another", either by accident or by design. It is a duty of the State to act in a way that this happens by design, if that "accident" does not occur. Government initiative may influence consumption and investment by taxation and the interest rate.

The other face of the problem is social inequality, "the paradox of poverty in the midst of plenty".[82] It is related to the different propensity to consume among different social classes: this propensity decreases with increasing income and wealth. The rich spend relatively less in consumer goods. Particularly in a society that is already rich, that already has a large stock of wealth available, that propensity is relatively weak, and the weakness of consumer demand is an inducement to reduce the demand for investments: the aggregate demand (for consumption and investment) is consequently low, and a reduction of production and employment will follow. In summary, investment and employment's growth does not depend on a low propensity to consume ("far from being dependent on the abstinence of the rich"), that is on higher savings, as classical economists explained, it is hindered by that. Until full employment is reached, an increase in the propensity to consume is an incentive to investment growth.

In the final chapter of his *General Theory* Keynes moves to his "notes of social philosophy". The first inference from his theory is related to inequality. This has been tackled through the scheme of direct taxation, which has however found severe limits in tax evasion and above all in the opinion—wrong, as seen above—that a high taxation discourages savings accumulation that is deemed necessary to promote investments. "The growth of wealth, so far from being dependent on the abstinence of the rich, as is commonly supposed, is more likely to be impeded by it".[83]

His note of social philosophy is: "I believe that there is social and psychological justification for significant inequalities of incomes and wealth, but not for such large disparities as exist today. There are valuable human activities which require the motive of money-making and the environment of private wealth ownership for their full function....It is better that a man should tyrannise over his bank balance than over his fellow-citizens...But it is not necessary for the stimulation of these activities...that the game should be played for such high stakes as at present. Much lower stakes will serve the purpose equally well, as soon as the players are accustomed to them".[84]

The second important inference, also having consequences on wealth distribution, regards the rate of interest. It is not correct to think that a high rate is conducive to higher investments through higher savings. Since interest is a factor of cost for the entrepreneur, additional amounts of investment will be realized until the marginal efficiency of capital—defined as the expected yield of additional capital—is equal to the market rate of interest.[85] It follows that this rate should be lowered up to the point where the expected yield implies a level of investment coherent with full employment. At that point, the expected yield will be so low as to cover little more than capital instruments' wastage and obsolescence, and "some margin to cover risk and the exercise of skill and judgement". The social consequence of low interest rates is related to their effects on the investors. The rich who enjoyed high returns from their savings will be deprived of such rent, that is of an income not gained by risk investments or by their work: "The euthanasia of the rentier". "I see the rentier aspect of capitalism as a transitional phase which will disappear when it has done its work".[86]

In Keynes' economic theory the determinants of the economic system are not savings and investment (as the classical theory suggested), but the propensity to consume, the marginal efficiency of capital and the rate of interest.[87] His economic philosophy implies government intervention in fields till then left mainly to private initiative, and an enlargement of State's traditional functions, in particular to increase the aggregate demand (by influence on the propensity to consume and to invest) and to lower the rate of interest, in order to make them compatible with the goal of full employment. On the other side, Keynes' aim is to safeguard the advantages of individualism, of the economic efficiency based on decentralization of decisions and private interests' interplay, provided that these advantages are contained within the above mentioned limits. In fact, when, thanks to those "central controls", the economy is close to full employment, the classical theory becomes applicable. This libertarian individualism remains important: "The authoritarian state systems of to-day seem to solve the problems of unemployment at the expense of efficiency and freedom".[88] And, with reference to investments, it is important that government intervention addresses the volume of investments, not their direction (which is up to the private initiative to decide:

"there are, of course, errors of foresight; but these would not be avoided by centralising decisions".[89])

Even recently, Keynes has been labelled as "planner".[90] Considering his philosophy as here described, this label is incorrect. An aggregate demand with full employment does not imply either nationalizations, nor production directions towards specific goods and services, nor fixing prices outside market schemes. In the *General Theory* are resolved his own perplexities as expressed in his 1933 article: the expansion of the State's role doesn't reach collectivism or planning; and he defends individual choices in the name of efficiency and rejects authoritarianism in the name of freedom. Are we far, perhaps, from the Croce's sentence, above mentioned, that "To a truly conscious liberal it sounds impossible to adhere to authoritarian and reactionary, or communist ideals, because liberalism includes all of them, within their acceptable limits"?

An aspect of Keynesian thinking that deserves particular attention is related to international relations. He is today remembered as one of the promoters of international cooperation, organized under the Bretton Woods System's banner. But it is necessary to mention a nationalistic attitude, as a reaction to the collapsing international order of the gold standard, an attitude that stresses the reactive capacity of his own country to the Great Depression and even approaches him to mercantilist ideas. There is an aspect, not emphasized, in Keynes' vision: his accent on the domestic character of his proposals, which is complementary to his refusal of the gold standard. It is not by chance that, in chapter 23 of the *General Theory* titled Notes on Mercantilism, he recalls, in analogy to what Friedrich List had written one century before, four points: (1) "Mercantilist thought never supposed that there was a self-adjusting tendency by which the rate of interest would be established at the appropriate level, rather thinking that an unduly high rate of interest was the main obstacle to the growth of wealth"; (2) "The mercantilists were aware of the fallacy of cheapness and the danger that excessive competition may turn the terms of trade against a country", hence the protection of the domestic market; (3) "The desire of the individual to augment his personal wealth by abstaining from consumption has usually been stronger than the inducement to the entrepreneur to augment the national wealth by employing labour on the construction of durable assets", hence the necessity to lower the interest rate; (4)

mercantilists were aware that protectionism might bring to war, but—Keynes writes—"their realism is much preferable to the confused thinking of contemporary advocates of an internationally fixed gold standard and laissez-faire in international lending, who believe that it is precisely these policies which will best promote peace".[91]

Keynes, in summary, is not hesitant in criticizing the "faulty theories" of the City of London, when they think that in order to maintain the rigid parity of foreign exchanges—that is, in order to maintain the equilibrium of the foreign accounts—the "bank rate", if necessary, has to be adjusted upwards, to levels totally inconsistent with full employment.[92] The gold standard supporters were unmoved. "But Mr Keynes would not even insist on a stabilization of the foreign exchanges. If he had to choose between a fluctuation in the price level and a fluctuation in the foreign exchanges, he would choose the latter".[93]

However, the cohabitation of international liberalism and national interest had not been a problem until Britain had been the conductor of the international orchestra, but things changed when the baton passed to American hands. Only during the Second World War Keynes moved towards the idea of a multilateral clearing union that would overcome the difficulties and complications of a large number of bilateral agreements (with Britain at the centre of her Empire); would have a supra national institution as the central clearing house; would be based on a new international monetary unit—the "bancor", to be issued by the clearing house to member countries against payment of quotas in gold and national currencies. This scheme would clash at Bretton Woods with the dollar-centred policies of the American Dexter White, who—as we know—ended up being the winner.[94] As we know, no international monetary unit was created, the dollar took the place as the main reserve currency, and the Bretton Woods system remained inherently unstable. The surplus, and then the debit, position of the hegemonic country, the United States, had as a consequence scarcity, and then excess, of international liquidity, and transmitted deflationary, and then inflationary, pressures on the rest of the world, until its demise in 1971.

These considerations show how feeble the border is between a vision based on a global liberalism and another based on the national interest, and how a liberal may find it difficult to reconcile the two visions under diverse circumstances. In our case, the awareness, matured after the First War, that the hegemonic role of Britain had inexorably come to an end, pushed Keynes to elaborate a system of international cooperation that might counterbalance the incoming American hegemony.

2.5 Beveridge's Welfare State

Still more than in Keynes', it's in Beveridge's works that a wider vision of the State's role is pursued. It is immediately clear that Beveridge's attention goes beyond the boundaries of economics and touches essential features of a liberal State. The goal of full employment is to be accompanied by the condition that all essential liberties are preserved, and only a democratic government can maintain and defend what he considers as citizens' essential liberties: freedom of writing, study and teaching; freedom of assembly for political and other purposes; freedom in choice of occupation; and freedom in the management of the personal income. It is the duty of the State to implement them. Therefore, this long list means excluding any totalitarian solution of full employment in a society completely planned and regimented by an "irremovable dictator": the necessity of socialism has yet to be demonstrated, Beveridge says. But, meaningfully, he does not include, in these essential liberties, that of private ownership of means of production: if experience showed that the abolition of private ownership is necessary for full employment, this abolition would have to be undertaken.[95] A liberal State would not be necessarily in conflict with a publicly owned productive structure (we may remember at this point Croce's ethical liberalism, and the non-necessary coincidence of economic and ethical liberalism).

In order to make those liberties effective—not a simple declaration of intent—the State has to provide not only well established public services as defence or police or justice, but also other services as free education, social security, national health service, infrastructures.[96]

Public finance, according to Beveridge, has a variety of sub-functions: to generate a distortion of resources for satisfaction of public wants (an objective recognized also by classical economists, but widened by Beveridge by enlarging the list of services that it's up to the State to provide); to correct the distribution of income and wealth; to use the fiscal instrument for income stabilization and growth: the distributional aspect seems to take priority over growth (this is the so-called "functional finance", see below). Even an unproductive public expenditure, which however generates employment, is preferable to a workforce obliged to idleness. It belongs to Beveridge the sentence, sometimes attributed to

Keynes, that "it is better to employ people on digging holes and filling them up again, than not to employ them at all".[97]

So far—Beveridge observes—two main principles have governed the State budget: to keep State expenditure down to the minimum necessary to meet inescapable needs, and to balance every year revenues and outlays. For the accomplishment of those wider objectives of insuring satisfaction of public wants in a framework of full employment, Beveridge thinks that public budget should be construed by determining "not merely the revenue and expenditure of government, but the estimated income and outlays of the nation as a whole".[98] Beveridge is a Keynesian, because according to both the State is the ultimate responsible for the level of total outlays (the Keynesian "effective demand")—private and public—consistent with a situation of full employment. Beveridge recognizes that larger public budgets are needed, because total expenditure, private and public, for consumption or investment—the national income must be equal to the amount necessary to insure that manpower is fully employed.[99] Within this macroeconomic framework, he lays down three rules of national finance, in order of priority: outlays should be directed to full employment; they should be directed by social priorities, as stated above; subject to the first and second priority, it's better to provide means for outlays by taxation than by borrowing.[100] Even admitting public deficits where necessary, Beveridge is reluctant to encourage them, because public borrowing means to increase income and wealth of rentiers: people having claims against the community without contributing with their own work.[101] Here, Beveridge seems to forget that an increasing amount of government debt was in the hands of working-class people, who are far from being defined as "rentiers".

In summary, Beveridge's ideas, and the "functional finance" whose principles would be developed by Abba Lerner,[102] have wider implications than Keynes' deficit spending, because they have a profound impact on the structure and functioning of the economic system. Post-war economic policies feel probably more Beveridge's then Keynes' influence. And Beveridge more than Keynes could be seen as the prime target of criticism by radically libertarian economists, and still more by German ordoliberalists (see Sects. 6, 7 and 8 in this chapter).

Lerner represents a further step towards an extension of the public sector. He stated, at the very beginning of his *Economics of Control*,[103] that control means deliberate application of whatever policy will best serve the social intent, without prejudging the issue between collective ownership and administration or some form of private enterprise. Three issues are before the control economy to solve: employment, monopoly and the distribution of income. There are dogmas both of the right—government not interfering with profit-making business—and of the left—which would establish 100% collectivism and outlaw any private profit-seeking enterprise as immoral; but a control economy can reap the benefits of the capitalist economy and the collectivist economy, and the resulting welfare economy will reconcile liberalism and socialism.[104]

The strong internationalism of Beveridge is visible in a courteous controversy between him and Keynes that goes back to the period of the Great Depression, when both took part, in 1931, in a cycle of conferences on *The World Economic Crisis and the Way of Escape*.[105] Keynes had invoked the adoption, by the United Kingdom, of a protective tariff, because—he said— "it is a necessary preliminary to world recovery that this country should regain its liberty of action and its power of international initiative".[106] Beveridge's answer charged Keynes with nationalism, based on the British pretence to act as a leader. "Well – said Beveridge – I am inclined to agree that we [the British] are [the leaders]...But if the justification for strengthening ourselves is that we are better internationalists, to strengthen ourselves,...by aping the foolish nationalism of others, destroys that justification".[107]

The metamorphoses of liberalism in the twentieth century show that one of its main features—"cosmopolitanism" (globalism)—can be lost or to a certain extent weakened. Nationalistic or socialist influences emerge according to different circumstances. With Beveridge, what seems to prevail is an idea of liberalism as an ethical concept before any economic efficiency's implication. This idea means an active intervention of the State in order to reach objectives as full employment and the provision of an extended series of public services. Without these objectives, freedom would be an empty concept, it could not be concretely enacted.

2.6 The Austrian School and Hayek's Liberalism

"There is nothing in the basic principles of liberalism to make it a stationary creed— Hayek writes— there are no hard-and-fast rules fixed for once and for all. The fundamental principle that in the ordering of our affairs we should make as much use as possible of the spontaneous forces of society, and resort as little as possible to coercion, is capable of an infinite variety of applications".[108]

This sentence is evidence of what we have stressed at the start of this chapter: the metamorphoses of liberalism in the twentieth century. In fact, the First World War, the crisis of Wall Street, the Great Depression and the related social and political developments, even new trends in philosophical thinking that separated concepts of ethical and economic liberalism, were reasons for a big re-thinking of well-established economic visions. But not all reflections went in the same direction: certainly, not all in the direction described in the above Sections (in particular, 3–5) of this chapter. Differently from the authors just mentioned (Keynes, Beveridge, or even Pigou), other liberal thinkers reacted to the political crises and to the collapse of the major economies with equal scepticism towards both ideas of an ample State involvement in the conduct of economic activity (which was criticized as a creeping antilibertarian socialism), and totalitarian ideologies, putting on the same footing fascist nationalism and Marxist socialism. The best epitome of this vision is represented by what is generally identified as the Austrian School and by the American Chicago School. Exponents of both were well represented in the Mont Pèlerin Society, an organization created in 1947, to elaborate principles aimed to create and preserve a free society. German ordoliberalism deserves a distinct mention, for its peculiarities.

We have not mentioned in the first chapter the political economist who is often included, with Jevons and Walras, in the top three representatives of the marginal utility theory, the Austrian Carl Menger.[109] The reason is that Menger occupies a peculiar position, being at the same time a major exponent of the Neo-classical School and the begetter of a pretty different stream of thought, the Austrian School of Economics. As we shall try to clarify, he appears more as a rebellious son of German Historicism than an expression of the new positive science in the field of economics.[110]

It is just time to mention him now, as the initiator of that Austrian School, which developed in the twentieth century, having Hayek as probably its major exponent, and gave a renewed moral standing to the economic liberalism. In this School is included a group of "liberist" economists which comprises, besides Hayek, authors as O. Morgenstern, F. Machlup, G. von Haberler, P. Rosenstein Rodan, L. von Mises: Austrian-born or Central European economists, who—because of their ideas—moved mostly to the United States or Britain.

Menger, with Jevons and Walras, reacted against the (mostly British) Classical School of Smith or Ricardo.[111] As we know, the Classical School supported the view of an objective theory of labour value, and did not give relevance to the subjective theory of individual utility. "One of the reasons why the classical doctrines had never firmly established themselves in Germany was that German economists had always remained conscious of certain contradictions inherent in any cost, or labour, theories of value"[112] (the Ricardian theory). Menger focussed instead on the individual and his utility, therefore contributing to build his own version of marginalism. Menger's path towards marginalism was, however, different from neo-classical economists', and cannot be explained without considering his cultural background: he, a graduate in Law in Vienna and Krakov, had first of all to free himself from the schemes of the Historical School of economics, then prevailing in Germany.

Well-known is Menger's harsh debate with the head of the Historical School, Gustav Schmoller. Schmoller criticized Menger because, in his opinion, Menger didn't do other than repeating the "wrong and obsolete fiction" of the British free-trade economists: a deductive method based on the assumption of elementary propositions regarding an abstract and average man.[113] Menger reacted to Schmoller: the error of the Historical School was that it considered the national economy—which is a complex of single individual economies—as, itself, an abstract, "a whole": a large economy in which the nation is to represent itself as the producing and consuming subject. The development of an economic system should, instead, be seen, according to Menger, as the unintentional result of the behaviour of a number of individuals operating in their own interest.

Having described Menger as an antagonist of both the (mostly British) Classical School and the German Historical School, it remains to be seen why he appears as a peculiar figure also among the neo-classical economists. Like them, he relied on individual utility as a subjective measure of value: exactly what neo-classical economists were doing elsewhere. But at the same time Menger took a well-characterized position.

It has been observed that, differently from Jevons and Walras, Menger favoured a humanistic approach[114] that does not belong to them. We shall not dwell upon his theory which—similarly to other neo-classical writers—is centred on a subjective idea of value, on marginal analysis, on methodological individualism; but his approach is also focussed on the purposeful human choice, on the act of preference as judgement and on the relationship between means and ends. Jevons and Walras rejected the means-ends relation, instead favouring the technique of modelling complex relations as systems of simultaneous equations in which no variable is cause of another variable. Menger saw instead, through the causal relation of means and ends, the time structure of production: the element of time had been neglected by the neo-classical economists, who had given a static mathematical exposition of the economic equilibrium (there is not a single mathematical formula in Menger's major work and, according to a comment, he might have been sceptic about the usefulness of mathematics as a tool of economic analysis.[115])

The Austrian School of Economics developed in the twentieth century, consolidating its own stance in the increasingly diversified field of liberalism, and antagonizing different liberal—as Keynesian—views. This School added vitality to the liberal idea through a radically libertarian credo, where a specific kind of ethics (in a way similar to Einaudi's vision, as described above) remains a basic component.

Friedrich von Hayek can be seen as the main exponent of this sort of twentieth-century liberalism. In opposition to neo-classical economists and to their natural parent—positivism—he takes distance from their "scientific" stance by making an explicit revaluation of "ideology", which he sees "simply [as] the analysis of human ideas and human actions". It is not by chance that he wrote a beautiful new Introduction to Menger's *Principles of Economics*.

Hayek makes a strong contraposition of social and natural sciences—just the opposite of the followers of the positivist philosophy. The former deal not with relations between things, but with the relations between man and things, or the relations between man and man. Their aim is to explain the unintended or undesigned results of the actions of many men. These actions—as studied by the social sciences in the narrow sense (used to be described—he writes—as the moral sciences)—are, in a conscious or reflected way, taken by the individual when he has to choose between various courses open to him. The approach of natural sciences is objective, of social and moral sciences is subjective, and the "facts" of the natural sciences become—within the social sciences— "opinions, ideas, concepts". As we have seen in Chapter 1, Hayek, in his polemic attitude towards positivism, arrives at assimilating Comte to Hegel, in their anti-libertarian stance, even putting Comte below the obscurantist Hegel.[116] This unwelcoming duo, who relies on simple laws to explain reality, is completed by Marx, who relies on both: Comte: natural laws; Hegel: metaphysical principles; Marx: materialistic interpretation.[117]

Within the framework of his largely anti-positivist attitude, there are at least two elements that differentiate Hayek's view from the neo-classical economists': (a) a theoretical different approach to the concept of rationality in economics; and (b) the role of the State in an evolving societal, political and economic context.

On the first point, concerning rationality, Hayek distanced himself from neo-classical marginalists, and denied that a rational economic order will result from the assumption that we possess all the relevant information, can formulate a rational system of preferences, and know the available means to put them into practice. If this were the case, the optimal solution for the best utilization of available resources (labour, capital, land) would be, indeed, just a logical deduction, best stated in mathematical form. However, these conditions for a rational order do not actually exist, since we have just "dispersed bits of incomplete and frequently contradictory knowledge", "the knowledge of the particular circumstances of time and place".[118] How to utilize this "knowledge which is not given to anyone in its totality"? According to Hayek, the free market is the most efficient economic arrangement, not because every economic agent has a complete, rational schedule of any possible alternative behaviour (uncertainty is unavoidable), but because the scattered pieces of partial knowledge are connected by the price system. Market provides the necessary connection between the economic agents, and prices are an objective information on the available resources. On the marketplace, a spontaneous order is created.

The rejection of a planning authority is the necessary *sequitur*: being individual preferences unclear and unknowable, any information about them cannot be used by the authority to govern the economy in a certain direction. A central plan is destined to failure because no vehicle can transmit to the authority what is, *per se*, uncertain and changeable.

The formation of the correct price requires a system based on competition. And this in turn requires a role for the State: this is the second element of difference from the neo-classical economists. To the role of the State— as guarantor of competition rather than as central planner— Hayek devotes a large part of *The Road to Serfdom*.[119] He does not reject the idea of planning if it is referred to the single economic agent, that is if it means to employ foresight and systematic thinking in planning man's common affairs, but the task of "the holder of coercive power" (the State) is confined to creating conditions that permit the individual to plan successfully. The liberal thinker is in favour of making the best possible use of forces of competition as a means to enhance individual planning, that is to coordinate human efforts.

Competition—he stresses—is not to follow a dogmatic laissez-faire: Hayek recognizes that the structure of the society has drastically changed in respect to the nineteenth century. Laissez-faire should be seen in a historical context and as a rule of thumb, based as it is on a passive acceptance of institutions as they are, as a "crude rule" in which the principles of economic policy of the nineteenth century were expressed. But those principles were "only a beginning", and to continue relying on that rule of thumb has done much harm to the liberal cause. There is room for a gradual improvement of the institutional framework of a free society. The problem—Hayek adds—is that this advancement has been slow: there is now a wide and unquestioned field of State activity.

"The functioning of a competition not only requires adequate organization of certain institutions like money markets, and channels of information – some of which can never be provided by private enterprises – but it depends, above all, on the existence of an appropriate legal system...designed both to preserve competition and to make it operate as beneficially as possible. It is by no means sufficient that the law should recognize the principle of private property and freedom of contract; much depends on the precise definition of the right of property as applied to different things".[120] Competition defined along these lines implies that no sort of agreement of syndicalist or "corporative" organization of industry can be permitted: a state of affairs, a monopoly, correctly opposed by both liberals and socialists.[121]

Hayek's *Road to Serfdom* was written during the Second World War, under the urge of political and military developments, even if it is the result of previous works.[122] It is obviously affected by that specific climate, by the enormous pressure coming from totalitarian states; it is a mix of theoretical and historical reflections and incitements to return to "the abandoned road" of liberalism of Adam Smith, Hume, Locke, and to individualism of Cicero, Erasmus, Montaigne, by relying on the spontaneous forces of the society, against any form of coercion.[123] This strict libertarian, free-market ideology is a guide to Hayek in order to ponder the issues of "planning and democracy" and "planning and the Rule of Law". And he is equally harsh towards "Western" and totalitarian economies. Let us look at these two issues.

On planning and democracy, Hayek's fundamental statement is that "democracy is essentially a means, a utilitarian device for safeguarding internal peace and individual freedom": an instrumental device, since he does not recognize society and public good as the centrepiece of democracy. The collectivist social goal, the general welfare, is realized through a single plan, whereby each individual need receives a certain rank, in a scale of values defined by the planner, which is a sort of complete ethical code. A common ethical code comprehensive enough to include a unitary economic plan is a reversal of the tendency to move towards an enlargement of the sphere of individual liberty. This code would be not only inconvenient from the point of view of individual freedom, but also logically impossible if it aimed at including the infinite variety of different needs of different people.[124]

Hayek follows a Benthamite approach to utility when he writes that the philosophy of individualism does not assume that man is egoistic or selfish, but simply that he has his own scale of values, which should not be subject to any dictation by others.[125] This vision is understandably on a collision course with the collectivist system, defined as "the deliberate organization of the labours of society for a definite social goal". Kinds of collectivism—be they fascism or communism—may differentiate on the nature of such a goal, but any collectivism is different from liberalism and individualism in its refusal to recognize a sphere of autonomy where individual ends are supreme. Since 1931 [the Depression]—he regrets—the United States and Britain—the "West"—have slowly moved towards socialism (this is a severe critique of the liberal economists mentioned above), even though we know that socialism means, in the end, slavery.[126]

Hayek then fixes a fundamental concept of a liberal State: the Rule of Law, as opposed to the arbitrary government. Under the Rule of Law "the government confines itself to fixing rules determining the conditions under which the available resources may be used, leaving to the individuals the decision for what ends they are to be used".[127] The rules are made in advance, as formal rules intended to be merely instrumental in the pursuit of people's various individual ends. The discretion left to the Executive Branch of government wielding coercive powers is consequently reduced as much as possible.

At the opposite end is the arbitrary government, whereby government directs the use of the means of production to its particular ends, through substantive and always provisional rules. The government provides for the actual needs of people and chooses between them, depending on the circumstances as they arise. As an example of arbitrary government, Hayek takes the case of Nazi Germany[128]: Nazis have always been intolerant of a merely formal justice, of the Rule of Law, that is of a law that has no view of how well off particular people ought to be, and want a socialization of law, attacking the independence of judges, and invoking the *Freirechtsshule*.[129] In Nazi Germany, the *Gerechte* State (the just State), advocated by the jurist Carl Schmitt,[130] is the substitute for the Rule of Law.

It is true—Hayek notes—that the Rule of Law tolerates economic inequalities. But, in a sort of trade-off between inequality and loss of individual freedom, Hayek's pendulum tilts towards the first. In his passionate defence of individual freedom—and aversion to collectivist welfare—he goes as far as to recognize that economic values are less important to us than many things precisely because in economic matters we are free to decide what we regard as marginal…while economic planning would involve direction of almost the whole of our life.[131] This notation of Hayek gives the essence of the liberal State, which must set citizens free to choose, not only [and not so much, one might add] in their economic choices, but more importantly in any strand of private and public life, when a decision has to be taken.

While a Crocean view might induce to think that an ethical liberalism can coexist with non-liberal economic structures (see above), Hayek is strongly against the possibility that democracy might survive if only the economic matters were directed by a superior authority. In this sense, it can be safely said that, with Hayek as well as with Luigi Einaudi, ethical, economic and political liberalism cannot be distinguished, they are just one idea: a position that put them in the stream of thought that goes back to the nineteenth-century liberalism, and takes the shape of a libertarianism which opens a wide gap between them and the liberalism of Keynes or Beveridge.

An acute observation is made by Hayek to motivate the rise of extreme-right totalitarianism, of the incumbent Fascist-Nazi threat. He notes that the socialist theory—Marxist or not—is dominated by the idea of a division of society into two classes with common but mutually conflicting interests: capitalists and industrial workers. This binary contraposition is made by socialists in the assumption that the middle class would disappear. But, according to Hayek, socialists have disregarded the rise of a new and very large middle class (made of clerks, administrative workers, tradesmen, small officials). Contrary to socialists' expectations, this new middle class, the petty bourgeoisie, survived and gained strength, even though its economic position was deteriorating vis-à-vis the industrial workers. Both classes—industrial workers and petty bourgeoisie—were associated by a shared hatred of the capitalist system, and in this sense, according to Hayek, they were both socialist, but the revolutionary ideals did not have appeal to this middle class, its idea of justice was different from that of old socialism. Fascism and national socialism—the political outcome of petty bourgeois class' hatred of liberal capitalism—are a sort of middle-class socialism. The conflict between these political movements on one side, and old socialism on the other, is to be seen as a conflict of rival socialist factions.[132]

This view of Hayek, singular as it might appear, can be compared to Marx's comments regarding the petty bourgeoisie: both writers fully understand the social and economic relevance of this class. Marx saw it as reactionary, adverse to socialism, and was convinced that it would finally disappear (see Chapter 1); Hayek on the contrary sees this class as strengthening and gaining power, and as a new rival faction of socialism itself. Hayek was undoubtedly right in stressing the non-transient importance of the petty bourgeoisie and its non-liberal, totalitarian ideology, but his assimilation of this ideology to socialism can be debatable, if by socialism we intend a revolutionary overthrow of the capitalistic class.

2.7 The Chicago School

The "Old" Chicago School has long been dimmed by the "New School"—the one championed by Milton Friedman and George Stigler, who both saw the old school as "interventionist", being its theory characterized by a firm set of rules, with which the market and its participants must comply. According to the Old one, the appropriate function of the State is not providing services nor carrying-out some economic activities, but that of giving a framework of rules within which the economic activities of both public and private economic agents can be freely performed. One of its major exponents, Henry Simons, explicitly states that his own is "a coherent scheme of practical ethics, a political-economic philosophy, or, if you please, a clear-cut ideological position…libertarian or, in the English-Continental sense, liberal". This scheme takes inspiration from—among others—Locke, Bentham, Smith and more recently Hayek: "Liberty as both a requisite and measure of progress".[133] Simons pays also attention to the distributive aspect of the economic system, which is however resolved in what he calls—similarly to Walras—commutative justice[134]: "each shall receive according as he (or it) contributes to organized, cooperative, joint production, or in technical economic language according to the productivity of his property, capital or capacity (including personal capacity)".[135]

Simons gives for granted his opposition to communism and fascism, but the true enemies of his ideas are "our liberal reformers and politically ambitious intellectuals…the naive advocates of managed economy or national planning" (it is not difficult to identify these reformers as the New Dealers).[136] "It is an obvious responsibility of the State …to maintain the kind of legal and institutional framework within which competition can function effectively as an agency of control…the so-called failure of capitalism (of the free enterprise system, of competition) may reasonably be interpreted primarily as a failure of the political State in the discharge of its minimum responsibilities under capitalism".[137] The responsibility of economic fluctuations belongs to the State that destabilizes the economic system by expanding and contracting the quantity of money in circulation (the monetary side of Simons' theory shall be considered later).

With the "naïve advocates of managed economy or national planning…we must agree on one vital point, namely, that there is now imperative need for a sound, positive program of economic legislation".[138] However, this programme goes against New Dealers' policies: legislation must state that government has few functions: to maintain the internal order, to wage war, to promote free trade as opposed to any form of mercantilism. To the well-known Rooseveltian freedoms—freedom of speech, of worship, from want, from fear—just one has to be added: freedom of enterprise, through minimization of State responsibilities.[139]

"The proximate objectives of a traditionally liberal economic policy, under modern conditions, may be defined in terms of the problems: first, of money; second, of monopoly and regulation; and, third, of inequality".[140]

About money, the increasing attention of Simons, and many others, is the obvious sign of the difficulty of replacing the old gold standard with new monetary arrangements, given the social and political implications of a "sound money". Money's management implies stable rules of the game well defined by law, aimed at controlling money in quantity and value, while any discretion in money management should be rejected. These rules should be a sort of extra-constitutional or quasi constitutional mandate. They would also require a reform of the banking system, which should separate the monetary function (which is of a public nature) from the "mobilization of funds for investment purposes", that is from credit (which is a private business).[141]

Monetary rules must also affect fiscal policy, because it is through it that they are enhanced; in other words, fiscal policy should not destabilize money. As a consequence, Simons has a critical view of public debt. When it is issued as a substitute for money, inflation can arise if investors' confidence is damaged. Money is not easily managed alongside debt (this sort of monetary constitution is also envisaged by Irving Fisher who, as a pure economist, does not linger on the philosophical vision that is the root of Simons' thought).[142]

With reference to the second objective, market regulation, the greatest enemy of a liberal democracy is monopoly, be that in the form of big corporations, industrial cartels, agencies for the control of prices, or also trade unions. Indeed, the best yardstick of economic efficiency is the price system. Prices must be freely determined on any market (including the labour market): the result of competitive purchases by persons free to utilize purchasing power as they please. Simons is therefore critical of trade unions, because through collective bargaining, they try to bring the level of wages above the level determined by competition, thereby reducing employment opportunities.

Mitigation of inequalities—this is his third point—is inconsistent with economic efficiency. It is true that, as a consequence of a system of free-market prices (including wages), individuals are in widely different income circumstances, but the "problems of inefficiency and of inequality…are, within fairly wide limits, distinct and independent".[143] Inequality is a separate problem that must be solved by progressive taxation.

As mentioned earlier, Simons is strongly critical of that kind of liberals who look at an active role of the State in the economy, whom he calls "collectivists". In reviewing their books, he attacks both the Keynesian Alvin Hansen and—even more—William Beveridge. Referring to his *Full Employment in a Free Society*, Simons writes that it "is written by a nominal Liberal, radical-reactionary in its substantive proposals, libertarian in its rhetoric", and complains that the book "may forecast or largely determine the course of British post-war policy". It is political philosophy more than economics. Recalling Beveridge's fundamental freedoms (see above, Sect. 3), Simons compares them to Nazi economic policy and ironically defines them as "A crusade against Want, Disease, Squalor and Ignorance, which is good if you like the pre-war German scheme as a national way of life"; a collectivist planning where there is nothing to enforce competition. Beveridge's work is nothing more than a "hyper-Keynesian scheme of tightly regimented economy, and extreme economic nationalism".[144]

From the fiscal and monetary perspective, Simons' criticism is addressed to the discretion given to the central bank: all the power—the issue and borrowing power—should be concentrated in the Treasury. The Treasury, in turn, should assure monetary stability under definite, coherent rules, with minimal intervention on the markets.

This radical, libertarian view could not be uncritically accepted even by a liberal economist as Lionel Robbins who, not many years later, will write: "The desirability of rules rather than authorities, to use the contrast so vividly posed by Henry Simons, is absolutely central to the main libertarian position…[but] I think it is a deficiency of the libertarian case…that even when it explicitly repudiates the superficiality of the extreme laisse-faire, it tends to suggest a conception of government that is too limited to the execution of known laws, to the exclusion of functions of initiative and discretion that cannot without distortion be left out of the picture". And he quotes "the sphere of finance": "It would be surely unwise… to assume that no situation could arise that could not be dealt with by purely automatic mechanisms".[145]

What has the "New School" of Chicago added to Simons' philosophy? Not a lot, other than an increased accent on "liberism". According to his main exponent, Milton Friedman, "government is essential both as a forum for determining the 'rules of the game' and as an umpire to interpret and enforce the rules decided on".[146] If we compare Simons' and Friedman' ideas, we can find similarities and differences. On the problem of wealth distribution, Friedman agrees with Simons on the principle that everybody should get a remuneration proportionate to his contribution to the production process, barring any form of egalitarianism. However, Friedman is contrary to taxation with progressive rates as an instrument of wealth redistribution ("I find it hard, as a liberal, to see any justification for graduated taxation solely to redistribute income"), preferring a flat-rate tax. High nominal tax rates seem "a clear case of using coercion to take from some in order to give to others and thus to conflict head-on with individual freedom".[147]

Regarding competition, State's umpire function means that it has to prevent that competition might be confused with freedom of collusion: no competitor can be left out of the market other than by selling a better product at the same price or the same product at a cheaper price (while in the "Continental" tradition—he observes—freedom of enterprise means that firms are free to fix prices, not to compete on the same market or to adopt practices to keep out potential competitors). But where monopoly has to be the final outcome as the most technically efficient solution, and three possible alternatives are available—public monopoly, private monopoly, public regulation of the market of a specific good or service—Friedman's albeit reluctant preference is for private monopoly, differently from Simons (who is inclined towards public monopoly) and the German ordoliberals[148] (who would prefer a publicly regulated market). Friedman's motivation is that the rapidly evolving technology might allow shifting from private monopoly to a situation of competition, while public monopoly—once established—would be more difficult to dismantle.[149]

Simons' monetary constitution takes with Friedman a more definite character. He thinks that gold standard—never fully enacted in its implicit automatism and, in fact, subject to governments' discretion—isn't any more adequate to current conditions, but even more inadequate is to give monetary responsibilities and ample discretionary powers to a group of technocrats, put together in an independent central bank: an arrangement that has brought only instability, measured by fluctuations in the money stock, or prices, or output. A liberal is indeed fearful of such a concentration of power. Rules instead of discretion: it is necessary "to achieve a government of law instead of men by legislating rules for the conduct of monetary policy that will have the effect of enabling the public to exercise control over monetary policy through its political authorities, while at the same time it will prevent monetary policy from being subject to the day-by-day whim of political authorities".[150] These rules should not address an optimal level of prices, which would leave too much discretional manoeuvring to the authorities, but the stock of money, which should grow by a stable percentage, quantified by Friedman at around 3–5% per annum.[151]

And here is the underlying motivation of his detachment from Simons: "Many earlier liberals…writing at a time when government was small by today's standard, were willing to have government undertake activities that today's liberals would not accept now that government has become so overgrown".[152]

2.8 Ordoliberalism, or Authoritarian Liberalism

The role of the State in the ordoliberal scheme is enough to distinguish German ordoliberals from Hayek and the "Austrians" in general. At first glance all of them might be seen as very similar to the ordoliberals, and certainly there was a bond of sympathy between them, linked as they were by their shared confidence in the efficiency of markets, in the system of prices as an indicator of value for products and factors of production, in freedom of market entry and in the emphasis on individual choices. But—as we shall see—there are differences. These differences emphasize ordoliberals' peculiarities not only in relation to the Austrians, but also to the new Chicago School, itself reluctant to recognize the central role of the State in the economy.

In short, the ordoliberals' vision is based on the recognition of the strength of the State at the very centre of the economic system. Their approach is coherent with the specifically German intellectual approach that we tried to summarize at some length in the Chapter 1 (Sects. 6–10), and is an explicit recognition of the wide role that the State was definitely assuming in governing national economies in the twentieth century. It is appropriate to add that—in a similar way to the German Historical School—the ordoliberal approach cannot be studied as a sort of "model", in the sense that an economist might attribute to this word; it is rather an essentially prescriptive scheme on the structure and organization of the economic system, within a well defined political framework. This approach requires a strict connection between economics and law: it is stressed with particular emphasis that the legal framework of an economic system should be carefully constructed, being essential to its proper working.

A question mark can be raised about whether ordoliberalism should be included within a broad definition of liberalism, or connected to an authoritarian nationalism. What has to be pointed out at the very beginning of this Section is that ordoliberalism cannot be seen as a monolith: some ordoliberals focus their attention on an omnipotent State ("The Leviathan was and had to be there"[153]), others on the efficiency of free markets. A corollary of the first feature is the State's overwhelming power to dictate law in the superior interest of the whole nation, as envisaged by the rulers, and the minimal political role attributed to individuals, as un-politicized entities that simply have to seek their well-being without begging for the State's support.

To understand ordoliberalism, we have just made a reference to the German intellectual framework, and here the name of Carl Schmitt comes to mind. Schmitt was an outstanding jurist and—while it is not our intention to dwell on his thoughts on the discipline of law and on the role of the State—a fact that cannot be neglected is that he was a Nazi State constitutional expert and ideologue. He shared with the early ordoliberals a distaste for liberal democracy, putting rather emphasis on a peculiar and apparently contradictory vision of a liberal-authoritarian State, which protects the market from requests of wealth redistribution.

Some words on Schmitt are necessary, because his way of reasoning is very close to the first ordoliberal thinkers.[154] He distinguishes "total State", as embodied by the Weimar Republic, and "authoritarian" State. Here, "total" means a pluralist democracy, where parliamentary representation reflects a homogeneity of rulers and ruled, and is no longer focussed on bourgeois interests; while government is accountable to mass emotions and passions. The Weimar Republic is critically seen as the emblem of the crisis of an unrestrained mass society in revolt, which had in fact "supplanted the liberal State". Too much democratic State had meant an excessive political and economic overload, and in this way an effective contradiction of liberal principles. A line of separation between State and society would prove useful to both: on the one hand, it would mean an effective ability of the State to govern, and on the other, a free exercise of labour-power by all economically active people, where all would be treated equally under the Rule of Law. The task of the State is to liberate the economy by depoliticizing socio-economic relations. The State must not be the target for welfare-seeking workers; rebellious proletarians must be transformed into self-reliant and willing exercisers of their own labour power: this is "the heroism of poverty, sacrifice and discipline". In summary, a free economy is not a natural order, but the result of a government practice. The State is the predominant category of political economy.

It was therefore necessary, according to Schmitt, to restore the State as an independent institution of authoritative decision-making (independent of the mass society). In abnormal times—like those lived under Weimar—no real democracy could be possible.

In a speech of November 1932, in the final stages of the Weimar Republic, entitled Strong State and Sound Economy, Schmitt argues that in the twentieth century all states tend to become "total", but Weimar was a "quantitative total state", incapable of resisting pressures coming from opposing quarters and parties; the total State that is needed is of a "qualitative" kind, having control over the army and the bureaucracy, while other areas are left to self-management and to the free economy: a new order, potentially corporatist and authoritarian, so as to preserve property, but at the same time, and in a somewhat contradictory way, an order that would defend the traditional liberal rights of man against the State as well as defending the State against the threat of liberal democracy: a depoliticized democracy, with a marginalized parliament.[155]

At the very start of the Third Reich, he writes that the new Enabling Act of 1933which marks the beginning of Hitler's Reich—while formally presented as a change to the previous weak and "neutral" Weimar constitution, represents a radical change: the Law has been decided by the parliament only in obedience to the people's will as expressed in the political elections just held; it is in reality a popular referendum, a plebiscite, recognizing Hitler as the German people's political leader. Freedom of propaganda, opinion, conscience and activity, and the ideological neutrality of the Weimar constitution are abolished. That constitution was "in no way capable of recognizing even a mortal enemy of the German people in order to abolish the Communist Party, the enemy of the State and of the people". Schmitt's reference to the people's will sounds familiar to our days' populists, as will be shown in Chapter 4 of this essay.

Regarding the State, Schmitt affirms a fundamental unity of the body politic, which is the result of three structures: the State itself, the Movement and the People. They are not in a parallel positions: the Movement is the dynamic structure and is embodied in the party, the single party of the German national socialist workers; it sustains the other two, penetrates and leads them. The State is the static member of this triadic structure: the organization of command, administration and justice. The People is the social and economic life of the nation, which grows under the protection and in the shadow of political decisions.

The entire liberal world has fallen. As in fascist Italy, the dead-end streets of liberal democracy are abandoned. The typical liberal democratic constitution—Schmitt remarks—was based on the opposition of two entities, be they State/society; or State/individual; or State power/individual freedom; or politics/private domain. Such a separation is meant to divide State power from society, so that the latter might control the former, as a defence of society against State power. The German triadic structure overcomes this division. In Germany, until the mid-nineteenth century, the State did not recognize that division, and had an overwhelming,

Hegelian, role. But even after that, with the advent of liberalism and positivism, the State remained in Germany an administrative State, with its class of public officials that was not an instrument, but an independent force of the State itself. The Hegelian vision therefore remained, and writers such as Adolf Wagner and Gustav Schmoller [the main exponent of the German Historical School of economics, see Chapter 1] kept alive that great German concept: the awareness that the cultured and incorruptible class of the German public officials makes it superior to bourgeois society.

There are similarities between Schmitt's lines of thought and the ordoliberal economic doctrine: the view of Weimar as a failure that results from State intervention in economic life, from a social and fiscal over-expansion, then followed by a deflationary policy, and, generally, piecemeal economic changes; a critical attitude towards mass democracy and a preference for an authoritarian government. Schmitt and early ordoliberals also keep the very characteristic way of seeing the working class as made up of single individuals with "free labour power", able to exercise their capabilities without reference to common interests and class solidarity, and therefore of seeing society as a set of depoliticized socio-economic relations. On the other hand, and in a very clear way, ordoliberals react against dirigisme, against the centrally administered system as advocated by Schmitt and realized by the Nazi government, and against the loss of personal freedom, thus vindicating the reasons for free markets.[156]

According to the ordoliberals, "creative destruction" of markets—embraced by Austrian economics—is not enough to ensure the dynamism necessary to the economy (for instance, the existence of big monopolies is due, von Mises thinks, to government's interference in the freedom of markets; on the contrary, for the ordoliberals, it is up to the government to resist monopolies created by unfettered markets). Ordoliberals think that only the authority of the State can exert the force necessary to create an efficient economic system (for the Austrians, this objective can only be reached by the private sector, through the self-interest of its components). Economic freedom rests on a strong State, which guarantees a social equilibrium, defined as a situation where the individual is protected against the hegemony of uncontrolled markets. Mass democracy may mean economic and social disorder.

Ordoliberalism was born in the context of the Great Depression, the crisis of the Weimar Republic and Nazi dictatorship. Beyond differences that characterize its individual supporters, it is generally considered as a neo-liberal alternative form of political economy to laissez-faire liberalism and to collectivism, in its various forms. It has been written that "the dictum that the free economy depends on the strong state is key to its theoretical stance".[157] But, at the same time, this relevance attributed to the State is far from the ideas of Keynes or Beveridge: again, another evidence of the metamorphoses of twentieth-century liberalism.

The central points of ordoliberal philosophy can be identified as follows:

> market competition, far from being spontaneous, is defined and protected by the regulations of the State: a strong State, very different from the limited, weak State of classical liberal thinking;
> only in a market based on competition, as regulated and protected by the State, is the entrepreneur able to operate, with his recognized vitality and innovative energy and leadership: he will not enter as such the political debate about market's structures and transactions.

The State must act in such a way as to de-proletarianize the social structures of capitalism. This de-proletarianization aims to empty the Marxist social structures of any content. "The solution to the proletarian condition consists in the constantly renewed effort to eliminate the proletariat by means of a social policy consistent with the market which, instead of imprisoning workers in the welfare state, facilitates their freedom and responsibility, making each akin to a propertied entrepreneur".[158] As said earlier, the worker becomes socially integrated in the production process. He keeps firm social and ethical values, rooted in tradition, family and community. The image of a de-proletarianized and self-confident worker approaches the ordoliberals' scheme to Einaudi's.

All this represents a strong overturn of positive economics, in favour of prescriptive economics: the problem is not to develop an analytical model to explain the real world, but rather to change the real world, by making it coherent with the ordoliberal model. This model sees political authority as the instrument necessary to establish a free economic system.

In 1936, an *Ordoliberal Manifesto* was published in Germany, signed by Franz Böhm, Walter Euken, and Hans Grossman Dörth.[159] According to a deep-seated orientation of German intellectual tradition (see Chapter 1), the authors address the disciplines of both law and economics but, separating themselves from the Historical School, they think that these two disciplines were effectively neglected during the nineteenth and twentieth centuries. This negligence was indeed due to the prevalence of Historicism: on the one hand, it had correctly observed, against the ideas of the Enlightenment, that no natural system of law and economics actually exists (as fully and rightly stressed by List, in the field of economics, and Savigny, in the field of law). But, relying on Historicism had exposed those disciplines to the risk of extinction, because of their relativism and fatalism.

Relativism is implicit in the assertion that law should be developed by the "inner silent forces" of society, not at the discretion of the legislator: the substance of law grows out of historical developments and jurist-made laws, also governing economic relations. In this way, thanks to this approach, "capitalism has always found ways and means to succeed *de lege, praeter legem et contra legem*". Indeed, if begetters of the law are those "inner silent forces", if law is generated by society itself and not by the will of the legislator, law itself is prevented from reacting against those forces (for example, this conception of a sort of creative power of judges did not hinder the creation of big industrial cartels, that is the denial of an efficient and competitive market).

Works by economists of the German Historical School of economics are seen by the ordoliberals as exercises in relativism, also from a methodological viewpoint. They failed because of their empiricism, which consists of observing and gathering an enormous amount of facts without noting their interdependencies. Economic reality, in fact, cannot be understood if it is considered as a mass of uncorrelated events. Their relativism prevented them from using classical political economy as constructed during the nineteenth century. They "did not know how to use the abstract thinking apparatus of political economy" and it was for them "impossible to arrive at any understanding of the interdependencies within the economic system".[160] They ended up in a confidence in progress, of a Hegelian flavour, justified by faith, not supported by a logical scheme.

Fatalism—authors of the *Ordo Manifesto* observe—is common to writers as diverse as Marx and Spengler, the first determinist, the second sceptical: according to both, things cannot be changed, they can only be observed. The whole of social, political and intellectual life cannot be seen as other than a "superstructure", superposed on a structure that evolves along its own laws, the "inner silent forces" mentioned above.

The ordoliberals' programme aims at the construction and organization of an economic system based on number of principles[161]:

> adopting a scientific attitude in the study of law and economics
> moving beyond the relativism of historicism
> at the same time, recognizing the importance of historical evidence
> understanding the constitution (structure) of the economy in order to decide how economic activity should be reorganized through legislation. In this regard, the problem of understanding and fashioning the legal instruments necessary for an economic constitution can be solved only if the legislator avails himself of the findings of economic research.

Ordoliberal thinking starts therefore from a criticism both of the "natural" system on which classical economics is based, and of historicist determinism, but finishes by grafting classical economics on to the tree of German historicism. This means that it takes from both what is considered convincing in their contributions.

The views expressed in the contributions made by ordoliberals are not unanimous: some of them insist on the central role of the State, others on the efficiency of a free, competitive market. These different visions bring us back to the two roots of economic thinking that we have tried to describe, in Schumpeter's footsteps, in Chapter 1: one based on the individual, nourished by the philosophy of the Enlightenment, and the other focussed on the State, as historically defined, and as described by German philosophers. Ordoliberals draw from both visions, but the second vision prevails. This is probably due to the fact that the rebirth of liberalism in Germany takes place in the years that precede and follow the Second World War, and in Germany the traditions of the discipline of economics had been going in a direction that was opposite to the liberalism of classical economic doctrine. Not by chance, Gustav Schmoller had ignored this doctrine as "hawkers' economics".[162] Even though ordoliberalism was critical of the Historical School, as we have seen, the ordoliberals were conditioned by that very historicism, and the role of the State was far bigger than in the classical doctrine.

Historicist and statist tradition is clearly visible in Euken's writings. Probably nowhere more than in an article of 1948[163]—where he wonders about which sort of economic system should be constructed in the defeated Germany. His approach is typically microeconomic. Euken observes that the rules governing the economic systems of industrial countries should ideally obtain the same results as those realized in a small closed subsistence economy. Anyone who governs this small economy should have a detailed knowledge of what is going on throughout the economy and be able to evaluate its utility. He should also be able to give instructions regarding the most efficient way of using all the factors of production. All the interdependencies of economic activity in that small economy are directly perceived by the ruler, who can properly take the appropriate decisions.[164]

In a similar vein, interdependencies exist in a big industrial country, but they are not easily detected in a complete and up-to-date way. What is then necessary is "some measure of scarcity", which would indicate which goods are in short supply and how factors of production should be combined to produce what is required. This "scarcity gauge" is given, for firms and households, by the price system, and on the basis of price the economic agents can calculate what is to be produced and the most efficient combination of the factors of production, in a way that is similar to a calculating machine. So far, Euken seems to follow the classical doctrine (as re-expounded, for instance, by Hayek). But, since prices are determined differently according to the different conditions of the markets concerned, they cannot be an indicator of scarcity throughout the economy. The interconnections between different elements in the economy make it necessary to see every act of economic policy in the context of the whole economic process. "An economic system has to control adequately the whole economic process in a reasonable way and in order to do this it is necessary that its individual components supplement one another".[165]

This scarcity gauge at a systemic level should however be designed as an instrument to make the system more efficient, not to reach full employment. Indeed, the objective of full employment might lead to an employment of labour in unproductive sectors, while in other sectors bottlenecks might arise as a consequence of the scarcity of available factors of production. Investments should be chosen under State control in the correct proportion, in every sector, industry or even specific regions or enterprises. The control of the whole production process and, through it, the achievement of full employment, is a wise policy; not so a policy that looks a priori for a full employment which masks or ignores the issue of efficiency. The ordoliberal State is a planner, not for social purposes but in order to avoid market malfunctioning.[166]

In this scheme, fiscal policy is side-lined: there is no room for it, that is for Keynesian, or "functional finance" purposes. In a perfect liberal order, there is no need for stabilization policies because the economic activity is stable by definition.[167] Therefore, Euken does not consider the use of fiscal policy for demand management purposes both in cyclical downturns and in the case of structural problems: even in this last case, only structural reforms are needed, operating on the supply side of the economy, that is by making supply more efficient, not by managing demand.[168]

If we look at the relationship between the fiscal system and the economic system, there is a striking difference between Beveridge's taxonomy, which implies an active, functional role given to the first, and the aseptic taxonomy advanced, a few years later, by an ordoliberal writer, Kurt Schmidt,[169] where no link is foreseen between public budgetary policy and employment, and—still more—no mention is made of the use of public debt to promote it.

The ordoliberals show equal reluctance to support an active role for monetary policy. In this regard, the first ordoliberals expressed, not by chance, a clear preference for the gold standard. Friedrich Lutz, in an article going back to 1935,[170] written during the last gasps of the old monetary regime, continues to stress the advantages of a system of fixed exchange rates, of containment of the money stock within the limits of the gold reserve, of an international distribution of gold reserves in relation to the evolution of the balance of payments, and of an automatic mechanism based on a few precise rules of the game, where absolutely nothing is left to management by central banks. A proper working of this system implies the exclusion of independent monetary policies—linked to the specific conditions of the economic cycle—and of protectionism. Lutz recognizes however the deep crisis of the gold standard: the gold loss of a certain country with a foreign accounts deficit is followed by a fall, difficult to accept socially and politically, in wages and prices and in the end by unemployment, in order to recover competitiveness. For this reason—he observes—this regime has been recently abandoned by the United Kingdom and by the United States (and it would be abandoned the following year by Italy and France). The decisive success of nationalistic ideas (we are—it is worthwhile repeating—in 1935) leads Lutz to wonder whether a monetary system "controlled at a national level" might be introduced, as an escape lane from the gold standard.

He envisages a series of technical measures to reach that objective,[171] but adds that, as a preliminary step, the more general problem of the alternative between a free economy and a planned economy should be solved.[172] This unresolved issue may explain why ordoliberal thinking on monetary policy never went beyond a generic "monetarism", meaning by this paying attention to keeping the monetary base under control through rules that preclude the discretion, politically manoeuvrable, of central banks, in order to obtain stable money (see Friedman, above). This position is accompanied by a sceptical attitude to the use of monetary policy to sustain, or curb, economic growth (a use of monetary policy that could be termed Keynesian), and instead by the affirmation of the neutrality of money, whose active management risks generating instability. In short, what is important to ordoliberal thinkers is not monetary policy, but a monetary constitution, based on a central bank not subject to political or partisan pressure and operating according to a few precise rules (a sort of gold standard without gold).[173] They particularly mistrust the expansion of the money supply through bank credit, a mistrust which even brought Euken to adhere to the Chicago School, from which the ordoliberals were, in other regards—mainly, the role of the State—rather distant.

Alfred Müller-Armack is more oriented towards the neoliberalism of the Austrian School, and therefore less focussed on the centrality of the State.[174] First, in any case he confirms that the concept of free competition has a central role, not to be identified with laissez-faire because it requires a series of institutional guarantees, aimed at preventing trade restrictions and controlling monopolies, oligopolies and cartels, to the benefit of consumers. In such a way the economic system is able to work properly and to perform at the same time a social function. Competition is a prerequisite of economic freedom that cannot be found or generated within the sphere of the private sector.

Müller-Armack is also interested in the Welfare State, but in a perspective that is very far from Beveridge's. The safeguards furnished by the Welfare State are to be maintained, but any public intervention has to be consistent with the market. This means an intermingling of market freedom and social equilibrium: a "social market economy", an expression made familiar by the German government's policies, particularly when Ludwig Erhard was Economics minister (1949–1963). In this regard, it is recognized that it is a duty of the State to intervene in the redistribution of output—through the State pension system, social insurances and various subsidies to less affluent classes—but social expenditure should not over-step the threshold at which the working of the competitive market and the production of income would be hindered. Regarding taxation, to comply with the same principle would mean that too high tax rates, designed to finance social expenditure, would damage the production of income. In a properly working market—he writes—the creation of new wealth would be sufficient and capable of tolerating a considerable redistribution of wealth without an excessive increase in tax rates. Again, no role is given to public deficit financing for the purpose of redistribution.

This theme is developed further by Wilhelm Röpke: the Rooseveltian "freedom from want" is "a negative concept", because it means that the needy have to rely on others—that is, to take from others—for their own sustenance. This also means that the State must use its power of coercion in order to oblige others to sustain the needy. But if taxation reaches excessive levels, the resources available are depleted, to everybody's disadvantage. In a free society, the same objective must be pursued mostly on a voluntary basis, through savings, insurance and voluntary contributions. Only in this way will the "proletarian form of existence" be overcome.[175] In the same vein, Müller-Armack thinks that to keep interest rates artificially low in order to facilitate credit to disadvantaged debtors is not consistent with the market, as well as to freeze rents on the whole property market without having regard to the degree to which lessees can afford rents, while a system of subsidized rents for the poor only would be consistent with the market.[176]

The stress placed by ordoliberals on political themes in a broad sense has prompted the question: what new ideas have they brought to economic theory? It has been pointed out that their themes—such as monetary stability, the market and its regulation, competition, and trade freedom—were concepts already familiar to economics, and that "the real reason [for their success] lies at the very heart of the philosophy of the social market economy…its theorists produced little in the way of concrete suggestions for the prevention of the excessive growth of the State".[177] This is a comment that can be only partly accepted. We take note that, on the one hand, we shall not find in their work, for instance, any deep analysis regarding the features of different types of markets, or any calculation of the multiplier effect of a certain expenditure, while, on the other hand, mainstream economics, which is analytically strong, is often uninterested in the institutional side, as an exogenous factor that has to be taken for granted. The phenomena that ordoliberals observe are the same as those analysed by mainstream economists, but from a different viewpoint: they are not interested in the lawlike regularities of behaviour that demarcate economics as a field of social analysis, and in constructing "models". As mentioned earlier, an "ordoliberal model" simply does not exist. They look at the prescriptive side, armed with instruments generally ignored by economists, such as history and law, and are interested more in an economic constitution than in active macro-management of the economy (macroeconomics is ignored). Whether their recipes were (are) conducive to economic welfare, is a matter of debate. But what is certain is that "the prevention of the growth of the State" finds in their theories conditions and limits, more structured and argued for than in other analyses by economists with a different background. And the result was a national supply-side strategy that utilized traditional cultural and institutional resources to assume a primary role on a European and global level (as even current developments in Europe clearly show; but this is a matter to be dealt with later on in this essay).

Notes

1. Baffigi (2009, p. 8).
2. If we focus mainly on its origin.
3. "When the facts change, I change my mind", Keynes—reportedly—said.
4. Keynes (1926, pp. 14–15).
5. Joan Robinson would then affirm that with Keynes "economics once more became political economy".
6. Skidelsky (1992, p. 224).
7. Trevelyan (1944, p. 557).
8. Stein (1990, p. 6).
9. This society, in existence since the late nineteenth century, took its name from the Roman Quintus Fabius Maximus, the *cunctator*, that is the slow moving but tenacious general. He would be a symbol of the inexorable, if gradual, movement towards socialism, as opposed to the diverse strategy, of sudden revolutionary changes.
10. 90 liras per UK pound, well above the prevailing market rate that had reached 125 liras per pound.
11. Blackett (1932, p. 96).
12. Croce (1973).
13. As distinct from the "Philosophy of the Spirit", which we will not dwell upon.

14. Croce (1973, p. 286). Joan Robinson defined value as “a metaphysical idea”; with the identification of value with the produce of labour (Ricardo, and then Marx), the metaphysical ideaRobinson says—becomes a “hypothesis” (1974, pp. 29–30).
15. At least in one case we have evidence of a relation between the two: Keynes commissioned to Croce an article for his series of reports on Reconstruction in Europe, for the Manchester Guardian, in 1922: A philosopher’s view of population. See Kelly (2019).
16. Croce (1973, p. 301).
17. Bodei (2003).
18. Schumpeter, in a similar vein, questioned whether perfect competition is a theoretical construction or a historical reality (1947, p. 107).
19. In this text, I stick where appropriate to the literal translation of the Italian word as an English neologism.
20. Croce (1973, p. 264). However, we might follow Croce’s approach, and see Adam Smith’s economic doctrine as “ethical”, because, in the *historical* circumstances of Smith’s Scotland (that time and place), it was perfectly attuned to pursuing an economic system that would definitely rid that country of previous feudal commercial practices.
21. pp. 259 and 264.
22. pp. 255, 256, 257.
23. p. 260.
24. pp. 262–266.
25. “The economists who use quantitative methods, bewitched by the evidence of their proceedings and not aware that theirs is a void evidence, rather than limiting themselves to the construction of their very useful schemes, increase the confusion by philosophising in an extravagant way: as we can see from one of the most shrewd and learned economists of our time” Pareto (p. 287).
26. “Liberistic”, adjective of “Liberismo”, “economic liberalism”.
27. Croce (2015, pp. 298–302) [originally published as a single essay, 1927].
28. p. 303.
29. Montesano (2003).
30. He will then explicitly speak of “nationalism” Croce (1955, p. 283).
31. pp. 284–285 and 288.
32. Croce (1941, p. 163).
33. The verse is from Ugo Foscolo’s poem “I sepolcri”, where he writes that Machiavelli showed the dire consequences of the Prince’s absolute and unrestrained power. The same did Marx—Croce writes—by showing the consequences of capitalistic profit.
34. Rathenau (1919, p. 62). Rathenau, co-owner and president of AEG, had been director of the German War Material office, at the War ministry

during the First World War. He would then be appointed Foreign secretary in the Weimar Republic, until his assassination in 1922.

35. p. 20.
36. p. 54.
37. p. 85.
38. p. 64.
39. pp. 68–69.
40. pp. 62–87.
41. Einaudi (1918, pp. 450–456).
42. Einaudi et al. (2006, pp. 5 and 7).
43. Einaudi (1972, p. 6).
44. Einaudi, *Lezioni* (1964, pp. 66–81). See also Baffigi, pp. 25–37.
45. Institute for New Economic Thinking. *The Italian Tradition*, www.hetwebsite.net/net/schools/italian.htm.
46. Einaudi et al. (2006, p. 17).
47. Robinson (1974, p. 72).
48. *The Economist* (2016).
49. Pigou (2013, p. 127).
50. Quoting Edwin Cannan.
51. p. 128.
52. Aslanbeigui, Oakes: Introduction: Reclaiming a Forgotten Master (Pigou, *The Economics of Welfare*).
53. p. XIV.
54. See Part II. On national dividend, Pigou follows Marshall, and criticizes Irving Fisher. On this topic, Keynes quotes Pigou and explains it in clearer terms (1936, p. 38).
55. See Part II, Chapters 1 and 2.
56. pp. 127–130.
57. pp. 134–135.
58. Hartford (2018). Hartford adds: "the economist William Nordhaus has estimated that during the second half of the 20th century, innovative companies generally managed to capture as profits just 3.7% of the social value they created; the other 96.3% went to others, largely consumers. For example, penicillin saves life for pennies". Whether this discourse can be valid for social media, it is debatable (see Chapter 4).
59. Pigou (2013, p. 192).
60. p. 5.
61. Macmillan, 1949 [1937].
62. p. V.
63. pp. 15–16. On distribution, he is indignant that 1% of persons over 25 own 60% of the total capital (p. 13).
64. This reminds, for instance, of the nationalisation of the electric energy in Italy in the 1960s.

65. Robinson (1974).
66. p. 73.
67. p. 80.
68. JMK to R. Harrod, 16 July 1938 (1973, pp. 299–300).
69. Keynes (1949, pp. 96 and 98).
70. Keynes (1925).
71. Keynes (1933) (Hitler had just seized power).
72. Keynes (1926, pp. 28–29).
73. On Schumpeter, see Chapter 3.
74. Keynes (1964, pp. 339–40).
75. Heibroner, Milberg (1995, p. 31).
76. According to Joan Robinson (1974, p. 65).
77. Skidelsky (2018, p. 386).
78. Jones (2013).
79. Concluding Notes on the Social Philosophy Towards Which the General Theory Might Lead. It's the 24th chapter of the *General Theory of Employment, Interest and Money.*
80. Chapter 3: The Principle of Effective Demand.
81. p. 372.
82. p. 30.
83. p. 373.
84. p. 374.
85. p 136
86. p. 376.
87. pp. 183–184.
88. p. 381.
89. p. 379.
90. Hoerber (2017, Chapter 7).
91. p. 348.
92. p. 339.
93. Hawtrey (1931, p. 102).
94. Steil (2013).
95. Beveridge (1944, pp. 22–23).
96. See Beveridge (1942).
97. Beveridge (1944, p. 147).
98. p. 135. *Full Employment* was published in 1944, having well in mind structure and methodology of a war budget.
99. See Part IV, and Appendix C of *Full Employment,* by Nicholas Kaldor.
100. Beveridge (1944) Part IV, Sect. 2
101. Beveridge (1944, p. 148). One has in mind the "euthanasia of the rentier", mentioned by Keynes.
102. Lerner (1944); (1951).
103. Macmillan, 1946.

104. Lerner (1946, pp. 1–4).
105. *Halley Stewart Lecture 1931.*
106. p. 80.
107. pp. 168–169.
108. Hayek (2008, p. 71).
109. He was actually born in Galicia, now Poland, but then (1840) part of the Austrian Empire.
110. One of his main works is (1976).
111. For this reason, Schmoller's charge against him as a classical economist was ill-directed.
112. Hayek, F. A.: *Introduction to Carl Menger's Principles of Economics*, p. 13.
113. Menger's work was dismissed by Schmoller as "merely Austrian"(!). Yagi (1997).
114. Klein, P: *Foreword to Menger's Principles*, p. 7.
115. This reminds of the phrase attributed to Joan Robinson: " I am not mathematically trained, therefore I have to think".
116. Hayek (1955, p. 203).
117. pp. 189–196.
118. Hayek (1945). See also the above quoted *The Counter-Revolution in Science, 1955.*
119. Hayek (1944).
120. p. 38.
121. p. 89.
122. See the *Introduction* to the Routledge edition of 2008, edited by Bruce Caldwell.
123. p. 13.
124. p. 65.
125. See Bentham, above (Chapter 1).
126. p. 13.
127. p. 73.
128. His book is written in the midst of the World War.
129. This legal school gives the judiciary's decisions a prevalence over formal law, at the risk of endangering the principle of law's certainty. The possibility of highly voluntarist and arbitrary decisions is potentially exploited by dictatorships.
130. On Schmitt, see Sect. 8 (ordoliberalism).
131. p. 91.
132. pp. 115–116.
133. Simons (1945, p. 1). This writing, as others quoted here, is included in *Economic Policy for a Free Society*, University of Chicago Press, 1948, published posthumous after Simons' untimely death.

134. A term used by Walras as opposed to distributive justice (see Chapter 1). This is not the only meaning given to the term. Adam Smith refers to commutative justice as "doing voluntarily whatever we can with propriety be forced to do" (*Theory of Moral Sentiments*, p. 334).
135. Simons (1945, p. 5).
136. Simons (1934, p. 41).
137. p. 43.
138. p. 41.
139. pp. 41–42.
140. Simons (1945, pp. 15–16); (1936, p. 79).
141. The Requisites (1936, p. 79).
142. Fisher (1935).
143. Simons (1934, pp. 46–47).
144. Simons (1945).
145. Robbins (1963, pp. 48–49).
146. Friedman (1982, p. 15).
147. p. 174.
148. See the following Section in this chapter.
149. pp. 26–28.
150. p. 51.
151. pp. 53–54.
152. p. 32.
153. Streek (2015).
154. See on this point Bonefeld (2016).
155. Caldwell (2005, pp. 365–366). Caldwell relies on a previous work by R.Cristi.
156. Peacock and Willgerodt (1989, p. 3).
157. Bonefeld (2012) (https://eprints.whiterose.ac.uk).
158. p. 12.
159. The Ordo Manifesto of 1936 (Our Task),in Peacock, Willgerodt (Peacock, A. 1989).
160. p. 21.
161. pp. 22–25.
162. Barry (1989, p. 106).
163. Euken (1948).
164. It has been observed that "*ordoliberalism is at heart a microeconomic model* that disavows macroeconomic policy becauseit treats countries, or even an entire currency zone, as if they were individual households. It makes sense for individuals to save when they are in debt, as the *proverbial Swabianhousewife* does in Germany. But if all individuals cut spending at the same time, the result can be a shortfall in demand that negates the benefits of microeconomic reforms. Once in a while it is better to break rules than all go under inlaw-abiding misery" (*The Economist* [2015]).

165. Euken (1948, pp. 28–29).
166. Bonefeld (2012, p. 5).
167. Zettelmeier (2017, p. 158).
168. Euken (1951).
169. Schmidt (1956).
170. Lutz (1935).
171. Open-market operations by the central bank, adoption of a gold-exchange standard in order to "save" the use of gold, exchange rate interventions by the central bank, creation of an international central bank (pp. 238–240).
172. p. 241.
173. An ordoliberal as Wilhelm Röpke calledfor a return to the gold standard (1951).
174. Müller-Armack (1956).
175. Röpke (1957).
176. Müller-Armack (1956, pp. 82–86).
177. Barry (1989) p. 121. Streek (2017).

References

Baffigi, A. (2009). *Luigi Einaudi. Teoria economica e legislazione sociale nel testo delle Lezioni*. Quaderni di storia economica della Banca d'Italia, settembre.

Barry, N. (1989). Political and Economic Thought of German Neo-Liberals. In W. Peacock (Eds.), *German Neo-Liberals and the Social Market Economy*. New York, NY: Pralgrave Macmillan.

Beveridge, W. (1942). *Report on Social Insurance and Allied Services*, HMSO.

Beveridge, W. (1944). *Full Employment in a Free Society*. London: Allen & Unwin.

Blackett, B. (1932). *Halley Stewart Lecture 1931. The World's Economic Crisis and the Way of Escape*. London: Allen and Unwin.

Bodei, R. (2003). Il ruolo dell'economia in Croce. *Economia politica*, 2.

Bonefeld, W. (2012). Freedom, Crisis and the Strong State: on German Ordoliberalism. *New Political Economy, 17/5*. (https://eprints.whiterose.ac.uk).

Bonefeld, W. (2016, August). Authoritarian Liberalism: From Schmitt to Ordoliberalism to the Euro. *Critical Sociology*.

Caldwell, P. C. (2005). Controversies over Carl Schmitt: A Review of Recent Literature. *The Journal of Modern History, 77*(2).

Croce, B. (1941). *Materialismo storico ed economia marxista*. Bari: Laterza.

Croce, B. (1955 [1925]). *Cultura e vita morale. Intermezzi polemici*, Nuova serie, XV, Liberalismo (p. 283). Bari: Laterza.

Croce, B. (1973 [1908]). *Filosofia della pratica. Economia ed etica*. Bari: Laterza.

Croce, B. (2015 [originally published as a single essay,1927]). *Liberismo e liberalismo. Etica e politica.*
Einaudi, L. (1918). La nuova economia. *La Riforma sociale, XXIX.*
Einaudi, L. (1964). *Lezioni di politica sociale.* Torino: Einaudi. Institute for New Economic Thinking. *The Italian Tradition.* www.hetwebsite.net/net/schools/italian.html.
Einaudi, L. (1972 [1924]). La bellezza della lotta. In *Le lotte del lavoro.* Torino: Einaudi.
Einaudi, L., Faucci, R., & Marchionatti, R. (2006). *Introduction to Luigi Einaudi, Selected Economic Essays.* London: Palgrave Macmillan.
Euken, W. (1948). What Kind of Economic and Social System? In Peacock & Willgerodt (Eds.), *Germany's Social Market Economy: Origins and Evolution.* London: Macmillan.
Euken, W. (1951). *This Unsuccessful Age, or the Pains of Economic Progress.* Edinburg: William Hodge.
Exams and Expectations. (2016, December 24). *The Economist.*
Fisher, I. (1935). *100% Money.* New York: Adelphi.
Friedman, M. (1982 [1962]). *Capitalism and Freedom.* Chicago: The University of Chicago Press.
Hartford, T. (2018, April 28–29). How to Put a Price on Social Media. *The Financial Times.*
Hawtrey, R. G. (1931). *The Gold Standard: Theory and Practice.* London: Longman, Green and Company.
Hayek, F. A. (1945). The Use of Knowledge in Society. *American Economic Review, XXXV.*
Hayek, F. A. (1955). *The Counter-Revolution of Science. Studies on the Abuse of Reason.* London Free Press of Glencoe: Collier-Macmillan.
Hayek, F. A. (2008 [1944]). *The Road to Serfdom.* London: Routledge.
Hayek, F. A. *Introduction to Carl Menger's Principles of Economics.*
Heilbroner, R., & Milberg, W. (1995). *The Crisis of Vision in Modern Economic Thought.* Cambridge: Cambridge University Press.
Hoerber, T. (2017). *Hayek vs Keynes. A Battle of Ideas.* London: Reaktion Books.
Jones, T. (2013). 'Reluctant' or Liberal Collectivist? The Social Liberalism of Keynes and Beveridge. *Journal of Liberal History, 78*(Spring).
Kaldor, N. Appendix C of Beveridge's *Full Employment.*
Kelly, D. (2019, April 29). Malthusian Moments in the Work of John Maynard Keynes. *The Historical Journal.*
Keynes, J. M. (1925, August). Am I a Liberal? *The Nation & Athenaeum.*
Keynes, J. M. (1926). *The End of Laissez-Faire.* London: The Hogarth Press.
Keynes, J. M. (1933, June). National Self-Sufficiency. *The Yale Review, 22*(4).
Keynes, J. M. (1949 [1938]). *Two Memoirs.* London: Rupert Hart-Davis.

Keynes, J. M. (1964 [1936]). *The General Theory of Employment Interest and Money*. London: Macmillan.
Klein, P. *Foreword to Carl Menger's Principles of Economics*.
Lerner, A. (1944). *Principles of Welfare Economics*. New York: Macmillan.
Lerner, A. (1946). *Economics of Control*. New York: Macmillan.
Lerner, A. (1951). *Economics of Employment*. New York: McGraw Hill.
Lutz, F. 1935. The Functioning of the Gold Standard. In Peacock & Willgerodt (Eds.), *Germany's Social Market Economy: Origins and Evolution*. London: Macmillan.
Menger, C. (1976 [1871]). *Principles of Economics*. Auburn: Ludwig von Mises Institute.
Moggridge, D. (ed). (1973). *The Collected Writings of John Maynard Keynes*, vol. XIV. London: Macmillan.
Montesano, A. (2003). Croce e la scienza economica. *Economia politica*, 2.
Müller-Armack, A. (1956). The Meaning of the Social Market Economy. In Peacock & Willgerodt (Eds.), *Germany's Social Market Economy: Origins and Evolution*. London: Macmillan.
Peacock, A. & Willgerodt, H. (1989). German Liberalism and Economic Revival. In Peacock & Willgerodt (Eds.), *Germany's Social Market Economy: Origins and Evolution*. London: Macmillan.
Pigou, A. C. (2013 [1920]). *The Economics of Welfare*. London: Palgrave Macmillan.
Rathenau, W. (1919). *L'economia nuova [Die Neue Wirtschaft, 1918]*. Bari: Laterza.
Robbins, L. (1963). *Politics and Economics. Papers in Political Economy*. London: Macmillan.
Robinson, J. (1974 [1962]). *Economic Philosophy*. London: Penguin.
Röpke, W. (1951). Interdependence of Domestic and International Economic Systems. In Peacock & Willgerodt (Eds.), *Germany's Social Market Economy: Origins and Evolution*. London: Macmillan.
Röpke, W, (1957). Welfare Freedom and Inflation, Reprinted in *Two Essays. The Problem of Economic Order. Welfare Freedom and Inflation*, University Press of America, 1987.
Schmidt, K. (1956). The Public Sector in a Market Economy. In Peacock & Willgerodt (Eds.), *Germany's Social Market Economy: Origins and Evolution*. London: Macmillan.
Schumpeter, J. A. (1947). *Capitalism, Socialism and Democracy*. New York: Harper and Brothers.
Simons, H. (1948). The Requisites of Free Competition (1936). In *Economic Policy*.
Simons, H. (1948). A Positive Program for Laissez Faire. Some Proposals for a Liberal Economic Policy (1934). In *Economic Policy*.

Simons, H. (1948). Introduction: A Political Credo (1945). In *Economic Policy for a Free Society*. Chicago: University of Chicago Press.

Simons, H. (1948). The Beveridge Program: An Unsympathetic Interpretation (1945), in *Journal of Political Economy, 53*(3).

Skidelsky, R. (1992). *John Maynard Keynes: The Economist as Saviour*, Vol II of Skidelsky's Biography of Keynes. London: Macmillan.

Skidelsky, R. (2018). *Money and Government. A Challenge to Mainstream Economics*. London: Allen Lane.

Steil, B. (2013). *The Battle of Bretton Woods: John Maynard Keynes, Harry Dexter White, and the Making of a New World Order.* Princeton-Oxford: Princeton University Press.

Stein, H. (1990). The Triumph of the Adaptive Society, in *The American Economist, XXXIV*, 1.

Streek, W. (2015). Heller, Schmitt and the Euro, in *European Law Journal, 21*(3).

Streek, W. (2017, May 4). Playing Catch Up. *London Review of Books.*

The Economist. (2015, May 9). *Of rules and order.*

Trevelyan, G. M. (1944). *English Social History: A Survey of Six Centuries, Chaucer to Victoria*. London, New York and Toronto: Longmans, Green and Co.

Yagi, K. (1997). Carl Menger and the Historicism in Economics. In P. Koslowsy (Ed.), *Methodology of the Social Sciences.* Berlin-Heidelberg: Springer.

Zettelmeier, J. (2017, November). German Ordo and Eurozone Reform: A View from the Trenches. In T. Beck & H. H. Kotz (Eds.), *Ordoliberalism: A German Oddity*? London: CEPR Press.

CHAPTER 3

Enemies of Liberalism

3.1 Nationalism and Corporativism

The twentieth century saw liberalism challenged by the nationalism and socialism. This was particularly relevant in the field of economic doctrines. In fact, liberalism's metamorphoses in the twentieth century were also due to their influence: liberal political and economic thinkers were often seduced by these doctrines, sometimes by the allure of a pervasive State, other times by the egalitarian impulse of a socialist society.

In the early twentieth century, and in particular after the First World War, nationalism meant on the one hand the completion of that process of independence of various European states, that had characterized the previous century. On the other hand, nationalism lost its liberal *élan*, and in larger, already well established states it took a strong turn towards authoritarianism, even supporting openly dictatorial regimes; in these states nationalism, as an economic doctrine, didn't do other than reaffirm the idea that the German Historical School of economics had already put forward: an economic system centred on an "ethical State". This commingling of authoritarianism and economic nationalism found a most accomplished expression in Italy: as we shall see, the Italian corporativist system was a stepchild of economic nationalism within a fascist framework.

After the Second World War, with the defeat of major nationalist and authoritarian powers, nationalism went on a declining path. It became sometimes a political model for underdeveloped areas of the world that

A. Roselli, *Economic Philosophies*,
Palgrave Studies in Classical Liberalism,
https://doi.org/10.1007/978-3-030-53317-5_3

wanted to get rid of their colonial past. Nationalism, however, has more recently made a strong comeback, as a reaction to the extended globalization accompanying the spread of economic liberalism, and to the Great Recession that followed the financial crisis of recent years. Generally focussed on the prevailing interests of the nation and potentially inclined towards mercantilism or protectionism, it shows a line of continuity with the old nationalism, but its features are still unclear, as we shall see later on, in Chapter 4.

As socialism is regarded, it had a notable influence on economic thinking of many authors of a liberal background, as we have seen in the previous chapter; but, on the other side, Marxist economists, the orthodox interpreters of the doctrine, remained essentially stuck to the verb of the master, in a sort of ideological inflexibility. Marxist economists Baran and Sweezy explicitly wrote of a "stagnation of Marxist social science".[1] Like Marx, they devoted their studies more to a wide and destructive criticism of capitalistic free-market regimes, than to adjust their thought to a deeply evolving social and economic environment, to the unavoidable changes even in socialist-oriented societies. Marxism suffered from the shortcomings and final collapse of the State which was socialism's major embodiment.

We shall consider the authoritarian nationalism of the first half of the twentieth century in Sects. 3.1 and 3.2, and Marxist socialism in Sects. 3.3–3.6. Section 3.7 is mostly devoted to two non-Marxist thinkers—Schumpeter and Polanyi—who made the fundamentally wrong forecast of an advent of socialism: a sort of socialism not actually pursued by a "necessary" revolution, but rather following the "necessary" exhaustion of the free market, liberal society: a sort of socialism by default. They ended up by being more (wrongly) deterministic than Marx himself.

Regarding economic thinking, Italy is perhaps the country that at the turn of the century was intellectually at the forefront in resuming the old ideas of the German Historical School, which was, itself, in early twentieth century on a declining path. Its theories gave however strength to Italian nationalists, willing to affirm in the international arena the position of their country, which was emerging from the recent struggle for its own independence: a position that Germany had conquered in not too distant years. Those Italian thinkers fought the positivist, individualist and utilitarian vision of neo-classical economists, and moved the focus of their reflections from the individual towards the all-absorbing ethical State, moving, so to speak, from Comte and Marshall to Hegel and Schmoller, from the vision of economics as a science to be studied as a natural science, to an inductive, historically rooted research of the specific Italian economic conditions. As just mentioned, Italy was indeed in a position similar to middle nineteenth-century Germany: "The least of the great powers",[2] but ambitious to gain that pre-eminent position that, in the rhetoric of the time, had been for so long time lost, after the glories of the Roman empire. And again similarly to Germany, Friedrich List's *National System of Political Economy* and economic protectionism gained traction within Italian academic circles.

In this context, if we have in mind the great Italian economists of the liberal tradition, a heated debate could not be avoided between protectionists and free traders. It was originally focussed on the high tariff that had been introduced in Italy in 1887, and had been followed by a strong increase of import duties on wheat and sugar. This protection had had uneven consequences on different sectors of the Italian economy. However, during the long tenure of Giolitti at the head of the Italian government, the relevance of those measures had been actually diminishing: most of them were excise duties (per unit taxes) and therefore—in a long phase of increasing price level—their effect had been lessened; in addition, the relative strength of the lira on the foreign exchange market contributed to make their burden less heavy.[3] Even if this evolution tended to give an upper hand to the arguments of the free traders, in 1913 the minister for Agriculture, Industry and Commerce, Francesco S. Nitti, appointed a Royal Commission to inquire the whole matter of the duty regime and trade treaties.

We shall not dwell on this debate, enlivened—particularly on the free traders' front—by some of the best minds of the Italian economic discipline—as Einaudi, De Viti de Marco, Luzzatto, Borgatta, Ricci, all liberal economists. With today's eyes, we can set that debate in a discussion between mainstream economists and those who were inclined towards the Historical School, whom the former were even reluctant to qualify as economists. The first group can be seen as carrying forward analytical arguments, with the second leaning instead towards a pragmatic approach, reflecting concrete sectoral interests and official positions.[4]

The lack of analytical arguments was, however, counteracted on the protectionist and nationalistic side by emphasizing issues that were gaining new strength, in particular the ideas that had characterized the German economic historicism: the centrality attributed to the State in governing the economy, the rejection of the liberal principles of the classical and neo-classical doctrine. On the political side, it was kept well in mind the protection granted to the German industry under emperor Wilhelm II. Italian nationalists gave particular emphasis to the authoritarian aspects of a protectionist policy, with a twist of thought that would then bring them on the fascist camp. A prominent figure in this regard is Alfredo Rocco, who, already in 1914, had laid the basis of what would be later called "corporativist doctrine".

In a text jointly signed by Alfredo Rocco and Filippo Carli, two principles are stressed: (1) methods of production have to be adjusted to the mass production. This entails—according to them—a rejection of free competition: "the competition regime is essentially a crisis regime", and the struggle to grab customers only means reciprocal destruction. What is needed is "solidarity", "associationism", to be enacted through industrial syndicates (cartels), which are indeed the result of "the general malaise of an unfettered competition, and overproduction": big industrial conglomerates, both horizontally and vertically integrated[5]; (2) National production has to be defended, not only by confirming, but also by reinforcing the protection of industry, in order to fill the current delay in respect to other more advanced economies: a defence advocated in particular by certain industrial sectors, as steel, shipbuilding, sugar. The authors are critical of the Ricardian theory of comparative advantages, because it nails poor countries to indefinitely maintain their model of production, without any chance of economic growth that would come from diversification of their economy (an argument clearly taken from List's writings).[6]

List, the theorist of protectionism, is seen by Rocco and Carli, just because of his battle against the Classical School, as the founder of the German economic science.[7] The main reason why German economic historicism deserves to be praised—according to these authors—is its rigorously empirical-inductive approach, based as it is on the study of the national economy of a specific people in a specific moment of its history. Against the "cosmopolitanism", the "worldly society" of the Classical School (the "globalism", in today's parlance), German economists had elaborated proposals made to measure for Germany of their own times, aimed at promoting State intervention in the economic and social fields. From this perspective, Rocco and Carli condemned both liberalism and socialism, which shared the idea of "disintegration"[8] of the national community, whose common purpose German historicists, and the two Italians, kept, on the contrary, in the highest regard.[9] Rocco and Carli write that "individuals [are to be seen] not anymore as an end, but as simple instruments and organs of the national society"[10] (it's like reading Hegel). Therefore they reject economics based on the individual, on Benthamite utilitarianism, on materialism, on internationalism. The main object of the economist's analysis must be "the study of the conditions of the Italian national economy". Rocco and Carli argue that the "causes of [its] inferiority",[11] which constrain its productive capacity and, in more concrete terms, make the extension of the 1887 tariff protection necessary, depend on both "natural" and "transitory" factors. The former are related to the national territory, largely sterile,[12] with scarcity of raw material, and unfit for easy communications; while the latter depend on lack of capital and entrepreneurial spirits, and on a shortage of managerial and technical capabilities.

This call for a strong customs protection responded to the interests not only of the heavy industry, but also of the military establishment. Not by chance, as a corollary to their study of the Italian development, a colonial war was strongly invoked by the two authors, in order to obtain the raw materials necessary for energy's national needs, a new space where to allocate the Italian workforce in excess, and to open new markets to national produce. It seems, in conclusion, that economic nationalism rests on protectionism, monopolistic concentration of production, colonial expansion.[13]

But the meaning of corporativism goes beyond the conduct of an economic nationalistic and protectionist policy, and cannot be grasped without its philosophical root: the Actualism of the philosopher Giovanni Gentile. He inveighed against the vision of State only doing ancillary activities to the benefit of the individual, and, in a Hegelian, anti-liberal perspective, saw the individual as inextricably connected to the State, very much far from the "abstract" man of the Enlightenment and liberal philosophy. "A corporativist economy would recognize the social character of production, with individual initiative governed by social needs and social goals",[14] in the superior interest of the nation.

Differently from the prevailing opinion that links corporativism to the Hegelian and statist tradition, the American historian James Gregor found in this approach an unexpected link with Rousseau's "General Will" and with the role of the State in the field of citizens' education, so that people can express themselves in a collective voice (see above, Chapter 1). This statist educational system would make individuals as uniform as possible in their values and aspirations, so that a harmony of the general will could be reached, and shared decisions taken. Government action would simply execute this general will, in a sort of "totalitarian democracy".[15] The Rousseauian vision that people's will cannot be delegated to parliament is central to the corporativist view of the State, and resurfaces in current populism (Chapter 4).

The corporativist idea is also central to Ugo Spirito's thought, a philosopher and ideologue of the fascist regime: the real world, which "is historically evolving,...has been removed by the economist from the always changing circumstances". The economic agent has been seen as "a naturalistic, botanical species: *homo oeconomicus*, naturally and scientifically analysable". "Against liberal economy we want to pit corporative economy. The first says that man is all what matters, and that society, or State, is only a guarantee for the individual; the second states that individual must be identified with the State, and that studying the individual means to study the State as an organism".[16] As a seal to these words, the entry of Enciclopedia Treccani titled "Fascismo", signed by Mussolini but probably written by Giovanni Gentile, reads as follows: "He who says liberalism means individual, he who says fascism means State". The inevitable result is that the artificial distinction between what is conceived as "public" and that conceived as "private" in the national economy is going to disappear.

In order to have a real fascist, Actualistic corporativism, Spirito envisaged a system of enterprise that would replace the liberal joint-stock company: an enterprise where the distinction between ownership and responsible management and between entrepreneurs and workers would disappear, in a community that would rest on collective interest, collective effort, collective rewards.[17] Whether this position can be interpreted just as a cover for industrial private interests, that is as a way to keep quiet the working class, or as a step towards a socialized—if not socialist—economy, is an issue on which we shall return in Sect. 3.2. There were, for certain, industrialists who feared a bolshevik evolution guided by regime's left-wingers. Others complained—between themselves—that the absence of workers' unrest and strikes was an advantage, but having to obey the regime's directives on their industrial projects was frustrating.[18]

Coherent with this openly anti-liberal economic philosophy is the idea of a specific model of capital–work relation within the corporative State. We have seen above (Chapters 1 and 2) how—to a classical economist—the equilibrium wage is the one that corresponds to "something more" than the worker's maintenance; how—to a Marxist economist, who relies on Ricardian foundations—there is an identification of the wage with the whole value of what is produced (and a worker's claim for the re-appropriation of what is subtracted by capitalist's profit); how—to a liberal of the twentieth century—wage has to be aligned with the enterprise's competitiveness, or—according to others—adjusted, with the State's intervention, to the worker's inferiority condition vis-à-vis the capitalist (since the bargaining power of the opposite social parts is different).

On their part, Rocco and Carli, whose goal is an "elevation of the working class", think that the equilibrium wage can be reached through the "corporation" ("Our old corporativism"—they write—that has been overwhelmed by jus-naturalistic (natural law) individualism, and by the French revolution). The agents of the national economy are just two: the State and the individual, and this last one—either employer or worker—has a social mandate, which means that he does not operate in his exclusive interest.[19] As a consequence, social conflicts, which express specific interests, must be overcome and reconciled in the interest of the nation. Class struggle does exist, but Marxist trade unionism is "antinational and anti-State".

In order to forbid class self-defence (we might say: a workers' independent syndicate), it is necessary to set up a system which makes it impossible. This system is made of two institutions: (1) Syndicates that put together employers and workers: only this kind of syndicate, legally recognized and brought under State's control, can legally represent all the workers and employers of a certain industry/sector; (2) Collective labour contracts: they are stipulated by these syndicates and bind all the persons who belong to that sector, members and non-members alike: indeed, the collective contract embodies the solidarity of all factors of production, and reconciles opposite particular interests, which must be subordinated to the superior interest of the national output (a specific judiciary—the Labour magistrates—has competence in the field of collective contracts.[20]). The collective contract would be an inter-classist solution to labour conflicts.

These concepts are written down in the Labour Charter of 1927.[21] The nation is an ethical, political and economic unit; it is a body which is above the individuals—singularly taken or grouped together—who are the nation's components. Corporations are State's organs which constitute the unitary organization of the production forces, whose interest they represent.[22] Structured along various production branches, corporations are the place where interest groups, which in the syndicates remain on parallel lines, can meet and resolve their differences. Corporations have both consultative and normative powers, can therefore dictate mandatory rules on work relations and production coordination. Private initiative is the more efficient to serve national interest, while State intervention takes place only when private initiative is lacking, or State's higher political interests come into play. The employers' syndicates are obliged to stimulate the increase or raise the quality of production, by decreasing costs. While, in a regime of free competition, wage tends to the level of production costs, in the corporative regime the worker can get more but not above the threshold beyond which others would be damaged.[23] In the opinion of Filippo Carli, the "corporative wage" would incorporate ethical and historical components, whatever this may mean.

What emerges from the corporativist system, is the opposite of a free-market economy: a State-controlled bilateral monopoly, as regards the labour market; and an oligopolistic regime, with cartels and consortia, for most of the other markets.

According to recent studies, through the corporativist system, income distribution was made less unequal; during the Depression of the 1930s, real wages were protected, albeit in a situation of decreasing employment and working hours. "It can be reasonably assumed that, without collective contracts' protection, things might have been much worse for the workers".[24]

3.2 Different Interpretations of Corporativism

As we know well, corporativism did not survive the historical experience of fascist Italy. It was, however, another turn—an authoritarian one—that nationalism took in the past century. Its interpretation may be interesting in order to check how a few ideas of its economic and social organization still affect nationalistic, or social-liberal economic philosophies of our times. Its interpretation is also useful to verify whether a "fascist, corporative economic policy" existed at all, as some studies suggest.[25] I shall mention here the leftist, and Marxian, view; the dirigiste view and the technocratic view. Later below, I shall briefly check what remained of corporativism in post-war, post-fascist Italy.

According to the first interpretation, big business (heavy industry and finance) actively supported the fascist movement and was the main beneficiary of the regime, in a *do ut des* social contract, by keeping the real wages not above subsistence level,[26] and by protectionist measures.

Corporativism was an instrument to protect industrial interests. The small bourgeoisie—caught in the middle between the great bourgeoisie and the proletariat—were victims of the Great War, inflation, the crisis of capitalism, and therefore frustrated and getting poorer. These people could not, however, go to the left, their goal was not the "class struggle"; on the contrary, they did not want to lose their social status albeit mostly apparent; they hated social disorder and had a strong concept of the nation: "pauperized but not proletarianized".[27] Again in a *do ut des* bargain, fascism gave them a strong lira (until it lasted) that benefited the middle classes as rentiers,[28] and an extended Welfare State: Fascism as a covenant between the great and the small bourgeoisie.[29] Its proclaimed anti-capitalistic stance was simply demagogy. And, of course, the ethical State was a fiction if not a mere swindle, on the shoulders of the working class.

Michal Kalecki gave a Marxist explanation of the big business's support of fascist—and Nazi—dictatorships.[30] He writes that, in a capitalistic free-market system, the opposition of the capitalistic class to large state intervention through policies of government spending rests on three reasons: the dislike of government interference in the problem of employment; the dislike of government spending directions, which could be extended to include nationalizations and provoke a crowding out of private investments; and the dislike of consumption subsidies, which go against the moral principle of the capitalistic ethics of "you shall earn your bread in sweat". Moreover and above all, in a situation of full employment thus created, the social position of the capitalist would be undermined by the consciousness of the working class, with strikes and social unrest and political tensions. The fascist or the Nazi dictatorships remove these capitalistic objections by putting the State machinery under the firm control of the big business: discipline in the factories and political stability are maintained by the "new order, which ranges from the suppression of the trade unions to the concentration camp. Political pressure replaces the economic pressure of the unemployment".[31]

Regarding dirigisme, Ugo Spirito noted that the political economy of the regime, liberal in its first phase, then State-socialist in the second (when big banks' bail-outs were enacted by the State), moved in the direction of "integral corporativism", a concept that goes "well beyond liberalism and socialism", through a critical departure from the liberal idea of the free individual, arriving to the identification of individual and State. Corporativism was resolving the contraposition of capital and labour through their unification in the superior interest of the State.[32] The fact that any distinction of owners, entrepreneurs and workers would melt in a system of collective interest and rewards, explains the fears, mentioned above, of important industrial leaders that corporativism might evolve into a sort of Bolshevism. Even though, as a matter of fact, fascist corporations appeared closer to the employers' interests, a forum of "concertation among producers",[33] a sort of bureaucratization of the economy was anyway the result.

The technocratic view is a derivative of the dirigiste interpretation, in the sense that it also relies on a heavy involvement of the State in the economy. Facing urgent and systemic problems, Mussolini paid just a lip service to corporativism and, also, put aside the fascist party, not trusting the competence and fearing the "rivalry of his freewheeling party chieftains".[34] Moving the focus of the decision-making process to the person of "Il Duce" himself, had, as a consequence, the rise of a group of technocrats, often outstanding personalities, only partly linked to the fascist party. The technocratic perspective has its institutional expression in the creation of more than 300 "enti pubblici" (quasi-State bodies), according to a new model of organization of a sectional public administration.[35]

These last two views, taken together, see corporativism as a "third-way" between economic liberalism and socialism. They can be reconnected to a specific Italian strand of thought, of "civil economics", that goes back to Enlightenment thought (Genovesi, Filangieri) up to Giuseppe Toniolo and F. S. Nitti. They follow a paradigm of common well-being, inter-classist cooperation, more equal income distribution, large State intervention. The *homo corporativus* would respond to objectives of rebalancing different social classes' interests and pursue a "mixed economy".

Regarding the survival of corporative ideas in the post-war Italian republic, it is possible to say that the emphasis on labour as a centre-piece of the economic system is still well visible: the Italian constitution, at its first article, states that "Italy is a Republic founded on labour"; in addition, the system of collective contracts is still in force. About State intervention in the economy, it should be born in mind that those quasi-State entities and financial institutions embodied, rather than the idea of a corporative State, a mechanism of economic development relying on an a-political technocratic elite. Even if this method was not immune from meddling through, collusive practices and political pressures on "independent" bodies, the institutional framework was solid and, in fact, long lasting, survived the fall of fascism and, again, characterized several decades of the new-born Italian Republic and its economy. What definitely ended with the fall of fascism was the protectionist attitude. Post-war Italy opened its frontiers to international competition: from this viewpoint, corporativism was definitely dead.

One might wonder whether an experience similar to Italian corporativism occurred in Nazi Germany. The answer is probably negative, and the corporativist experience remained a typical Italian product. In the same period of time ordoliberalism represented in Germany the real new intellectual development in the field of economic philosophy. And if a link existed between the profoundly illiberal Carl Schmitt and ordoliberalism (see Chapter 2), no such link can be found between him and the Italian fascism. "Fascism, in pursuing anti-democratic goals, prefers to rely on the ideological support of the Actualism of Giovanni Gentile and on the ethical State, much more self-restrained and reassuring than the vertiginous and extremist Schmittian thought".[36]

3.3 Marxist Economic Philosophy After Marx: No Change

Between economic philosophies and theories on the one side, and economic institutions and policies on the other, a two-ways relation has constantly existed. In the previous chapters we have seen how liberalism profoundly influenced politics and economics between the nineteenth and the twentieth centuries, being in turn affected by the dramatic events of the First World War and the Great Depression, and by the achievements of socialism and nationalism in the first decades of the 20th.

Regarding the Marxist doctrine: had it, in the course of last century, some kind of evolution, particularly in the light of trends of Soviet economy, that is of the country that wanted to embed the very idea of its begetters? It seems that for a long while Marxist economists did not devote many efforts to develop the Marxist vision beyond what emerges from Marx's and Engels' works, and to adjust this vision to the changing circumstances of the real world, both of free-market and socialist economies.

Socialism—in its Marxist version—remained in the twentieth century a static ideology, compared to the dynamism of liberalism, agitated in different directions by continuous intellectual rethinking of previous or competing visions. Some factors can be mentioned in this regard.

The absence of a similar, self-critical attitude is at least partly due to the fact that Marxism is a doctrine in the narrow sense of the word: the historical materialism is an interpretation of social and economic reality that does not admit deviations, not to mention alternative perspectives. Reading Marxist economists—even those more open to a benevolent, if critical, view of liberal thinking (of economists of the Classical School, in particular)—one cannot avoid the impression that, for them, Marx's doctrine has a really sacred content, it is a "credo", almost an act of faith: deviations are acts to be stigmatized. This almost Christian view of socialism as an incoming kingdom of God led often to dismiss the idea that a socialist society might be afflicted by some essential contradictions that characterize the capitalistic society even in its most advanced stage of social inclusion: an idea deemed incompatible with Marxist theory.

During the 1930s, when major capitalistic economies were still stuck in the aftermath of the Great Depression, while the Soviet Union was enjoying a relatively benign, uninterrupted phase of growth, Sidney and Beatrice Webb hailed communism as a new civilization: "This fundamental transformation of the social order—the substitution of a planned production for community consumption, instead of the capitalistic profit-making of the so-called 'Western Civilization'—seems to me [sic] so vital a change for the better, so conducive to the progress of humanity to higher level of wealth and happiness, virtue and wisdom, as to constitute a new civilisation". And communism didn't appear to them so far from Christian values, because the new institutions were "not contrary to the living philosophy of the Christian religion".[37] Political leaders of capitalistic democracies—they added—considered that philosophy as the foundation stone of the society, but it was in fact very far from the root impulse of a profit-making society.[38]

The Webbs are sometimes seen as "Stalin's useful idiots", but this is what a liberal philosopher as Bertrand Russell wrote in 1920: "The fundamental ideas of communism are by no means impracticable, and would, if realized, add immeasurably to the well-being of mankind".[39]

Another explanation of the inflexibility of the Marxist doctrine can be given even in terms of a Marxist perspective. It gives essential importance to the "structure" of the society, as opposed to its "superstructure" (see Chapter 1): one might argue that Marxist thought was—has been—unable to adjust to changes occurred over time in the very structure of the capitalistic society, that is in its modes of production. They were changing in many aspects: in the deeply evolving technology, in the relations of capitalists, managers and workers, in market structures, in the relative importance of different sectors of the economy and social classes. With specific reference to the nature of the capitalistic enterprise—the centre piece of the capitalistic system—Schumpeter argued that "the process of industrial change was not correctly understood by Marx...with him, the mechanism [of industrial change] resolves itself into mere mechanics of mass of capital. He had no adequate theory of enterprise and his failure to distinguish the entrepreneur from the capitalist...accounts for many cases of non sequitur and for many mistakes".[40]

Another aspect of the capitalistic structures not considered by Marx was later pointed out by two Marxist economists, Baran and Sweezy. They observed that Marx had focussed his attention to a structure of capitalism that was already outdated at the time of his writing: "Marx treated monopolies as remnants of the feudal and mercantilist past", and saw competition as the prevalent form of market in nineteenth-century Britain. But "they [the monopolies] were becoming a permanent feature of the system; and also his [Marx's] successors failed to explain or sometimes even to recognise their existence".[41] These large-scale enterprises, just because of their significant share of an industry's output, as monopolistic or oligopolistic firms, generate an up-trending structure of prices and full control of production and investment volumes, in a way that is "nothing short than devastating to capitalism as a rational social order",[42] and in contradiction with the price structure as emerging from a non-existent perfect competition regime. Monopoly capitalism thus generates a tendency of surplus—defined as "the difference between what society produces and the cost of producing it"[43]—to rise. However, according to Baran and Sweezy, the structure of capitalism does not have an adequate mechanism of surplus absorption, a lack that is statistically visible in the figures of unemployment and under-utilization of available resources. This in turn is cause of stagnation, only contrasted, so far, by epoch-making technical innovations and military and imperialistic policies.[44]

The theme of monopolistic structures of capitalism is a constant of Marxian thought, but it was Schumpeter (of which Sweezy had been research assistant at Harvard), who in his *Capitalism, Socialism and Democracy*[45] denied the relevance of competition for capitalism to flourish, and rather attributed to the "creative destruction", enacted through large-scale enterprises, its continued strength (see below, Sect. 3.7).

We shall develop this theme of the ever evolving "modes of production" later on, but for the moment enough is to observe that, this evolution notwithstanding, a Marxist might put in evidence that an essential and continuing contraposition of interests between the owner and the labourer is still present in a capitalistic society. The changing weight of entrepreneurs and owners inside the firm, technological displacement of labour by machinery, the enlargement of the services sector, the ability of workers to start businesses of their own, "the conversion of insecure workers into confident consumers" would not be enough to get rid of an essential struggle of social classes.[46]

This importance of the evolution of the "structure" was not appreciated by Marx. Moreover, if Marx's criticism of the capitalistic production had its flaws, the way how the productive structure would concretely operate in a socialist society escaped his attention. It was observed, by a Marxist economist, that "the founders of scientific socialism, Marx and Engels, devoted all their efforts to the analysis of the capitalistic economy. They made only a few highly generalized remarks about the socialist economy. As a matter of principle, they refused to enter into the problem in greater detail, out of fear of proving more utopian than scientific".[47]

This eschatological and deterministic view was perhaps one reason why the process of transition from capitalism to socialism—which was in Russia abrupt, not only in terms of time - was neglected as a field of inquiry. The initial phase—the Bolshevik "War communism"—was the harshest, and far from gradual, introduction of a socialist society, followed by an equally abrupt reversal to the opposite policy, the New Economic Policy-N.E.P., in turn abolished after few years. Moreover, the revolutionary events that took place in 1917 had occurred in a country whose social and economic structure was far from that envisaged by Marx as a mature environment for a successful revolutionary outcome.[48] The socialist revolution was accomplished, in few months, earlier than expected by Marx, and in a country still far from the advanced capitalism's industrial phase. According to him, a prerequisite for socialist upheaval was a sufficiently developed industrial structure and a motivated and self-conscious proletariat: conditions well far from those prevailing in tsarist Russia. This circumstance made the organizational problems of a transition towards socialism particularly complicated.

The main issue for Marxist economists, in the really uncharted territory of political and economic alternatives that was wide open before them, was if, and to what extent, the economic "laws" of a capitalistic society would be valid in a socialist system. Their reflections were constrained by the intellectual framework set up by Marx, but could not remain unaffected by the actual situation of the Soviet economy at the time of their writing. It is only in the second half of the twentieth century that some rethinking of the Marxist doctrine emerges. "Just as in the eighteenth century, a radical change in socio-economic organization is engendering a radical change in the nature and function of economics", a Marxist economist, Ronald Meek, wrote in 1964.[49] This rethinking was deemed necessary in order to take account of the increasing structural weakness of the Soviet economy.

Marxist socialist doctrine remained disconnected from the concrete conduct of Soviet economic policy. As Edward Carr wrote: "The fulfilment of the eschatological promises of Marxism was delayed, like the Second Advent, far beyond the original expectations of the faithful".[50] In particular, policy evolved along lines that had rather to do with the evolving political and economic circumstances. In fact, Soviet policy has been compared to the conduct of a war economy of a capitalistic country. Essentially, this policy evolution followed endogenous forces aimed at building a national power over many decades through a planned command economy, based on a pervasive intervention of the State, public ownership of means of production, monopoly of foreign trade: "Socialism in one country", according to Stalin's and Buckharin's theory, rather than a coherent design, of a permanent and universal revolution, as envisaged by Marx.[51]

This dichotomy between an uncompromising ideology and the concrete evolution of Soviet policies over the years is well illustrated by a sympathetic observer, Rudolf Schlesinger, who writes in 1947: "It may be unreasonable to expect the leaders of the USSR openly to declare that there has been a quite natural change, not only of politics, but even of dominating ideas since the days of 1917. So the public abroad is faced with two contradictory assertions: that of the (mainly Trotskyte) critics that the Soviet regime has abandoned its original aims and conceptions [and] has degenerated, and that of the regime itself which not only maintains that it has been true to those original conceptions, but in order to prove its case even tries to interpret its past in the light of the present".[52]

In the same vein, within this framework of a command economy, "there has been a series of Soviet economies over the years, each significantly different from the others". The organization of the economy changed accordingly, while "Communist ideology [was] interpreted and reinterpreted to justify these organizational shifts".[53]

On balance, Soviet government brought mass production and mass armies, increased education, created better opportunities for women, but also—in a sort of profit and loss account—caused failures in the fields of better productivity and extended welfare, and—more importantly—profound losses in terms of famines, mass killings, use of forced labour.

Regarding GDP real growth, if we compare—with all the uncertainties of this kind of comparisons—GDP levels in 1913,[54] just before the war and the Revolution, and in 1991, at the end of the Soviet Union, GDP stood in 1991 at slightly over 8 times the level of 1913. In the same period, the US economy grew more than 11 times. The American GDP in 1913 was 2.2 times larger than the Russian one; in 1991, it was 3.1 times larger. From this viewpoint, the Soviet attempt to reach and overcome the arch-enemy country was far from successful. But if we limit our comparison to the period 1913–1939 (the year of outbreak of the Second World War), the conclusion is different, because the divergence in size of the two economies shrank, in respect to 1913, albeit slightly, to 2 times only. This narrowing of the divergence can be, at least partly, explained by the collapse of the American economy during the 1930s: -29% between peak and trough, while the Soviet economy escaped the Depression, with a continuing GDP increase all over the 1930s.[55]

The main phases of the evolution of Soviet economic policies in the 74 years of its power, from the revolution of 1917 to its collapse in 1991, can be summarized as follows.[56]

The Bolsheviks in Power

After his promises given during the revolution, Lenin, in 1917, wiped out landlord holdings, giving legality to the spontaneous peasant land seizure, and so sanctioning the spread of private property, in an un-Marxist move. But, in the presence of a serious starvation and of a strong anti-Soviet reaction—the White Armies and the ensuing civil war—any attempt to collaborate with what remained of the capitalist class came to an end, and the system of "War Communism" was introduced, putting everybody and everything at the service of the State's fight for military and economic survival: all factories were nationalized and trade was made a State monopoly; the working of the market-place based on the use of money was largely disrupted. A system of barter, wages paid in kind, forced requisition characterized the phase of War Communism. But production collapsed, in the midst of roaring inflation due to continued over-issue of paper currency.

The N.E.P.

In 1921 War Communism was junked by Lenin who, in a total reversal of course, introduced the New Economic Policy-N.E.P., which approved and encouraged self-interest as an incentive to economic activity, seeking to restore forms of free markets. "Without capitalists, but with the most progressive labour legislation in the word, the State-owned factories worked better than in private hands". This policy gave notable results, even though it was only in 1928 that the GDP of the USSR reached its pre-war level.[57]

The Stalin Era, and Then Khrushchev: Extensive Capital Accumulation

Following Lenin's death in 1924, Trotsky and the left-wing of the party objected strongly to the N.E.P., urging a return to full economic planning and State-induced, rapid industrialization. The choice was for a high rate of accumulation and consequently for a strong containment of consumption. Peasants, the great majority of the country, would bear the burden of this industrialization through a compression of their real wages. Right-wing policies, which put emphasis on the agricultural sector, were defeated, and under Stalin—who had succeeded against Trotsky in the struggle for Lenin's succession—the just mentioned process of strong industrialization resumed with vengeance, also in view of what was considered a forthcoming, inevitable international conflict. Investment in instrumental goods for industry was a priority, while the diversification of consumer patterns was not a relevant goal before the 1970s (under Stalin, the respective percentages of instrumental versus consumers' goods only increased, from 60.5% and 39.5% in 1928—the first year of the Five Year Plan—to 68.8% and 31.2% in 1950).

Planning was defined by Stalin as "not forecasts, but instructions". The central planning organ was the Gosplan (State Planning Commission), in charge of the administration of the price system and the definition of goals of physical production. Managers of State firms were accountable to the State, not to customers, being incentivized by volumes of production, not by costs. The production potential was defined by the stock of fixed capital, and the availability of circulating capital and workforce, not by cost minimization. Prices were fixed by the planning authority in relation to wages, in such a way to achieve full utilization of plants (the Keynesian "effective demand" problem was therefore considered as non-existent). Volume's objectives and price fixing by planners led to exaggeration of firms' performance, or shortages and customers' queues, with black market and privilege as a consequence, even though a relative equality of incomes was formally assured.

Land ownership was extensively collectivized since the 1930s (cooperatives as Kolkhozes, State farms as Sovkhozes). Also with an impulse of Western technology, industrial output rose substantially over the 1930s. As mentioned earlier, the Soviet Union escaped the worst of the Great Depression that ravaged most Western countries.[58] At the outbreak of the war, in 1939, Soviet GDP stood at a level around 85.5% higher than in 1928, a remarkable achievement.

After the hardships of the Second World War, the rapid expansion of the economy resumed, favoured by many years of domestic tranquillity and international peace. The Soviet Union—like other free-market countries—recovered from the war relatively quickly, to heights of economic development never seen before in the history of that country.

The government relied, as before the war, on the growth of heavy industrial production more rapid than the output of consumer goods; emphasis continued to be on defence and capital investments.

While, until the death of Stalin in 1953, the output increase resulted primarily from an increase in the amount of resources devoted to production, from 1953 to 1961 there was a remarkable increase in productivity. "A major theme in Soviet planning and public exhortation [became] the need to increase productivity of labour and other resources",[59] through improved technology and wide use of incentive payment schemes for workers.

From 1955 up to his demise in 1964, Khrushchev gave a new impulse to the economy, trying to reach a better balance between the production of industrial and consumer goods. However, given the emphasis on investment and investment goods, the consumer goods percentage continued to decline (still in the 1980s the military capabilities of the Soviet Union, built on a strong arms-oriented industrial complexes, continued to be disproportionate to its economic size). Khrushchev also gave incentive to the agricultural sector, affirming that the fight against Western capitalism had to be won not through war, but by a productivity race that would give Russians a higher standard of living, while much of the Stalinist system of coercion of Soviet workers was dismantled.

Intensive Capital Accumulation. Slowdown

Since the end of the 1960s, the economy suffered from a depletion of reserves of agricultural labourers and of natural resources. Economic policy shifted to an intensive capital accumulation, aimed at minimizing costs and increasing efficiency. This effort was substantially unsuccessful, due to technological delays and militarization of the economy which led to a sort of confiscation of innovation by the military industry. At the same time, there was a deterioration of the workers' discipline, encouraged by a de-Stalinization process, a more open political system, and wage pressure coming from a situation of full employment. Abandoning previous schemes of an insulated command economy, foreign trade—for a long while a relatively minor sector of the economy—increased, with exports pushed by oil and gas, and arms. But this exposed the economy to structural external vulnerability.

Perestroika

Gorbachev, party's Secretary general from 1985, had two goals: to revive the economy, and to raise the standard of living of the population. He started by softening central planning, by decentralization of decisions and workers' participation in enterprise management. Some laws have to be quoted as particularly relevant: the law on Individual labour activity of 1986, which started an effective private sector of the economy; the law of State enterprise of 1987, which gave autonomy to State firms, making central plans indicative and not mandatory. Price system ceased to be controlled by the Gosplan, moving the economy towards a market mechanism; at the same time, a deeper integration with the world trade was pursued. The lessened discipline in the labour sector was fought by introducing workers' self-management, but that was not enough: strikes continued, and inflation grew. The law on Cooperatives of 1988 favoured the development of a managerial class that really behaved according to the mechanisms of a capitalistic economy, and the extension of their activity from the real economy to the financial intermediation marked a further step towards a market economy. With a law of 1988, foreign trade was also de-centralized.

A class of affluent managers of firms substantially privatized (the "oligarchs") "played a central role in the collapse of the USSR by financing the pro-capitalistic coalition and deepening the economic imbalances". Huge imbalances in wage structure and in foreign accounts, which depleted the Soviet Union of gold and foreign exchange reserves, were the final blow to the Union, which came to an end on 25 December 1991. After the collapse, that class of managers would have taken great advantage from the shock therapies of post-Soviet Russia in the 1990s.

3.4 Adjusting and Interpreting Marx

The problem of the "economic calculus"—that is of assuring the equilibrium between availability and use of any good through a market mechanism—was not adequately examined by Soviet planners. This inadequate attention was coherent with an economic system that, in perspective, would make of the price mechanism an obsolete instrument. It should be noted, however, that planners were aware of this problem. Stalin himself made two relevant remarks in a small book, in 1952[60]:

- full nationalisation would not be possible in agriculture, where "collective farms should [rather] be placed on the modern technical basis of large-scale production, not expropriating them, but on the contrary supplying them with first-class tractors and other machines". This would imply the coexistence of State-owned industries in towns, and cooperative and collective farms in the countryside. Between these two sectors, "exchange through purchase and sale [that is, a market-price mechanism] should be preserved for a certain period, it being the form of economic ties with the town which is alone acceptable to the peasants. And the Soviet trade—state, cooperative and collective farms - should be developed to the full, and the capitalists of all types and description [that is, private owners of the means of production] ousted from trading activity".[61]
- "of course, when instead of two basic production sectors, the State sector and the collective-farm sector, there will be only one all-embracing production sector, the right to dispose of all consumer goods produced in the country, commodities circulation, with its

'money economy', will disappear, as being unnecessary element in the national economy".[62]

In two sectors the mechanism of market prices would remain operating, at least for a while and although within a planned economy: the consumer goods market (where consumers were left free to choose goods in which to spend their income), and the exchange ratios between cities and countryside (where the exchange operated between State industries and cooperative farms). It would have been, according to Stalin, an error if the hasty abolition of market prices contributed to aggravate the above mentioned problems of overproduction and shortages.

The rigid framework of the Marxist doctrine remained unchallenged until some serious cracks appeared in the organization and conduct of the Soviet economy.

It can be interesting to compare three successive approaches to Marxism, by Maurice Dobb, Oskar Lange, and Ronald Meek. Dobb's approach that we consider here is related to the situation of the 1930s, when the advancement of the Soviet economy continued, relatively undisturbed by the long Great Depression of the capitalistic world. The process of accumulation of capital, favoured by large availability of resources and manpower, is the background of Dobb's theorizing. He wants to stress few points: the hiatus between the capitalistic and the socialist systems, which is impossible to fulfil through an adjustment of the former, and even less so in the opposite direction; the contraposition of the ex-ante coordination of economic activity under socialism, and the only ex-post inadequate coordination of the market system; and the fact that the issue of wealth distribution is eliminated at the root in a socialist system, by resolving the antagonism of competing social classes. The second one—by Lange—of the late 1950s, can be read against the coming economic difficulties surfacing under Khrushchev's leadership. Lange deals with continuing social conflicts despite the abolition of social classes, the relevance—even in a socialist society—of the concept of economic "value", to be assessed in monetary terms, and the necessity to decentralize economic decisions. The third—by Meek—, of the 1960s, is a sort of invitation to re-think in similar terms the economic problems facing socialist and "western" liberal countries: at the same time an implicit denial of the hiatus mentioned by Dobb in the 1930s, and almost a reduction of the whole economic discipline to a sort of de-politicized social engineering, valid in both liberal and social economic systems.

Writes Dobb, in 1937: "The growth of the Soviet economy in recent years, moreover its capacity for maintaining a steady 'boom' rate of expansion over a decade, the large-scale constructional efforts which it has achieved, and its substitution of a state of scarcity for surplus in the labour market, have not only quickened interest, study and controversy, but have provided a concrete basis of comparison which before was lacking".[63]

The direct coordination of the constituent parts of the system can be never attained in a capitalist society, "by reason of the atomistic property rights on which [this] system rests".[64] In the field of investments, in a capitalist system the act of investment is guided by profit expectations, and these are affected—in addition to the expected demand for the product and future technical innovation—by factors of which the entrepreneur is mostly ignorant: rival acts of investments, acts of investment which are complementary to his own, amount of savings and investments in the whole system, future capital accumulation. These last two are of major importance and the least understood, but in a socialist system they become a problem of distributing labour between various types of production: the relative decision is made by a single authority, to avoid inconsistency provoked by the independence of separate decisions. Presumably, the determining relations controlling the economic activity will be predominantly of a technical/statistical character (this relevance attributed to the technicalities of the production process will be stressed by later economists, who end up by observing an asserted similarity of the concrete working of free market and socialist economists, in a sort of ideological neutrality: see, below, Lange and even more Meek).

In a capitalist economy, "laws" have the form of stating that, given certain conditions of nature and technique and certain consumers' preferences, producers will behave following certain value-relations. In a socialist economy, their guide will be to behave according to a certain purpose. This must be seen as a postulate, albeit not arbitrarily determined but conditioned by the new type of social organization and selected on the basis of the concrete situation. Given that postulate (purpose), the economic law will not be any more the Ricardian/Marxist law of labour value.

In a class society, capital accumulation is subject to a limit which retards it, the limit being the resistance to approach a condition of full employment in the labour market, because the wage-rise shrinks the capitalist's surplus-value. A socialist society overcomes the issue of the distribution of surplus: no ethical inquiry is anymore necessary about this distribution, thanks to the abolition of capitalistic profit. In a socialist society profit ceases to be an income category (the only income is wage income) and an economic incentive, and the sole incentive will presumably be to increase wages to the higher extent: the limit is set only by existing productive powers and considerations of future productive equipment. "This is—concludes Dobb—to march in the best tradition of Political Economy".[65]

This uncompromising view gives way to a more nuanced perspective in the reflections of the Polish economist Oskar Lange, in late 1950s. After the death of Stalin and the accession to power of Khrushchev, writing in 1959 he shows the difficulty that the Soviet economy faces in order to go beyond the previous rigidities of a command economy, and to adjust to the emerging needs of a society in evolution.

The most relevant concepts emerging from Lange's reflection seem to be the following: the persistence of social conflicts in a socialist economy between different social "strata" rather than between "classes"; the enduring relevance of the Ricardian/Marxian "law" of labour value and of values expressed in monetary terms; the necessity to strengthen self-government and production incentives in the enterprises, in order to achieve efficiency and avoid bureaucracy.

This can of course be questionable. The substitution of the term "stratum" for "class" means that there are no owners of the productive structure in a socialist society. But the lack of profit incentive meant adding more bureaucracy than efficiency (as the above mentioned evolution of the Soviet economy amply demonstrates).

Lange's discourse is done within the framework of the Marxist doctrine and its typical language, and having in mind Stalin's remarks mentioned earlier in this Section.[66] He observes that it is incompatible with Marxist theory to believe that the advent of socialism has solved all the problems of the new social and economic organization, as if all social contradictions in human life would automatically disappear in a socialist society. The advent of socialism is not the "realization of the Kingdom of God".[67] Lange adds that any theoretical generalization should take into account not only the accumulated experience matured in previous decades in Russia, but also the more recent vicissitudes of other European socialist countries, and China.

Following the doctrine of historical materialism, Lange looks at the Marxist contradictions (contradictions meant as increasing incompatibility over time between economic magnitudes and institutions) that are the moving force of social development. They are two:

- the first emerges between the development of productive forces—labour employed into a mechanism of production, combined with resources according to the state of technical knowledge—and the class struggle characterizing the relations of production between labourer and capitalist;
- the second is the contradiction between modes of production related to each type of social organization (slavery, feudalism, capitalism, socialism, communism) and the superstructure of the economy, as the juridical and political system raised over a specific mode of production, with its corresponding forms of social, political, intellectual life.[68]

The first contradiction in a capitalist society appears in the relations of production, taking the form of a class struggle of opposing interests of workers and capitalists; in a socialist society, in the absence of capitalists, it disappears as such. But the problem reappears with the second contradiction, regarding the adjustment of the superstructure to the new modes and relations of production. In this process of adjustment, the interests of the different social groups existing in the superstructure—which, as mentioned earlier, Lange calls "social strata" to diversify them from "social classes"—may collide, for instance with reference to methods of economic management, or political organization. Beating vested interests in the superstructure, still lingering notwithstanding the abolition of the capitalistic relations of production, while not implying a social revolution, requires an overcoming of frictions between different social strata.

Regarding the economic laws, Lange—confirming, again, Stalin's view—disregards the opinion of many Marxists (Rosa Luxemburg, Nikolaj Bukharin among them) who think that political economy, as science of capitalism, has no need to survive in a socialist society. By taking distance from Dobb, Lange writes that economic laws still exist, the only difference being that they should express the working of a different, free society, the socialist one. The economic law which organizes the economic system depends on the existing relations of production. Under capitalism, those relations are based on the contradiction between social classes, and private ownership of the means of production exists for the owner's profit; the socialist mode of production overcomes that struggle and ownership exists for the satisfaction of human wants.

Also, in a socialist society the laws of value and monetary circulation continue to operate in order to determine the price of commodities that are exchanged between different owners. There are different forms of socialist ownership, not just one, that is the national ownership. Just a single national ownership (an all-including State sector) could have been possible if Russian economy had been a well developed capitalistic economy; but the need to maintain a non-State sector of the economy arises from the fact that the affirmation of socialism happened in a not fully developed capitalistic society, where non-capitalistic forms of production (as small commodity production through cooperatives) still survived. These particular historical conditions make opportune not to move directly to national ownership. In addition, also in a socialist society individual ownership will continue to exist as consumer ownership (the remarks quoted in this paragraph are directly taken from Stalin's text).

But, how commodities are exchanged within nationalized sectors, that is, without a change of ownership? Transfers within the nationalized sectors are priced by imputation. It is "an accounting process reflected backwards to the means of production which are used to produce them"[69] [the goods that are actually exchanged]. As long as this law operates, a socialist planning board could use the resulting price to input the appropriate prices for capital goods produced and exchanged in the nationalized sectors. By using this "imputation", socialist planners could construct a system of equations of costs and revenues, and solve the system for the efficient quantity of any good exchanged in the nationalized sectors, to be produced in such a way as to minimize costs.

Then, there are laws affecting the superstructure of the management of a socialist economy (see above Lange's reference to "strata"). Under socialism the only mode of social interaction is planning, directed by the purpose of social welfare. The socialist firm must act as a trustee of the general social interest, and must be a self-governing body. Therefore, planning requires maintaining incentives and opportunities to rationalize the use of the means of production. Allocation of goods through planning must be reconciled with the respect of the law of value, to avoid that interaction of administrative allocation and bureaucratic resistance from some strata prevents workers from influencing the use of the means of production; an effective democratic participation is needed, however avoiding that, for instance, the objectives of the plan are fixed too low, in order to get premiums of production more easily; or that they are only slightly fulfilled so that they shall not be raised too much the following year.

Writing in 1964, Robert Meek reflects on the history of economics, and observes—in a sort of positivist mood—that the whole economic history is made of an attempt to free economics of value judgements, that is to move from normative economics to positive economics[70]: starting from Adam Smith, economists wanted to assume a passive attitude towards the distinction between what the economic life is and what it ought to be. The economic system appeared as a gigantic machine, whose objective interrelations could be described as "laws". The new science wanted to cut-off moral values, value judgements. Moral and political views were seen as excrescences upon that machine.

Nevertheless—Meek adds—value judgements returned, in fact, into economic analysis: not for mere human frailty, but for more profound reasons: the machine studied by the economists is a very complex one, and there cannot be a single explanation as valid for any part of it. Hence, alternative explanations are needed, and ideological, moral and political, considerations are the motivation of the choice of one of them. Without them, the results of our analysis would remain of a limited validity: "an uncomfortable knowledge".

But, in the last 10/20 years—Meek continues—two tendencies are emerging, to remove ideological biases:

- The evolution of certain mathematical techniques, designed to assist in the solutions, by private and public managers, of difficult problems of economic choice;
- The affirmation of welfare economics, as a set of rules by which various economic situations, available to a society, may be ordered and compared as to their desirability.

Both situations, which are even more frequent, imply economic choices where price mechanism, as the focus of the economic investigation, cannot be expected to work.

As a consequence of these tendencies, "the breakdown and destruction of that complex machine is evident", Meek points-out, both in

Communist countries and in the West, where planning techniques, and large and complex public enterprises, tend to prevail, creating a convergence of economic policies. The result is that economics is being transformed—independently of the type of economic system—into a science of economic management, of social engineering, of engineer efficiency. Economics came to be regarded and taught as a problem-solving subject, a bit like engineering. Similar tendencies emerged in western academia. For instance, George Shackle argued that, from the input–output analysis by Wassily Leontief in the early 1930s, a scheme of "indicative over-all planning or "the Social Accounting Matrix" could be constructed as "a complex productive web of industries supplying and drawing upon each other, when the final 'bill of goods'...could be calculated...at one stroke (even though that 'stroke' consisted in the solution of a great system of equations"). In these schemes of coherence, embracing the whole economy, economics has the best hope of justifying itself at a tool of the human mind able to match, though not to imitate, the achievements of the natural sciences".[71] Economic history was irrelevant, as it was by definition out of date.

What is the role of value judgements in this situation? According to Meek, and Shackle, very small, it seems, just because of the prevailing "engineer efficiency". But again, the criteria of efficiency, common to socialist and capitalistic economies, can be valued differently in diverse economic systems, and which should be adopted? The role of ideological biases remains, Meek concludes.

Not considering the inconclusiveness of the solution, the observations of Meek are relevant because, on the one side, they point out to a transformation of the economic science into a sort of (apparently) non-ideological economic management, largely operating through mathematical techniques. This is an anticipation of trends of the economic discipline that would emerge in the final decades of the century; on the other side, they are revealing the difficulties that purely Marxist schemes were encountering in the interpretation of evolving socio-economic structures, even within the Soviet system.

The introduction of computers for economic planning reinforces a non-ideological approach to economic issues, where blurring are the boundaries between free-market and socialist economies. Market is not anymore seen as a transitory device to full socialism,[72] while economic planning becomes fashionable even in market economies, generally between the post-war 1940s and the 1960s. Lange stresses the importance of computer-driven mathematical techniques, which may close the ideological gap between liberal and Marxist economists. "Mathematical programming assisted by electronic computers becomes the fundamental instrument of long-term economic planning, as well as of solving dynamic economic problems of a more limited scope. Here, the electronic computer does not replace the market. It fulfils a function which the market never was able to perform".[73]

The slowdown of the Soviet economy towards the end of the 1960s and the acceptance of forms of market economy, and on the other side an increasing critical attitude towards capitalism in Western liberal economies, lead economists of both sides to compare their respective experiences and to try an attempt—which would in the end prove sterile—to move towards extensive planning in capitalistic economies, and more autonomy in entrepreneurial decisions in the socialist ones.

This rapprochement is well exposed by Joan Robinson. "History has seen two methods of carrying out the accumulation necessary to install scientific technology. The first, which has been in operation for almost two centuries, relies upon individual acquisitiveness; the second, which has been in operation for less than half a century, relies upon socialist planning".[74] The fruits of accumulation are now available—she writes—but in each system institutions and habits of mind are putting obstacles in the way to their rational enjoyment. In capitalistic countries, egalitarianism, which has been set up thanks to the democratic process, is defeated by legal arrangements favouring property and by the acceptance of the class structure, necessary to foster accumulation. Now, private property has become "otiose": shareholders, and rentiers alike, are devoted to the lucrative business of swapping securities among them without giving an effective contribution to the productive process. Economic development is not constrained by lack of private savings (here is an echo of Keynesian economics): industry draws from itself the necessary resources through amortization funds and retained profits. But the great independent corporations cannot be relied upon to secure continuous full employment and a consistent pattern of development. Private industry's independence prevents the economy from creating organs of control, in the general interest. A democratically decided programme—a "national planning"—is necessary, to overcome the systematic bias in the pattern of production of goods and services which can be sold piecemeal, so as to provide scope for profit, and to address production towards goods of collective consumption, which has to be financed by taxation.[75]

With reference to socialist countries, the problem—Robinson writes—is the opposite, even with the same goal of enjoying the fruits of accumulation: to move production from the sector of heavy industry, and to take care of consumer interests. This is prevented by a system of command from above which deprives the individual manager of authority and initiative, making planning both rigid and clumsy, and a fetter upon further progress. Changes towards stimulating the light industry and agriculture have to be made centrally, but in detail more space has to be given to individual enterprises, overcoming "the exaggerated horror of risk". Adjusting the price system from cost accounting and production goals of physical terms, to market demand, would avoid piling up of unsaleable goods in the cellars of shops.[76]

In fact, large part of the debates that followed in the 1970s, not only within the Soviet academia, but also through their discussions with economists of non-socialist countries, reflects on one side the intent of socialist economists to make their system more efficient at a micro-level, albeit in the Procustean bed of the Marxist doctrine, on the other side the uneasiness of "Western" economists, facing the difficulties of stagnant output and inflation, and abandoning the "Keynesian consensus", after the long period of growth and stability that had followed the Second World War. It took a certain time for it to be realized that it was actually over.

The closing remarks of an international conference devoted to these themes, by prof Michael Kaser of Oxford, emphasized that "The clearest conclusion that this conference has reached is that the market mechanism has not solved social problems and externalities, though it admitted a rather wide divergence of view on whether they can be corrected by price adaptation or by planning. At the other extreme all insisted—Kaser concludes—on the value and actual application of micro-planning".[77]

3.5 Dobb's Criticism of Free-Market Economics. Sraffa's Reconciliation of Classical Economics and Marxism

In economic philosophy's terms, the hostility of Marxist economists is addressed more to the marginal utility theorists of neo-classical economics than to the Classical School. According to Marxists, the Classical School theory of labour value does not appear so outdated as the marginal utility economists pretended. Marxist economists think that the theory of labour value, unable to explain the working of a socialist economic system, remains a useful instrument to understand the capitalistic society, and acknowledge that theory as the starting point of Marxian analysis.

Maurice Dobb looks at the political economy of capitalism. We know—he observes—that a scientific theory must be based on a specific abstraction, which has to be appropriate to the researcher's interest. But a general abstraction must in turn contain a sufficient dose of realism, the risk being that what the abstraction gains in breadth, it loses in depth, so that the corollaries deducible from the abstraction will be of a limited meaning: even if presented as "laws" of the real world, these corollaries are empty of real content. It is better to keep foot on the ground, than being lost in the "precision of algebraic formulation".[78]

That dose of realism means to keep into account "the productive relations and the property and class institutions of which they are the expression"; neo-classical economists did not do that, and arrived at generalizations—"laws"—deemed valid for any type of exchange economy. In a class society, ideas that were derived from that society tended to assume a "fetishistic character" (in Marx's words): they may have played a positive role of enlightenment as weapons of criticism against ideas and institutions of a previous epoch, but later have become reactionary and obscurantist, and the representation of reality resulted veiled.[79]

The reality—Dobb adds—is that the so-called "laws" of economics must not be based on the subjective aspect of economic interrelations, as individual desires and choices—as the neo-classical, marginal utility economists do—but on the more fundamental relations and modes of production. Class relations were completely forgotten by the economic doctrine when the new industrial capitalism emerged in the course of the nineteenth century, giving new awareness to the industrial proletariat. Marx's political economy is the analysis of this social and economic reality, and Marx's thought traces a dividing line between the Classical School of Ricardo and the marginal utility theorists. By that time economics became, as Marx writes, a "vulgar" discipline.[80]

The utility, neo-classical school retreats in pure formalism, impotent to deliver substantial judgements on problems that are peculiar of a certain kind of society. Economics becomes a sort of "algebra of human choice", an "empty shell". Dobb's vision of society is not in terms of individuals but of social classes, and this is valid in the political and the economic sphere as well.

In the political sphere, the State, according to the traditional theory of politics, is the expression of the "general will",[81] resulting from the autonomous will of free and equal individuals. Likewise, in the economic domain, "the majority of economic writings refers to the rule of the consumer [the consumer's free choice] because there is as market". But this is an "idyllic picture" (which hides the class structure of the society), as painted by the capitalistic Press in the field of politics, and by the advertisement industry in the field of economics. In the first, the atomistic character of the social body (the utility-guided individual of the neo-classical economists) is the antechamber of dictatorships: writing in 1937 about Nazi Germany, Dobb's view is that to think differently "is as naively as seeing Herr Hitler and his Totalitarian State as the product of a popular will because he held a plebiscite". In the second field, the market's autonomous valuations under capitalism are illusory and represent, themselves, a very high degree of authoritarianism. Consumer choices, apparently free, are in reality the expression of the difference of economic and social status and of the "dependence of ownerless upon owner".[82]

An essential harmony of interests between classes denies the existence of a Marxian surplus-value and of labourer's exploitation, and becomes "a simple case of *petitio principii*".[83]

With the Marxist economists of the twentieth century, the modes of production and the class structure of the society remain the starting assumption for economic theorizing; and the fundamental approach to wealth production and distribution—the labour value theory—is not substantially altered.

The view of the structure of society in different classes and the theory of the labour value permits a rapprochement of Marxism to the Classical School. As mentioned, both classical economists and Marxists see the structure of society as divided into social classes. But the former think that these classes, in their respective roles, contribute to create a condition of optimal well-being otherwise non-attainable, and therefore see this social structure, even being a result of a historical evolution, as valid "in all times and places". The latter see this structure, just because historically determined, as specifically positioned in terms of time and place: the social and economic structure of capitalism, which evolves into a new socialist society once the proletariat overthrows the capitalistic class.

Within this class structure of the society, both Ricardo and Marx recognize that a commodity's value rests on the labour necessary to produce it. This is immediately evident in a primitive subsistence economy, where the total produce is just what is needed to maintain, year by year, the level of production as it is, and where the labourer takes control of the whole process of production and gets the whole produce of his labour. In this society, the relative equilibrium prices of commodities would tend to be equal to the relative quantities of labour required to produce them (this is the classical theory—or "law"—of labour value). Marx agrees with this analysis: these are what Keynes called "the Ricardian foundations of Marxism".[84]

When a capitalistic class enters the scene, and a surplus over subsistence is yielded, net product has to be distributed between participants in the production process, in particular between the worker and the capitalist. The classical law of value might continue to operate if the whole net product went to the worker: prices would continue to be determined as above and no profit would emerge: an impossible assumption in a capitalistic economy. On the other side, net product cannot be entirely accrued to the capitalist: in a society of non-slaves, a capitalistic society, the labourer sells his labour-power to the capitalist at a price (wage), and wage cannot be zero.

In this case, prices diverge from the quantity of labour employed in production. Adam Smith gave a formal, non-resolving answer: this net product would be divided between factors of production according to their respective contribution to the process of production, resulting in their "natural price" (Chapter 1); but, how this natural price might be assessed? And how commodity prices would be consequently determined? What is the relation that links prices, wages and profits? In particular, is the net product divided between the factors of production in a casual way, or does it respond to a certain "law"? Are there ethical considerations to consider? Is there a class that takes more than what she deserves in relation to her productive contribution? These points had remained undefined within the Classical School. Joan Robinson wrote: "we need to know the prices to value the surplus that is to be divided. This was the problem that flummoxed Ricardo".[85]

Marx had solved the problem in a radical way. He introduced the concept of "surplus-value", as the amount of work appropriated by the capitalist. In the words of Marx, "the surplus-labour of labour-power is the inexpensive labour of capital and thus forms super-value for the capitalist, a value which costs him no equivalent return" (see also Chapter 1). But—even with Marx—the relation between super-value, wages and means of production and, consequently the commodity's price, remains unresolved.

Marxist economists have approached the work of the Italian economist Piero Sraffa, of Cambridge University, as evidence of a continuity between Classical and Marxian thought: a way to reconcile Classical School's economics and the Marxist doctrine, and the appropriate adaptation of Marx's scheme to a modern capitalistic society.

His main work was published in 1960: the result of long years of reflections concentrated in a pretty compact book, where mathematics is the predominant form of expression.[86] Some mainstream economists saw Sraffa's book as a Ricardian interpretation of society: there is a link between his editorship of a critical edition of Ricardo's works[87] and his own research interests. Others criticized Sraffa's scheme as abstractly logical but not responding to verifiable experience.

Far from discussing the controversial "model" produced by Sraffa (worth repeating, this is not a history of economic thought), we want here to highlight, behind the veil of his reasoning, the "notes of social philosophy"—to use Keynes' terminology—that can be inferred from his work. But to do so requires few hints of his line of thought.

His theoretical purpose is to fill the gap that Ricardo and Marx had left unexplained: to find the logical connection that links wages, profits and prices, or—put in another way—to solve the problem of determination of prices and, with it, the problem of income distribution between wages and profits, in a different way from neo-classical economists.[88]

His assumptions[89] are:

that outputs of certain industries are to constitute the inputs of others: what is input in an industry is the output of another. Each sector of the economy cannot work other than by connecting with other sectors;

that—in line with the Classical School—value is independent of individual utility, and therefore of the concept of "demand": not only Sraffa's work does not even enter the marginalists' arguments of the neo-classical theory[90]; but it also neglects the macroeconomic relevance of aggregate demand in Keynesian thought[91];

that "his" economic system does not depend on changes in the scale of production or in the proportion of factors of production: in this way, he is not involved, again, in questions related to changes in "marginal product";

that the return is constant: the rate of profit—defined as the ratio of profit to the means of production (that is, to the owner's investment)—has to be the same in any industry: it is distributed all over the economic system in proportion to the means of production employed in the productive process.

Sraffa looks at Marx's elaboration of the theory of labour value. He makes however an adaptation to Marx's scheme. Marx had written that the "variable capital"[92] is the worker's contribution to the production process, and that it is divided into two parts: the "labour capital", paid to the worker as a wage, and the "surplus value", which is the rest, expropriated by the capitalist. Sraffa does not distinguish between labour-capital and surplus-value (implicitly rejecting the Marxist view that profit is an expropriation of what is due to the worker), and rather uses the concept of "net product", which includes both.

In a capitalist society, this net product is divided between the worker as wage and the capitalist as profit. In the light of the assumptions mentioned earlier, the critical point to examine is—according to Sraffa—the different proportion in which labour and means of production (input, as just said) are employed in each industry, because the profit emerges as a result. Profit is not an expropriation of the worker, as in Marx, but is a residual value that can be determined when we know: (a) the wage, which is seen as resultant of social struggles; and (b) the proportion labour/means of production.

If this proportion is different in different industries, in order to have the same rate of profit, given a certain level of wages, the profit has to be higher where the means of productions are in bigger proportion in relation to labour.

But this is not the conclusion, according to Sraffa, because any commodity is produced by using means of production that are, in turn, commodities produced through labour and means of production combined in different ratios. Therefore, "the relative price-movements of any two products,...come to depend...not only on the proportion of labour to means of production by which they are respectively produced, but also on the proportions by which those means have themselves been produced, and also on the proportions by which the means of production of those means of production have been produced, and so on."[93]

The problem that "flummoxed Ricardo"—the deviations of prices from labour value—can be solved therefore by observing that the rate of profits over the economy as a whole is determined as soon as we know the ratio of the net product (wages and profits) to means of production, and the proportion of net product going to wages. Or, in other terms, when the proportion of the net product going to wages is given, the average rate of profit depends upon the level of the ratio of net product to means of production.

We shall not dwell further into Sraffa's reasoning. He appears to deprive Marx's theory of the ideological component and to build a model of the working of a capitalistic society that responds to economics as a "science". Similarly to Walras or Pareto, he does not see any form of expressing his theory other than in a sequence of equations: a habit, or necessity, so to speak, that would become increasingly widespread in economics. As mentioned, his theory met critical voices from his colleagues at Cambridge, their criticism being based, rather than on abstract consistency, on empirical verifiability.[94]

But this would be a partial reading of his model. Sraffa had a culturally solid liberal background; he was however dissatisfied with how capitalism effectively worked in countries where liberal ideas were interpreted as pure protection of vested private interests, and grew increasingly sympathetic towards socialist ideas, being particularly close to Communists' position (Gramsci's, in particular)[95] and to Marxist economists in Britain (as Dobb).[96]

His ideological component is well visible when—in a Marxian way—he thinks that the capitalist's profit, the reward of capital as a specific factor of production, is the result of the interaction—or fight—between the owner of the means of production and the worker who lends his force to him. In practise, his vision fits well into a generally critical attitude towards the actual working of a capitalistic society within the institutional framework of a democratic political system. This vision would give theoretical underpinning to leftist political movements and to highly unionized workers, in the increasing tensions between capital and labour which characterized the late 1960s and the 1970s.[97]

3.6 Liberal Criticism of Marxism

The figures of capitalist, landowner and labourer, and the corresponding categories of profit, rent, wage, are well firm in Adam Smith's work, and this "distinction of ranks"—to quote his words in *The Theory of Moral Sentiments*—is the basis of the "peace and order of society".[98] The same relevance of social classes, but in the opposite direction—that is to show the exploitation of the worker by the owner of the means of production—is kept in the Marxist doctrine.

With the affirmation of the utility-guided, individualistic and classless neo-classical thinking of the turn of the century, the class-centred orientation of both Classical School and Marxism disappears. And during the twentieth century, liberalism of any shade does not deal with the basic issues of the economic organisation in terms of different social classes. It remains class-blind, perhaps under the influence of the democratic political values underlying twentieth-century liberalism.[99] The position taken by liberal economists on Marxism should therefore be evaluated by keeping in mind that social class is not explicitly part of their vocabulary. This does not mean that liberalism of the twentieth century does assume a classless society, it only means that its reasoning is not based on that distinction.

Another point to have in mind is that each of the different streams of thought (metamorphoses) of liberalism in the twentieth century has its own attitude to Marxism: we have on one side economists who stress the wealth distribution issue, and on the other economists who rely on product maximization, on wealth production and on the individual's freedom of choice: Keynes' or Beveridge's position vis-à-vis Marxism cannot be the same as that of Hayek or von Mises or Friedman.

As mentioned above, Keynes quite firmly stated that his major work would mean a destruction of the "Ricardian foundations of Marxism", but his attitude towards Marxism was more benevolent than neo-classical and libertarian economists. In Schumpeter's words, there was "no such gulf between Marx and Keynes as there was between Marx and Marshall and Wicksell".[100] In the General Theory, there are just passing mentions of Marx. Elsewhere, his criticism is not based on an essential irrationality of the socialist economic system, on its logical impossibility to reach a situation of equilibrium in the economic system, but on the inability of Marxist socialists of his own time to understand the evolving "structure" of capitalism, that is that capitalism as described in the Capital has greatly changed: current capitalism is barely a remembrance of the old one. Stalin—Keynes writes—"look[s] backwards to what capitalism was, not forward to what it is becoming.[101] That is the fate of those who dogmatise in the social and economic sphere where evolution is proceeding at a dizzy pace from one form of society to another...for one reason or another, Time and the Joint Stock Company and the Civil Service have silently brought the salaried class into power. Not yet a Proletariat. But a Salariat, assuredly. And it makes a great difference". About communism, Keynes ironically writes that "offered to us as a means of improving the economic situation, it is an insult to our intelligence. But offered as a means of making the economic situation worse, that is its subtle, its almost irresistible, attraction".[102]

More leaning towards socialism is Beveridge, whose proposals, as contained in *Full Employment* (Chapter 2), are "neither socialism nor an alternative to socialism:...A conscious control of the economic system at the highest level—a new type of budget which takes man-power as its datum—adequate sustained direct demand for the products of industry—organization of the labour market—these are required in any modern society".[103]

A radical libertarian as von Mises launches a very different attack on Marx's socialism, and this can be better understood if we have in mind what liberalism is, according to him. "Liberalism has never pretended to be more than a philosophy of earthy life...It has never claimed to exhaust the Last or Greatest Secret of Man. The anti-liberal thinking promises everything".[104] In fact, only two visions are contending the social and economic organization of society. On one side, there is liberalism and market economy; on the other, the following list of societal organizations: Welfare State, Socialism, Nazi and Fascist regimes, New Deal, even—in a later edition of his work—Peron's Argentina, all under the embracing banner of "full socialism", their rivalries notwithstanding.[105] And, later, "Our own civilisation rests on the fact that men have always succeeded in beating-off attacks of the re-distributors", where redistribution is "the slogan of socialists".[106] Notwithstanding his apparently diminutive meaning of the concept of liberalism (a sort of "earthy" matter), his concept is such that only liberalism gives real content to the idea of democracy: "democracy without liberalism is a hollow form".[107]

As regards Marxism, von Mises, confirming a widespread judgement that is common to liberal and Marxist economists alike, stresses that on purpose Marx did not devote attention to the organization of a socialist economy. According to von Mises, "the purpose of prohibition to study the working of a socialist community...was really intended to prevent the weakness of Marxist doctrines from coming really to light in discussion regarding the creation of a practicable socialist society".[108]

But von Mises is one of the few economists who provided with clarity the explanation of the impossibility of establishing a proper economic accounting under socialism. He observed that in any economy transactions are made in terms of a general medium of exchange, and not in terms of subjective use-values (that is, in terms of value judgements about a certain good's utility). What a socialist economy wants to achieve is the substitution of calculations in kind for calculation in terms of money. This is an illusion and rational production of goods becomes impossible. In the production of a certain consumer good, a supply chain of intermediate goods must be created, through all the establishments engaged in the process of production. The "command of a supreme authority would govern the business of supply", but the economic administration would have no real sense of direction in making the choices regarding how much to produce and in which manner to combine the production of those intermediate goods. In the long chain of production of a consumer good through a series of interconnected factories that produce the intermediate goods, there is "no means of ascertain whether a given piece of work is really necessary, whether labour and material are not being wasted in completing it". Which of the alternative processes of production is more satisfactory? The quantity produced can be compared, but not the expenditure incurred in its production, and it must be the smallest expenditure. What is necessary is a calculation of value in terms of money, not a technical calculation of use-value.[109]

Not by chance, when in the late 1950s, in front of the increasing difficulties of a proper functioning of the Soviet economy, Oskar Lange turned to the subject of economic accounting in a socialist economy, he recognized—quoting among others Ludwig von Mises—that socialism could not avoid a metre of calculation that went beyond physical measurements. As we have seen above (Sect. 3.5), he had to resort to the complicate and inefficient method of valuing transfer of goods in nationalized sectors "by imputation".

3.7 Socialism by Default: Religion, Schumpeter and Polanyi

We have seen, at the very start of this essay, how Schumpeter explained the origin of political economy. He reconnected this discipline to two roots: philosophical studies that focussed on man as a social entity, whose activity should be studied on the basis of empirical observation and explained by means of a cause-effect relation; and the views of people whose interest, rich in business experience, is mainly concerned with practical, daily matters pertaining to their economic activity.

More or less in the same years of Schumpeter's reflections, other thinkers paid increasing attention to this second root, that is to the actual working of the capitalistic system, to the concrete experience of business-oriented people who put the system into practice. This was happening when capitalism's affirmation and growth, particularly in Western economies, was having enormous consequences on output production and distribution, on social relations, on political structures and normative activity. In Germany, Max Weber, studying society's capitalistic structure, tried to give an answer to the following question: which sort of psychological conditions made the development of modern capitalistic civilization?[110]

The answer, according to Weber, should be found in the religious Protestant revolution of the sixteenth century that generated the movements giving birth to capitalism as we see it. Those conditions were indeed the result of a new attitude that religious people showed in carrying out their daily duties, in particular their business activity. The first capitalists adopted a code of economic conduct and a system of relations, defying sharply different, old and consolidated schemes of social ethics, and pre-existing conventions and laws that had the support of Church and States as well. Protestant asceticism interpreted business and labour as a divine "calling", to be observed through one's personal ability and initiative. This calling was not seen as a condition in which the individual was born, as such to be passively accepted, but as a route chosen by the individual, to be pursued with responsibility. It was "what is most characteristic of the social ethic of capitalistic culture and is, in a sense, the fundamental basis if it". Calling was an obligation to be fulfilled "no matters…whether it appears on the surface as a utilisation of [the individual's] personal powers, or only of his material possession".[111] The pursuit of wealth was "not merely an advantage, but a duty". New moral standards canonized as economic virtues what was before condemned as vices.[112]

"The *summum bonum* of this ethic, the earning of more and more money, combined with the strict avoidance of all spontaneous enjoyment of life, is above all completely devoid of any eudaemonistic, not to say edonistic, admixture".[113] This made the specific, modern Protestant capitalism radically different, not only from capitalism of other ages and places (from China, to India, to the classical world, to the Middle Ages), but also from crude utilitarianism, according to which honesty, punctuality, industry, frugality are only an unnecessary surplus.

How this religious attitude to economic activity came to change the pre-existing economic structure? Relying on the individual's initiative religiously pursued, Dutch Calvinists opposed any form of monopolistic, politically privileged capitalism which represented the basis of a Christian-social ethical foundation...The Puritans, likewise, in the same spirit "repudiated all connections with large-scale capitalistic countries...as an ethically suspicious class, and took pride in their own superior middle-class business morality".[114] They were, specifically, passionate enemies of state's privileged capitalism, exalting individualistic impulses of rational behaviour, contributing to industries born outside the assistance of established, public powers: the contrast of two forms of capitalism was in parallel with contrasts of a religious nature.[115]

This original impulse, however, was then fully secularized, became the zeal of modern capitalism, assuming a hedonistic form, detached from the original religious impulse. In a Faustian way—Weber writes quoting Goethe—the acquisition of material wealth becomes the primary goal of life, while the divine "calling" is totally lost. "The Puritans wanted to work in a calling; we are forced to do so. For when asceticism was carried out of the monastic cells into everyday life—continues Weber with almost Marxian accents[116]—, and began to dominate wordly morality, it did its part in building the tremendous cosmos of the modern economic order. This order is now bound to the technical and economic conditions of machine production which today determines the lives of all individuals who are born in this mechanism", perhaps..."until the last ton of fossilized coal is burnt".[117]

"In the field of its highest development, in the United States, the pursuit of wealth, stripped of its religious and ethical meaning, tends to become associated with purely mundane passions".[118]

Schumpeter, who includes Weber in the German Historical School of Economics (see Chapter 1), paid no more than a scant attention to his thesis. In a footnote of his *History of Economic Analysis*, he explains that Weber's methodological error consists in the adoption of the "method of Ideal Types": Weber puts the "Ideal" Feudal Man against the "Ideal" Capitalist Man, presents the capitalist's New Spirit—a different attitude to life and its values, born out of the Protestant Reformation—as transition from the former to the latter Type. Schumpeter writes that this is a "spurious problem", to be dismissed: this sort of ideal transition has no counterpart in the sphere of historical facts. "He [Weber] set out to find an explanation for a process which sufficient attention to historical details renders self-explanatory".[119]

As mentioned earlier, Weber had concluded that capitalism would last "until the last ton of fossilized coal is burnt", that is: indefinitely. Joseph Schumpeter, in *Capitalism, Socialism, and Democracy*[120], after having observed that any attempt at social prognosis, if based on facts and arguments, is scientific in its final results, concluded that capitalism could not survive.

Schumpeter's central idea, that capitalism will die of its own success, is indeed presented not as an ideological, pre-analytical position, rather as a scientific view, based on facts and arguments that support certain inferences (admittedly—he writes—hard to prove as a Euclid's theorem). He is not an ideological Marxist, but his conclusion is the same as Marx's. He fell victim to determinism, the abhorred term for every economist, who is however most prone to follow it.

The fact that an acute social analyst and great economist yielded this prediction, and that—at least so far—the experience seems to be in conformity with Weber's prediction, raises doubts about the scientific character of Schumpeter's prognosis, or about economics as a science, or at least leads to narrow the scope of science proper—that is, of experimentally and logically supported conclusions—within the economic discipline[121]. Experience appears to support the historical insights of the German School.

He starts by writing that capitalism's story is one of incremental output, without substantially affecting wealth distribution. The success of capitalism, in terms of welfare, is not due to a wider range of goods and services produced (Louis XIV would have remained perfectly happy even without the invention of the electric bulb, being able to spend in unlimited quantities of candles, and to have at his disposal all the servants attending to them[122]), but to making easily available goods and services at cheap prices to larger and larger strata of population.

Schumpeter then asks whether the capitalistic structure of society was favourable to its successful performance. About this, he starts by observing that the bourgeois society is moulded on an economic foundation: success is identified with economic success. The prototype of the successful man is the entrepreneur, whose activity, according to British classical economists, even performed in self-interest, is geared to the interest of all. A gulf between self-interest and interest of all, however, remained unexplained, and two strands of thought developed to fill that gulf. The neo-classical approach, based on perfect competition and product maximization, theorized a state of equilibrium "in which all outputs are at their maximum and all factors fully employed".[123] A second strand, however, criticized this view: perfect competition is the exception; monopolistic competition and oligopoly prevail. In addition, under the conditions envisaged by neo-classical economists, that equilibrium would generally be inconsistent with maximum output and full employment (interestingly, on this point no reference to Keynes is made by Schumpeter).

The relevant fact is that, even in those conditions that make "entirely imaginary a golden age of competition", in that sort of structure, that is in an environment of large-size concerns in quasi-monopolistic condition, the rate of output growth continued unabated: "A shocking suspicion that big business has to do with increased standard of life". This proves that capitalism is never a stationary state of equilibrium: rather, it is an evolutionary process, a "process of creative destruction",[124] the contrary of a state of permanent lull. The impulse of capitalism comes from new consumers' goods, new methods of production, new markets, new forms of industrial organization, not from a condition of perfect competition on the market, reputed as good at all times.

Why this structure, based on large enterprises and on a far from perfect competition, has been so successful? Schumpeter looks at economic and political history and mentions five "exceptional circumstances" favouring growth and better standards of life: a benevolent government action, which, after the phase on unfettered capitalism (after circa 1870), raised new fetters—as systems of social security—but not much to damage the preceding trend; new discoveries of gold, which, in a regime of gold standard, permitted adaptive monetary conditions and policies; increased population; new discoveries of sources of raw materials, as coal, oil; and the force of new technologies.

These favourable conditions, though, do not lead—according to Schumpeter—to maintaining a favourable prognosis for its future. "[Actual] capitalist performance is not...relevant for prognosis...Hence, I am not going to argue, on the strength of that performance, that the capitalist intermezzo is likely to be prolonged. In fact, I am going to draw the exactly opposite inference".[125] Why?

In line with the evolutionary state of capitalism, two factors, adverse to capitalism, have been in operation. The first, on which both Marx and Keynes would agree, goes under the label of "Theory of vanishing investment opportunity",[126] according to which, and broadly speaking, those exceptional factors mentioned above would gradually cease to operate (Schumpeter has no confidence in "pump priming" through public expenditure in investment, even in deficit).

Then, and more importantly, there is the "Evaporation of the substance of property",[127] which has in turn two components: the industrial side and the consumers' side.

About the first factor—investment opportunities—Schumpeter thinks of a state of satiety of wants and absolute technological perfection, with a consequent mechanization of progress that would affect entrepreneurship and capitalist society: a state which is far from us, but whose perspective is observable already. Capitalism, as evolutionary process, could not survive. Here is the accent on a distinction of roles that is rather blurred in Marx's vision: the entrepreneur and the bourgeoisie.

The entrepreneur' function "does not essentially consist in either inventing anything or otherwise creating the conditions which the enterprise exploits...consists in getting things done"[128]; it is a factual function—the entrepreneur as a doer—that loses importance when his job becomes a sort of routine. Economic progress tends to become depersonalized and automatized, "bureau and committee work tends to replace individual action".[129] This is "the obsolescence of the entrepreneurial function".[130] The entrepreneur is not, *per se*, a social class, but the bourgeois class absorbs him and his family and connections.

And what about the bourgeoisie? Schumpeter sees it—beyond "the precincts of purely economic considerations", as "the cultural component of the capitalistic economy...its socio-psychological superstructure", in Marxian terms.[131]

The former is a small but essential part of the latter; but, at the same time, the bourgeoisie depends on the entrepreneur. "Between, there is the bulk [of] industrialists, merchants, financiers and bankers: they are in the intermediate stage between entrepreneurial venture and mere administration of an inherited domain".[132] The giant industries are more and more made of these administrators, while the entrepreneur tends to vanish. The vanishing entrepreneur draws his social class into his own decline and death.

Regarding the second factor of capitalistic decline, the evaporation of the substance of property, it means, first of all, the "Evaporation of industrial property".[133] The modern businessman, entrepreneur or managing administrator, "rational and unheroic", gradually acquires the psychology of the salaried employee working in an increasingly bureaucratic organization: his will to fight is not anymore the will of the creative destroyer; the modern corporation socializes the bourgeois mind, and will eventually kill the entrepreneur's roots. But the bourgeoisie cannot save itself by taking the lead of the government: it has never been accustomed to govern: "the ledger and the cost calculation absorb and confine".[134] The capitalist process, after having destroyed the institutional framework of the feudal society, destroys at the end itself.

Connected to the first "evaporation", is the "Evaporation of Consumers' property"[135]: the disintegration of the family, going *pari passu* with the progress of capitalism, makes the amenities of the bourgeois home less obvious than are its burdens; hospitality, rather than home reception, is "increasingly shifted to the restaurant or club".[136] Work and savings for wife and children fade from the moral vision of the businessman; this hedonistic component is a negative factor for capitalist efficiency. Family used to be the mainspring of the profit motive. This leads to "a different kind of *homo oeconomicus*...who cares for different things and acts in different ways;...from the standpoint of his individualistic utilitarianism, the behaviour of that old type would in fact be completely irrational".[137] The time-horizon of the businessman shrinks to his life expectation.

The gradual disappearance of capitalistic "values" brings to a critical attitude towards capitalism itself. The bourgeoisie finds that "his [critical] attitude does not stop to the credentials of kings and popes: but attacks private property and the whole scheme of bourgeois values".[138] Life is taken out of the idea of property. Ownership becomes dematerialized, disfunctionalized and absentee. There is an extra-rational driving power and capitalism faces a trial where judges have already expressed a sentence of death. However, grievances and attacks would not suffice to generate an active hostility to social order. There must be groups that organize resentment, nurse it and give it a voice. The final attack to capitalism will come from the "intellectuals", whom the very bourgeois class nourishes and defends, by giving them the role of expressing its own discontent and frustration. They have a vested interest in social unrest, even not having concrete responsibilities in the conduct of public affairs. They are not professionals, have no direct responsibility of first-hand knowledge for practical affairs, generally are not politicians, but have the role of political advisers. They invoke freedom, a freedom that bourgeois class may dislike, but the "freedom which the bourgeoisie disapproves cannot be crushed without also crushing the freedom it [the same bourgeoisie] approves".[139] Schumpeter concludes: "There is not so much difference as one might think between saying that the decay of capitalism is due to its success and saying that it is due to its failure".[140]

Schumpeter's "vision"—because in no other way than as a vision can his thought be defined—appears correct, and prescient, when he deals with a well-entrenched decline of bourgeois values in the decades following his book (in particular, what he labels "evaporation of consumers' property"), but he seems to have totally missed the subsequent resurgence of capitalistic "values", of the "creative destruction" we are witnessing, in new forms. Whether this development can be seen in a Marxian way—as a sign of capitalism's evolving "structures" or as a powerful influence of evolving "superstructures", of the economic philosophies of Neoliberalism—we will see in the following chapter.

Karl Polanyi's critical attitude towards economic liberalism is rooted in a Christian vision, and his political and economic analysis of the liberal order leads him to envisage the advent of a spiritual socialism, the first signs of which—Polanyi notes—can be already detected in a number of disconnected initiatives, some going back to the nineteenth century: a sort of socialism well far from the doctrine of Marxist socialism.

His major work, *The Great Transformation. The political and economic origins of our time*,[141] is more or less contemporary of Schumpeter's, *Capitalism, Socialism and Democracy*. Both were published during the early 1940s, when the urge of fighting dictatorships was mixed up with a radical re-thinking of established economic and political views, with a particularly uncertain future ahead (fascism is the objective of harsh comments in both books, but particularly in Polanyi's). Both reserve scant or null attention to Keynes, whose magnum opus had been published a few years before. Liberalism is clearly under strain in both books. Both are characterized by deep historical insights into the evolution of the capitalistic system and see its final unsustainability. Both consider some sort of socialism as the result of a gradual but inevitable process, even though both do not see Marx as a decisive key to explain the issues of their own time. Socialism will not be—in either view—the outcome of the proletariat revolution against the privileged class.

The concept of "class", well present in Schumpeter, is absent in Polanyi, who relies on "society". Society risks self-destruction by the forces of free-market economy. The latter author has a sort of moral inspiration that is totally absent in the former: the author's value judgements are, with Polanyi, unreservedly and broadly expressed, and contrast with Schumpeter's "scientific" approach: Polanyi would never see the boredom of the bourgeois class and the exhaustion of the entrepreneur's animal spirit as the main factor of capitalism's demise. He attacks the core of the liberal society, seen as an expression, or a derivative, of the self-regulating market, and antithetic to the substance of democracy. He criticizes the widely shared view that our society started approximately with the publication of Adam Smith's Wealth of Nations and that previous cultures are irrelevant to an understanding of the problems of our age. His analysis of the nineteenth century is therefore carried out not because civilization starts from there, but for the reason that the current (twentieth century) problems cannot be understood without looking at a typical feature of that century: the self-regulating market system. Polanyi sees the self-regulating market as the "matrix" of the whole liberal system, and the liberal State as its creation. Since then onward, classical economics "haunted the science of man, and the reintegration of society into the human world became the persistently sought aim of the evolution of social thought". The attempt of Marxism to reconciliate society and humanity was unsuccessful, just because of the too close adherence of Marx to Ricardo[142] (the "Ricardian foundations of Marxism", as Keynes wrote, should here be reminded).

It is well known his scheme of explanation of the nineteenth century's prevailing political and economic structure, which assured the "Hundred Years Peace". It was characterized by four institutional arrangements: on one side, the balance-of-power system and the liberal State, based on political and national institutions; on the other, the monetary regime of the gold standard and the self-regulating market, which are, both, economic and international institutions.[143]

A pivotal role was then performed by haute finance, as embodied by the Rothschild family. They were subject to no government, symbolized the abstract principle of internationalism, responded to the States' needs of the time by having in any State agents commanding the confidence of governments and investors.[144] Even not being designed as an instrument of peace, haute finance's influence, exerted on national governments, was itself a factor encouraging peace: a general war could not be functional to the smooth working of the international monetary system, the gold standard, upon which international trade and credit would flourish.

The essential problem with this economic system (Polanyi seems to think of the liberal political system as a "superstructure" of the economic one, almost in a Marxian way) was economic liberalism's misjudgement of social wants, seen only from the economic viewpoint. Man's behaviour is not solely economic. This misjudgement was not by chance: once established, the market system can work properly only in the absence of outside interference of any kind. This system is "controlled, regulated, and directed by markets alone; order in the production and distribution of goods is entrusted to this self-regulating authority"[145] (there is no need to stress that this vision of the homo oeconomicus had already been put under strains even by liberal thinkers, who—according to different strands of thought—pointed, point and will point, to non-economic motivations, irrationality in choices or other factors influencing his actions).

In order to work properly, the liberal system needs three tenets: that labour should find its price on the market; that the creation of money should be subject to an automatic system (gold standard); that goods should be traded internationally without preferences or hindrances. The Industrial Revolution, free labour contracts stipulated under no worker's protection, abolition of protective duties are terms that define society's submission to the self-regulating market. Man, and significantly nature, were subjected to laws of supply and demand, dealt as commodities, as goods produced for sale. The subordination of social wants to the laws of the market does not mean that the separation of the two spheres existed in every type of society at all times. "Normally, the economic order is merely a function of the social, in which it is contained. Neither under tribal, nor feudal nor mercantile conditions was there…a separate economic system in the society. Nineteenth century society…was, indeed, a singular departure".[146]

Polanyi indulges in a benevolent view of past societal structures (sort of laudator temporis acti), where barter rather than market exchange, mercantilism rather than free trade seemed to respond more directly to social needs and equality: "the greatest number of poors is... to be found in those [nations] which are the most fertile and the most civilized".[147] Economy, in Polanyi's words, must be embedded in non-economic institutions: this means that acts of production and distribution should be performed as a discharge of social obligations.[148]

The subordination of social wants to free-market systems could not last without a self-destruction of the social structures. Even free market and free trade and competition required, as a consequence, outside intervention to be workable. Marxism itself was—according to Polanyi—a "liberal myth": in Marxism, actually, the liberal economic outlook found powerful support. He rejects the view that public intervention is the result of "collectivist conspiracy"; public intervention and subsequent restrictions on laissez- faire started in a spontaneous way, as a realistic self-protection of society, in countries of a widely dissimilar political and ideological configuration.

In the nineteenth century the expansion of the market economy started being counteracted by a reaction against the market dislocation "which attacked the fabric of society". Robert Owen—whom Polanyi sees as a towering figure foretelling an incoming, different society—gave a true Christian insight by saying that market economy, if left to evolve according to its own laws, would create great and permanent evil. As a reaction to liberalism emerged the need for social protection: protecting legislation, restrictive associations.

Liberalism of the nineteenth century was therefore not destroyed by the First World War, nor by a proletariat revolution, nor by small- and middle-class fascism; not by the Marxian tendency of the profit rate to fall, nor by underconsumption or overproduction, that is by Keynesian insufficient demand. Liberalism was destroyed by the strains and stresses created by the conflict between market and the elementary requirements of an organized social life, by society's reaction in order not to be annihilated by the self-regulatory market.

Polanyi's definition of socialism: "Socialism is essentially the tendency inherent in an industrial organization to transcend the self-regulatory market by consciously subordinating it to a democratic society".

This sort of new socialist society may develop along different lines, with a unifying factor: labour, land and money (the three tenets of society) will be liberated from the constraints of the self-regulating market: the nature of property will undergo a deep change.

With religious accents, Polany concludes by writing that three facts represent the "consciousness of Western man": knowledge of death, of freedom, of society. The first is revealed by the Old Testament, the second by the teachings of Jesus, the third comes from our own living in an industrial society: no great name is attached to this last one, but Robert Owen. The British manufacturer turned social reformer was the nearest to a full understanding of what living in our society means. "He recognized that the freedom we gained through the teachings of Jesus was inapplicable to a complex industrial society. His socialism was the upholding of man's claim to freedom in such a society. The post-Christian era of Western civilization had begun, in which the gospel did not any more suffice. And yet remained the basis of our civilization".[149]

Polanyi's ideology ends up by envisaging a sort of nuanced, not clearly defined, socialism, where the religious component prevails and leaves undetermined—because not deserving special attention—the issues of output maximization and distribution, to the advantage of "a distinctively human relationship of persons which in Western Europe was always associated with Christian traditions".[150]

His rather singular vision can, on the one side, be seen as an anticipation of the political and economic organization of the social-democratic State, a sort of prefiguration of the welfare State of the post-Second World War world; on the other, as a utopian society that the experience of two centuries has cancelled as a realistic alternative. A criticism of Polanyi's work is indeed that this socio-political (not economic) role performed by society's actors does not explain why they are engaged in production and distribution activities, that is the motivation of those activities.[151]

Notes

1. Baran and Sweezy (1966, p. 3).
2. To quote the title of a book by R. J. B. Bosworth.
3. Fenoaltea (2011, p. 136).
4. Fenoaltea (2011, pp. 136–137).
5. Rocco and Carli (1914, pp. 29–32). The ideas are almost verbatim the same as expressed by Rathenau (see chapter II).
6. Rocco and Carli, pp. 24–25.
7. Rocco and Carli, p 27. For the influence of List on Rocco, see Gregor (2005, pp. 43–48).

8. Rocco and Carli, p. 6.
9. D'Alfonso (2004, pp. 124–127).
10. Rocco and Carli, p. 5.
11. Rocco and Carli, pp. 49–51.
12. "Uncultivated land, to be exploited, is a gay phantasy of our liberals and socialists".
13. D'Alfonso, pp. 131 and 136.
14. Gregor, p. 117.
15. Gregor, p. 119.
16. Spirito (1939, p. 99).
17. Gregor, pp. 131–133.
18. Conti (1986, p. 431).
19. Rocco and Carli, pp. 56–57.
20. Ministerial report to the Chamber of the Deputies on bill 1926/563, related to the discipline of collective contracts (in 1939, there were around 8500 of them).
21. As reported in De Felice (1968, pp. 542–547).
22. Corporations were, however, created only by a law of 1934.
23. This is the interpretation given by Papi (1958, vol. I, p. 457).
24. Negri Zamagni (2019).
25. Toniolo (1980).
26. Ciocca (2007, p. 203).
27. Guerin (1939, p. 28).
28. Ciocca, p. 223.
29. Sylos Labini (1975).
30. Kalecki (1943).
31. p. 425.
32. Spirito (1933, pp. 97 and 101) and Gregor (2005, chapter Six).
33. Ciocca, p. 215.
34. Paxton (2004, p. 122).
35. Merlini (1995, p. 48).
36. Galli (2010, p. 12).
37. We shall see this Christian inspiration also in Polanyi (Sect. 3.7 of this chapter).
38. Webb (1944, pp. XXXVII and L).
39. Russell (1920, p. 90).
40. Schumpeter (1947, p. 32). That distinction of roles is emphasized in the book as a reason of collapse of capitalism (see Sect. 3.7).
41. Baran and Sweezy (1966, pp. 3 and 4). The book has an epigraph: *The Truth Is the Whole* (Hegel). Almost to stress, if needed, the Hegelian philosophical origin of Marxist doctrine, and his sometimes "obscure" language (Schumpeter).
42. Baran and Sweezy, p. 56.

43. p. 9.
44. Chapter 8.
45. Schumpeter (1947).
46. Streeck (2016, pp. 2–3).
47. Lange (1959, p. 1).
48. However, Lenin was convinced that what Marx had said in his essay on the constitutional and political aspects of the Paris Commune of 1871 applied with equal truth to the Russian Soviet of 1917. See Webb (1944, p. 9).
49. Meek (1964, p. 95).
50. Carr (1958, vol. 1, pp. 21–22).
51. "The process of degeneration from the pure ideal took on specifically Russian forms in a Russian context...this process, subtle and undeclared, was well advanced when Stalin first propounded the hybrid doctrine of 'socialism in one country'" (Carr, ibid.).
52. Schlesinger (1947, p. 10).
53. Schwartz (1968, p. 2).
54. We take 1913 because the GDP level is not available for 1917, the year of the Revolution.
55. Maddison (2003, Tables 2b and 3b).
56. See Harrison (2017) and Schlesinger (1947).
57. Maddison, Table 3b.
58. Ukraine was however affected by famine and Soviet repression of dissident intellectuals.
59. Schwartz (1968, p. 26).
60. Stalin (1972).
61. p. 13.
62. p. 15.
63. Dobb (1937a, p. 270).
64. Dobb (1937a, p. 271).
65. Dobb (1937a, p. 338).
66. Lange (1959).
67. p. 2.
68. Marx (n.d. [1867], vol. I, Part I, pp. 50, 58, 94, 251).
69. Lange, p. 9.
70. Meek (1964).
71. Shackle (1963, p. 194).
72. "The market is institutionally embodied in the present socialist economy". See Lange (1967, p. 160).
73. Lange, p. 161.
74. Robinson (1967, p. 176).
75. pp. 176–178.
76. pp. 178–181.

77. Kaser (1971, p. 254). The experience of national planning in some major European economies was negative.
78. Dobb (1937b, p.131).The theme of economic "laws", as characterising economics as "science", has been a recurring object of debate, anytime there are difficulties to adjust them to the economic reality. When this happens, what was a "law" is degraded to "regularity". Notable examples of faulty economic laws are the "invariable distribution of income" (Pareto, chapter I), and the "Phillips curve" (which we shall mention at chapter 4). 30 years after Dobb's writing, Axel Leijonhufvud, observed that "the sharp distinction…is one of the devices economists use in order to effect a clear separation of Economics from the other social sciences disciplines – and to put the problems of the latter in the ceteris paribus dustbin". He adds that this is a pernicious distinction if we consider its artificiality, and that it is only thanks to the "drastic abstraction" of pure economics from the totality of other social sciences that economists have been able to go "far ahead" of those social sciences in theoretical construction. Only this abstraction and shared paradigms have allowed economics not to simmer on interminable discussions and conflicts (1968, pp. 233–234).
79. Dobb (1937b, p. 132).
80. Marx (nd [1867]), p. 57
81. Dodd's implicit reference is to Rousseau's General Will, see chapter I. It is questionable that Rousseau's thought can be seen as the "traditional theory of politics and of the State".
82. Dobb(1937b, pp. 177–178.)
83. Dobb, p. 182.
84. Which Keynes wanted to "knock away". Letter to G. B. Shaw, 1 January 1935 (1973, pp. 492–493).
85. Robinson (1972, p. 200).
86. Sraffa (1960).
87. Sraffa (1951–1955: vol. I–X, and 1973: vol XI–indexes).
88. Roncaglia (2009, p. 453).
89. Apart from the first, which permeates the whole book, these assumptions are in the book's Preface.
90. Sraffa writes that the identification of the concept of value with marginal utility is "notoriously an invention of bourgeois economists, post-marxist and anti-marxist" (2017, p. 3).
91. Roy Harrod wrote a favourable review of Sraffa's book, only complaining that in his text there is no reference to "demand", according to the Ricardian, classical tradition (1961, p. 783).
92. As opposed to "constant capital", the machinery.
93. Sraffa (1960, p. 17). See also Meek (1961).

94. The uniform rate of profit over the industry, for instance, is offered by Sraffa in a way that is logically rigorous, but historically deaf. See Napoleoni (1963, p. 201).
95. See Naldi (2000).
96. Sraffa (2017).
97. See Napoleoni (1963, pp. 194–201); more recently, Mazzucato (2018, p. 70).
98. *Theory of Moral Sentiments*, p. 331.
99. Heibroner and Milberg (1995, p 118).
100. Schumpeter (1947, p. 112).
101. As we can see, the inability to catch the evolving structures of capitalism was—is—a recurring criticism of the Marxist thought.
102. Keynes' intervention on *The New Statement* and *Nation* (1934, pp. 34–35).
103. Beveridge (1944, p. 206).
104. Von Mises (1951, p. 48).
105. p. 13.
106. p. 51.
107. p. 76.
108. p. 29.
109. p. 120.
110. Weber (1930). See the *Preface*, by Tawney, R. H., p. 1b. Tawney is the author of *Religion and the Rise of Capitalism*, John Murray, 1926.
111. Weber, p. 54.
112. Tawney, *Preface*, p. 2.
113. Weber, p. 52.
114. Weber, p. 179.
115. Weber, pp. 302–303.
116. Weber was "appalled" by modern capitalism (Gregory [2012, p. 241]).
117. Weber, p. 181.
118. p. 182.
119. Schumpeter (1954, p. 80).
120. Schumpeter (1947). See in particular Part II, "Can Capitalism Survive?"
121. We shall not deal here with Parts III and V of his book, where Schumpeter is critical of socialism itself, which risks damaging the gains of capitalism and freedoms of liberal democracies.
122. p. 67.
123. p. 78.
124. pp. 82–83.
125. p. 130.
126. Chapter XIV.
127. p. 156.
128. p. 132.

129. p. 133.
130. p. 131.
131. p. 121.
132. p. 134.
133. p. 158.
134. p. 137.
135. p. 158.
136. p. 159.
137. p. 160.
138. p. 143.
139. p. 150.
140. p. 162.
141. Polanyi (1957).
142. Polanyi, p. 126.
143. Polanyi, p. 3.
144. "The metaphysical extraterritoriality of a Jewish bankers' dynasty domiciled in the capitals of Europe", p. 10.
145. p. 68.
146. p. 71.
147. p. 103.
148. Heilbroner (1988, pp. 17–18).
149. p. 258.
150. p. 234.
151. Heilbroner, p. 18.

References

Baran, P., & Sweezy, P. M. (1966). *Monopoly Capital. An Essay on the American Economic and Social Order*. New York: Monthly Review Press.

Beveridge, W. (1944). *Full Employment in a Free Society*. London: Allen and Unwin.

Carr, E. H. (1958). *Socialism in One Country, 1924–1926*. London: Macmillan.

Ciocca, P. (2007). *Ricchi per sempre? Una storia economica d'Italia*. Torino: Bollati Boringhieri.

Conti, E. (1986). *Dal taccuino di un borghese* (p. 431). Bologna: Il Mulino.

D'Alfonso, R. (2004). *Costruire lo Stato forte. Politica, diritto, economia in Alfredo Rocco*. Milano: Franco Angeli.

De Felice, R. (1968). *Mussolini il fascista. L'organizzazione dello Stato fascista 1925–1929*. Torino: Einaudi.

Dobb, M. (1937a). *The Question of Economic Law in a Socialist Economy, in Political Economy and Capitalism. Some Essays in Economic Tradition*. London: Routledge.

Dobb, M. (1937b). *The Trends of Modern Economics, in Political Economy and Capitalism. Some Essays in Economic Tradition*. London: Routledge

Fenoaltea, S. (2011). *The Reinterpretation of the Italian Economic History, from Unification to the Great War*. Cambridge: Cambridge University Press.

Galli, C. (2010). Carl Schmitt nella cultura italiana (1924–1978). Storia, bilancio, prospettive di una presenza problematica. *Storicamente, 6*.

Gregor, A. J. (2005). *Mussolini's Intellectuals. Fascist Social and Political Thought*. Princeton and Oxford: Princeton University Press.

Gregory, B. S. (2012). *The Unintended Reformation. How a Religious Revolution Secularized Society*. Cambridge: Belknap Press of Harvard University Press.

Guerin, D. (1939). *Fascism and Big Business*. New York: Pioneer Publishers.

Harrison, M. (2017, May). *The Soviet Economy: Its Life and Afterlife* (Warwick Economics Research Papers, n. 1137).

Harrod, R. (1961). Review of Production of Commodities by Means of Commodities. *The Economic Journal, 71*(284).

Heilbroner, R., & Milberg, W. (1995). *The Crisis of Vision in Modern Economic Thinking*. Cambridge: Cambridge University Press.

Heilbroner, R. L. (1988). *Behind the Veil of Economics. Essays in the Worldly Philosophy*. New York: W. W. Norton.

Kalecki, M. (1943). Political Aspects of Full Employment. *Political Quarterly, 14*; reprinted in Hunt, E. K., & Schwartz, J. G. (Eds.). (1972). *A Critique of Economic Theory*. Harmondsworth: Penguin.

Kaser, M. (1971). *Planning and Market Relations. Proceedings of a Conference Held by the International Economic Association at Liblice, Czechoslovakia*. London: Macmillan.

Keynes, J. M. (1934, December). Intervention in *Stalin-Wells Talk. The New Statesman* and *Nation*.

Keynes, J. M. (1973). Letter to G.B. Shaw, 1 January, 1935. In D. Moggridge (Ed.), *The Collected Writings* (Vol. XIII). London: Macmillan.

Lange, O. (1959). The Political Economy of Socialism. *Science and Society, 23*(1).

Lange, O. (1967). The Computer and the Market. In C. H. Feinstein (Ed.), *Socialism, Capitalism and Economic Growth. Essays Presented to Maurice Dobb*. Cambridge: Cambridge University Press.

Leijonhufvud, A. (1968). *On Keynesian Economics and the Economics of Keynes*. New York: Oxford University Press.

Maddison, A. (2003). *The World Economy. Historical Statistics*. Paris: OECD.

Marx, K. (n.d. [1867]). *Capital. A Critique of Political Economy, Vol I*. Moscow: Progress Publishers (Marxist.org).

Mazzucato, M. (2018). *The Value of Everything. Making and Taking in the Global Economy*. London: Allen Lane.

Meek, R. (1961). Mr. Sraffa's Rehabilitation of Classical Economics. *Scottish Journal of Political Economy, 8*(1), 119–136.

Meek, R. (1964). Value-Judgements in Economics. *The British Journal for the Philosophy of Science, XV*(18).

Merlini, S. (1995). Il governo costituzionale. In R. Romanelli (Ed.), *Storia dello Stato italiano dall'unita' a oggi*. Donzelli: Roma.

Naldi, N. (2000, October). The Friendship Between Piero Sraffa and Antonio Gramsci in the Years 1919–1927. *European Journal of the History of Economic Thought, 7*(2).

Napoleoni, C. (1963). *Il pensiero economico del '900*. Torino: Einaudi.

Negri Zamagni, V. (2019, December 12). *Quanto corporativa fu l'economia italiana negli anni 1930?* Paper presented at the conference Economia ed economisti del periodo fascista, Accademia Nazionale dei Lincei.

Papi, G. U. (1958). *Principii di economia*. Padova: Cedam.

Paxton, R. O. (2004). *The Anatomy of Fascism*. London: Allen Lane.

Polanyi, K. (1957 [1944]). *The Great Transformation. The Political and Economic Origins of Our Time*. Boston: Beacon Press.

Robinson, J. (1967). Socialist Affluence. In C. H. Feinstein (Ed.), *Socialism, Capitalism and Economic Growth. Essays Presented to Maurice Dobb*. Cambridge: Cambridge University Press.

Robinson, J. (1972). Prelude to a Critique of Economic Theory. In E. K. Hunt & J. G. Schwartz (Eds.), *A Critique of Economic Theory*. Harmondsworth: Penguin.

Rocco, A., Carli, F. (1914). I principi fondamentali del nazionalismo economico. In *Associazione nazionalista italiana: Il nazionalismo economico*. Bologna: Paolo Neri.

Roncaglia, A. (2009). *The Wealth of Ideas. A History of Economic Thought*. Cambridge: Cambridge University Press.

Russell, B. (1920). *The Practice and Theory of Bolshevism*. London: University of Books.

Schlesinger, R. (1947). *The Spirit of Post-War Russia. Soviet Ideology 1917–1946*. London: Dennis Dobson.

Schumpeter, J. A. (1947). *Capitalism, Socialism and Democracy*. New York and London: Harper and Brothers.

Schumpeter, J. A. (1954). *History of Economic Analysis*. New York: Oxford University Press.

Schwartz, H. (1968). *An Introduction to the Soviet Economy*. Columbus: Charles E. Merrill.

Shackle, G. L. S. (1963 [1990]). General Thought-Schemes and the Economist. In J. L. Ford (Ed.), *Time, Expectations and Uncertainty in Economics. Selected Essays of G.L.S. Shackle*. Brookfield: Edward Elgar.

Smith, A. (1853 [1759]). *The Theory of Moral Sentiments*. London: Henry Bohn.

Spirito, U. (1933). L'economia programmatica corporativa. In *Capitalismo e corporativismo*. Firenze: Sansoni.

Spirito, U. (1939). Politica ed economia corporativa. In *Dall'economia liberale al corporativismo. Critica dell'economia liberale*. Messina-Milano: Principato.

Sraffa, P. (1951–1955 and 1973). *David Ricardo. Works and Correspondence*. Cambridge: Cambridge University Press.

Sraffa, P. (1960). *Production of Commodities by Means of Commodities. Prelude to a Critique of Economic Theory*. Cambridge: Cambridge University Press.

Sraffa, P. (2017). *Lettere editoriali (1947–1975)*. Torino: Einaudi.

Stalin, J. V. (1972 [1952]). *Economic Problems of Socialism in the U.S.S.R.* Peking: Foreign Press.

Streeck, W. (2016). *How Capitalism Will End?* London: Verso.

Sylos Labini, P. (1975). *Saggio sulle classi sociali*. Roma-Bari: Laterza.

Toniolo, G. (1980). *L'economia dell'Italia fascista*. Roma-Bari: Laterza.

Von Mises, L. (1951). *Socialism. An Economic and Social Analysis*. New Haven: Yale University Press.

Webb, S. B. (1944 [1935]). *Soviet Communism. A News Civilisation*. London: Longmans, Green and Co.

Weber, M. (1930 [1905]). *The Protestant Ethic and the Spirit of Capitalism*. London: Allen & Unwin.

CHAPTER 4

Neoliberalism

4.1 Keynes' "Classical Situation"

Which sort of liberalism was emerging from the Second World War? Neither the individualistic, radically libertarian ideas put forward by Hayek, nor Chicago School's theories, based on rules that would limit authority's discretion in monetary management. It was rather a Keynesian vision, which went even beyond the field of economics, to support an approach that would favour a large role of the State in country's social life. The Welfare State was being established, in fact leaning more on Beveridge's design than Keynes' macroeconomics.

This broad configuration took different shapes, according to the peculiar situation in which countries had exited the war, and their previous experiences. For instance, in Britain the Labour government of the immediate post-war years took action to implement the Welfare State along the lines drawn by its begetter, in a political climate inclined towards benign views of socialist developments elsewhere. The British economy was largely managed through administrative controls. Even if this policy could be explained as the adoption of necessary but temporary devices in the difficult circumstances of post-war period, in the economic profession some thought that controls should be a permanent feature of macroeconomic management.

In Italy, after the fall of fascism and the defeat in war, economic reconstruction could be carried on in a free market; but at the same

A. Roselli, *Economic Philosophies*,
Palgrave Studies in Classical Liberalism,
https://doi.org/10.1007/978-3-030-53317-5_4

time the presence of the State covered a large part of the economy, and dirigiste policies continued to be followed, a continuation of practices established in the pre-war period (see Chapter 3). In the economic profession, research and teaching continued to rely on neo-classical schemes, even though the elders were still influenced by corporativism, and only the younger were intellectually seduced by Keynes. In France, economists were engaged in indicative planning. German economists and policymakers largely relied on that peculiar form of economic liberalism that is ordoliberalism (Chapter 2).

It is important to notice that in some major countries large sections of the public, and of the intellectual elites, leaned towards extreme forms of socialism, still attracted by the experiences of the Soviet Union. The Sputnik launch, in 1957, was widely seen in the West as evidence of technological advancement and scientific superiority (particularly *vis-à-vis* the United States), and powerful was the lure of an apparently more egalitarian and well educated society, while only slowly the economic shortcomings and the appalling social consequences of the Soviet regime (see Chapter 3) became evident to outside observers.

Still strong as a form of political struggle in several liberal democracies (communist parties still took a large share of the electorate during the 1970s), socialism's ideological appeal became, however, dimmer. Indeed, Marxist socialism gradually disappeared as an alternative political and economic ideology, while the accomplishments of a free liberal society, in terms of technological innovations, spectacular economic growth, rising standards of living, and limited government, were evidence that the liberal *Weltanschauung* was prevailing over rigid nationalism or Marxism.

In the economic discipline, Marxian studies still flourished for a while, also thanks to important and brilliant economists, whom we have mentioned in Chapter 3, but—in parallel with the economic decline of the Soviet Union—Marxist economists tended to find an escape route, abandoning Marxian ideological premises, and to see economics as a sort of neutral science of economic management, of social engineering, which would in the end approximate schemes of advanced socialist economies to those of free-market economies. The triumph of liberalism meant that the economic discipline was more and more identified as the study of capitalism.[1] This mainstream economics tended to dislodge alternative forms of economic thinking. It was reinforced by political and economic developments of the final decades of the twentieth century. The possibility of a structural collapse of the capitalistic order appeared remote while, as a left-leaning thinker has written, the unlimited production and accumulation of productive capital confirmed that the market could assure the conversion of "the private vice of material greed into a public benefit", and the insecure workers of the free-market system were converted into confident, affluent consumers, "even in the face of the fundamental uncertainty of labour markets and employment".[2]

On the opposite side of the debate, nationalist ideology, discredited by the defeat of the major countries that had pursued its more authoritarian version, survived (sometimes mixed with a Marxist approach: perhaps an evidence of their common statist origin) as a political and economic ideology, but was generally seen in a limited perspective: as a possible driving force for underdeveloped, often newly created countries, to accelerate their economic development. Left-leaning economists devoted many reflections to the economies of underdeveloped countries. This nationalistic and socially inspired perspective was characterized by a widely shared preference for public or State enterprise over private undertakings; by policies aimed at substituting domestic production for imports, and by a refusal or reluctance to admit investment of foreign capital, unless it could be fully controlled by the national government. The liberal view, according to which reliance on a competitive market price would be preferable to government control and ownership; that economic efficiency would be best served by the Ricardian comparative advantage principle; and that domestic capital in underdeveloped countries was scarce and therefore a bottleneck to growth, was generally dismissed with arguments that, in the end, would find their main support in Friedrich List's protective *System of Political Economy*, if not in Marx's *Capital*.[3] In fact, nationalism would be characterized by policies—often badly conceived—mainly concerned with redistributing income rather than increasing it, and by an emphasis on what is called "psychic" income, in the form of pride in the nation, or—even worse—in an ethnic group, even to the detriment of material income.[4] We shall find some of these features in the revival of nationalism in our times, in economically advanced countries, as will be shown in Sect. 4.6.

The widespread liberal outlook, reinforced by well known, radical changes in politics which occurred in a few important countries, particularly in the United States and the United Kingdom, received an unofficial but extremely well publicized blessing from a too famous essay by Francis Fukuyama.[5] This claimed that the "total exhaustion of viable systematic alternatives"[6] was evidence of the triumph of Western liberalism. What is somewhat intriguing in Fukuyama's writing is that he frames his vision in an ill-conceived Hegelian perspective,[7] that is in the works of an author who made the entire course of history dependent on the idea of the State (Chapter 1), that very idea which—as a liberal—Fukuyama looks at with suspicion, to say the least.

Interestingly, however, while Fukuyama sees the ideas of fascism—centred on a strong State that forges new people on the basis of national exclusiveness—as a promise of unending conflicts and disastrous defeats, he does not reserve a similar negative opinion for nationalism, *per se*: "it is not clear that nationalism represents an irreconcilable contradiction in the heart of liberalism…Only systematic nationalisms of the latter sort [such as National socialism, Fascism] can qualify as a formal ideology on the level of liberalism or communism…nationalist movements do not have a political program beyond the negative desire of independence from some other groups of people and do not offer anything like a comprehensive agenda for socio-economic organization"[8]: this sounds plausible, in the light of nationalism's current revival (in Sect. 4.6 of this chapter a bleaker interpretation of Fukuyama's essay is presented).

Regarding liberalism, a distinction between different views must however be made within that wide span of time which encompasses around 60 years of political and economic history, between the Second World War and the outbreak of the financial crisis at the start of our century: under the wide wings of economic liberalism, large ideological shifts have occurred. This distinction, perhaps still unclear when Fukuyama wrote his essay (1989), is important, because these shifts opened the way to very difficult developments—in terms of economic growth, social inequality and financial stability—in early twenty-first century. These developments have, in turn, raised new questions, still unanswered.

As mentioned at the start of this chapter, in the immediate post-war decades, within the liberal vision, Keynes' approach was seen as prevailing and marking a point of departure from other, generally more libertarian strands of thought. Keynes' thinking, as we have observed in Chapter 2, was seen sometimes as leaning towards socialism, a sort of social liberalism that included a managed market economy, the goal of full employment, and a welfare society; but it maintained the principal individualistic features of a free capitalistic society: in fact, Keynes thought that his *General Theory* would point the way to the very survival of capitalism, after the Great Depression. Notwithstanding the unending revolutions and counter-revolutions that have agitated the economic discipline after Keynes, Keynesian thought, in its wider sense, is sometimes represented as the last point of reference, or standard model, that for a while maintained a large consensus not only within the economic profession, but also in any society inspired by liberal democratic values.

The Keynesian consensus represented the kind of agreement that Schumpeter calls "classical situation".[9] It was not the first, and for sure will not be the last case of a classical situation. Schumpeter does not give a formal definition of this expression, although recurrent in his *History of Economic Analysis*, but his clear reference is to the achievement of a substantial, widely shared agreement in economic thought (in this sense, we might speak of a "classical" consensus with reference to any discipline): an agreement that is reached, more or less broadly, after a period of struggle and controversy in the economic profession and, perhaps more widely, in the way in which society looks at economic matters. Schumpeter writes that a typical classical situation is characterized by the fact that the "leading works" that give it its character, exhibit "a large expanse of common ground" and suggest "a feeling of repose". This well established consensus creates, "in the superficial observer, an impression of finality—the finality of a Greek temple that spreads its perfect lines against a cloudless sky".[10] What in this essay we prefer to name a vision, an ideology—as the explicit, or implicit, point of reference of the economist who elaborates his own theoretical scheme—becomes a "classical situation" when a sufficiently widespread consensus is reached not only on his theoretical construction, but above all on his ideological premises.

The complacency with which one can look at a classical situation cannot lead us to think that ideas and theoretical constructions which are at the basis of the "temple" are really "final", unbound from specific situations defined in terms of time and place (this is probably the main factor that separates a classical situation in moral sciences from the same kind of situation in physical sciences).

Before Keynes, this sort of classical situations emerged, for instance, with the Classical School of late eighteenth–early nineteenth century, and then with the highly abstract theorizing around marginal utility, apparently indifferent to social and political considerations, of neo-classical thinkers of the end of the nineteenth century and later: a period when the most perfect equilibria of social mechanics were dreamt of.[11]

In fact, in a longer perspective of historical change, every classical situation, in the field of economics, has, inside it, the seeds of its own evolution into something different (signs of decay, breaks in the offing, writes Schumpeter): a new classical situation that radically alters previous objectives and methods of research.[12]

What is of interest now, is to see:

a. which "signs of decay" or "breaks in the offing" were visible, to later observers, in Keynes' *General Theory*;
b. which new philosophical attitudes, and revolutions or counter-revolutions in the discipline of economics, came out of them;
c. if a new "classical situation" resulted from these movements, which characterized the last decades of the twentieth century.

Each of these three points is developed in the Sections that follow. In very general terms, it is worth while stressing again that liberalism occupied the whole territory of political, institutional and economic theorizing, but a sharper libertarian stance emerged, increasingly resting on individual selfishness. This vision went wider than the field of economic philosophy and thinking, extending to the body politic and social life.

4.2 Demise of Keynesian Consensus

Regarding the "breaks in the offing" that were detected in Keynes' work, the criticism of Keynes stems in part from some developments of an economic and social character, which occurred in the period following the Second World War, and in part from an attack on Keynes' analysis, at first directed specifically against the role of inflation in Keynes' *General Theory*, and then against the "wreckage" of "that remarkable intellectual event called Keynesian Revolution".[13]

On the first point, some developments in public finance, labour relations and government activism, must be mentioned:

- a wider role for welfare economics, as envisaged by Beveridge, and the enactment of a "functional" public finance (see Chapter 2): they were generally accompanied by a strong expansion of government budgets and of deficit spending. These developments had a deep impact on the economy: not really Keynesian, because deficit spending was advocated by Keynes in a situation of under-employment of resources, of insufficient effective demand, such as that prevailing in the 1930s. Keynes was convinced that an equilibrium with under-utilization of resources might be more than an accidental possibility, but he argued that when there is full employment "as nearly as is practicable, the classical theory comes into its own again from this point onwards".[14] In the post-Second World War period, for instance, in Britain, the belief that the immediate post-war boom might be temporary and that the economy would relapse into high unemployment persisted for long, giving room to spending more public money; moreover, the unemployment of resources remained notably high in other countries, and wealth distribution unbalanced. But the push to welfare economics sometimes outstripped financial sustainability, with a high subsidy component and perverse incentives. The influence of party politics was, in this regard, not negligible;

- the habit of "concertation" in contracting wages and other work conditions, between employers and employees, often brokered by the government: this stronger bargaining power of labour contributed to the creation of a work environment—in terms both of wage levels and employment rates—which, as just observed, was rather far from the enduring stressful conditions of labour market of the pre-war period. These industrial relations, which might recall the Italian corporativism of the fascist era, in a sort of connivance of capital with labour, became frequent, mostly in Italy (under the guidance of Christian-democrat/Socialist parties governments) but also elsewhere (in Britain this policy was already a feature of the Churchill administration in early 1950s, and later Labour and Conservative governments found themselves forced to adopt corporativist solution when in government[15]);
- a growing activism of governments, particularly in Europe, not to be confused with the macroeconomic policies of the welfare state, mentioned above: this activism took different shapes, for instance through the "social market economy", inspired by the ordoliberal credo, as in Germany (Chapter 2), or the "mixed economy" in Italy, where quasi-governmental institutions created under fascism continued to survive and prosper in the post-war period. This government activism actually incorporated the dirigiste, technocratic tendencies already well visible in the fascist regime, and was, in fact, one of the driving forces of post-war economic recovery

> (Chapter 3). This activism, which only vaguely might be associated with Keynesian interventionism, appeared to may libertarian observers an obvious infringement of the very core of liberalism, where the adjectives "social" or "mixed" would coexist uncomfortably with the noun "market".

On the second point—the theoretical attack on Keynes—from an analytical point of view inflation had not been a central point in Keynes' *General Theory*. Inflation is seldom named in that work. The most relevant mention of inflation is probably when he points out to an apparent asymmetry between the effects of deflation, and inflation, on effective demand: "For whilst a deflation of effective demand below the level required for full employment will diminish employment as well as prices, an inflation of it [of effective demand] above this level will merely affect prices".[16] He had in mind the depressed business conditions of the 1930s and a monetary regime sufficiently stable to disregard inflation as a specific source of instability.

After the war, the domestic component of inflation reflected a monetary regime of discretionary, manipulative "fiat" money,[17] affected by the political and social developments mentioned above. In addition, the sudden jump in energy prices in the early 1970s—evidence of changing geo-political conditions—had a significant effect on the external component of inflation, a component equally irrelevant in the context of the *General Theory*.

As a matter of fact, inflationary pressures in the 1970s were accompanied by a slowdown in output and unemployment: a combination—the "stagflation"—that would be hard to explain in Keynesian terms.

Without going into details of Keynesian economists' doctrines in the post-war period, it appeared that this lack of attention over inflation could be covered by the model given in the late 1950s by the economist A. W. Phillips. He saw a long-term tendency of the wage rate (and, by inference, of the price level) being related, in a stable and inverse relation, to the rate of unemployment. The "Phillips curve" was not in Keynes' *General Theory*, and was introduced "not without opposition by some Keynesians".[18] And it appeared to be at odds with the situation of the early 1970s, when, as just mentioned, stagflation meant high inflation and high unemployment, in a context of falling or stagnant output. That correlation, even if apparently supported by historical statistical evidence, could not be demonstrated in the current context. It was academically discredited, as a "law-like" or "regularity" which could not stand up to empirical evidence.[19] There might be arguments to support Phillips's thesis but—beyond academic debates—what is more relevant was the changing political and intellectual climate of those years.

A caustic, but acute analysis by the Canadian economist Harry Johnson—an analysis that, if it ever needed to be deployed, would be enough to give evidence of the intermingling of ideology, theory and changing social and economic circumstances—shows how "signs of decay" and "breaks in the offing" in the Keynesian "classical situation" were exploited by a different vision, and theoretical construction.[20]

According to Johnson, the factors that had accounted for the success of the *General Theory* can be ascribed on the one hand to the existence of an important social and economic problem—unemployment and depression—which the previous orthodoxy (the neo-classical economics) had been unable to solve, instead evidencing general confusion and obvious irrelevance; on the other, to its superior social relevance and intellectual distinction (appealing to the youthful iconoclasm of younger generations of economists), even though Keynes actually incorporated in a novel and confusing fashion some valid elements of the traditional theory.[21]

Johnson observes that Keynes' revolution became established orthodoxy—a "classical situation", we can say—mainly through the work of his followers. They (which means the profession at large) elaborated Keynes' analysis, developed in a given set of historical circumstances, into "a timeless and spaceless set of universal principles[22]...and so established Keynesianism as an orthodoxy [itself] ripe for counter-attack".[23]

It is no wonder that in an environment, in which inflationary concerns were taking the place of mass unemployment as the central issue for policymakers and economists,[24] a revival of interest in money would not be unexpected. The criticism of the *General Theory* stimulated initially a renewed attention to already established, alternative theories and, then, new researches based on individual's behaviour. Both developments give further evidence that economic theorizing is never really "final" and remains inevitably connected to specific social and intellectual conditions that may prevail in certain times and places. However, the "monetarist counter-revolution", and subsequent theories (which go on the whole under the name of New Classical Economics: see Sect. 4.4), were not only a matter of renewed scientific interest in the behaviour of monetary aggregates and in individuals' rational choices; they were also evidence of a shifting of the prevailing economic ideology against the Keynesian orthodoxy.

The widely accepted view is that this powerful intellectual change can be labelled under the title of neoliberalism. A comprehensive and acceptable definition of this change has been provided: "Neoliberalism is in the first instance a theory of political economic practices that proposes that human well-being can best be advanced by liberating individual entrepreneurial freedoms and skills within an institutional framework characterized by strong private property rights, free markets, and free trade. The role of the state is to create and preserve an institutional framework appropriate to such practices".[25] Neoliberalism can therefore be seen as an attempt—certain, not the first in political and economic history—to reverse the encroachment of the State in our daily life.

On the economic side, an important—if not particularly new—specification is that neoliberalism is not only characterized by a non-interventionist stance, but is built on the presumption that each agent cares only about his utility and does not care about the utility of others. This is stated as a "positive" claim, a "scientific" assertion. In front of this claim, the sentiment of "sympathy", which I mean also as "trust", of Adam Smith—which is the foundation of a well-functioning free-market system—becomes wishful thinking.

Neoliberalism has various implications, sometimes subsumed under the expression "market fundamentalism": regarding working relations between employer and employee, their respective contractual strength is put on the same level; concerning market organization, neoliberalism enforces a Darwinian concept of prevalence of the fittest and more efficient, up to the extreme of voiding the same concept of market and to the paradoxical emergence of rent positions; international trade relations are governed by a globalism that denies forms of national or regional protection under any circumstance; fiscal and monetary policies have to be coherent with (or constrained by) rules that imply their substantial neutrality in respect to the smooth working of unhindered markets.

Referring to the United States, Paul Samuelson, in 1997, characterized its economy as the "Ruthless Economy", and its labour as a "Cowed Labour Force". The first feature, marked by a retreat from an unlimited welfare State, told the "same story", as applied to post-Reagan America, or to the "extreme case" of Britain's Margaret Thatcher, or to most of Western Europe, Scandinavia, or Australia. The second feature, the Cowed Labour Market, was referred to an intimidated labour force as an indication of how "uncertain income receivers have become", but also to "the employers race in the same rat run, too. Ruthless competition, which constantly demands, 'What have you done for me lately?', is what puts all of us into a kind of visceral anxiety".[26]

The following two sections are devoted to the political side and the economic side of neoliberalism.

4.3 Philosophical Attitudes: Economic Constitutionalism

The first aspect to consider, to explain the move away from the Keynesian classical situation, is the pervasive, powerful intellectual change that, in the second half of the twentieth century, affected political theorizing about government and the economy. It was a long strand of thought that developed in a continuity with Hayek and the "Austrians", that is that group of economists, many of Central-European origin or descent,[27] who asserted the necessity to preserve—or to come back to—social and economic structures focussed on the individual operating in a free-market economy, while maintaining a sceptical attitude to State intervention, seen as a road to authoritarian, paternalistic or even liberticide regimes (see Chapter 2). This change gave capitalist economic systems a marked libertarian stance.

In order to put neoliberalism in its intellectual context, it is worthwhile reminding two strands of thought. Both developed in the second part of the twentieth century, and it is possible to see them as competing schemes. At the cost of some oversimplification, they rely, respectively, on "sympathy" and "selfishness". The basic difference is that "the libertarians restored the rights to individual, but not the obligations".[28] "In the most extreme versions, money [became] the measure of wellbeing, and justice [was] nothing more than efficacy".[29] Notwithstanding certain apparent similarities, these two approaches saw the organization of society in very different ways, and it is immediately clear that the second viewpoint has prevailed.

We refer here to the contractualism of John Rawls and the contractarianism of James Buchanan. Both can be seen as political theories of government legitimacy and as moral theories about the origin or legitimate content of moral norms. The legitimacy of political authority is rooted in the consent of the governed. This consent consists of a mutual agreement that gives legitimation to moral norms.[30] In both—Rawls' and Buchanan's—philosophies, a social contract, ethically grounded, is indeed the basic link between the members of a society, and is the justification for their living together. So they both belong to liberalism, broadly defined.

However, if we enter the field of economics proper, the effective relevance of Buchanan's thinking has been certainly higher. There are two reasons for that:

- we would not be able to find in Rawls a connection to specific theoretical approaches in economics, his thinking is more attuned to the political organization of the State than to its economic system, while in Buchanan there is an obvious *sequitur* from political thinking to economic consequences.[31] And his political and economic thinking is more attuned to the prevailing circumstances of his time.
- But, more importantly, the model of liberal society that Rawls might suggest was suffering the same sense of crisis and demise that, in the economic field, was characterizing Keynesian economics.

In both cases, we are far from any State-oriented philosophy, while man in his individuality is the centre of the philosopher's attention. If we go back to the philosophical roots of social contract theories that are the background of both, two names come to mind: Immanuel Kant and Thomas Hobbes. Kant is behind Rawls' reflections, Hobbes behind Buchanan's.

Kant has a fundamentally benevolent view of man acting in society, whose ethics is expressed in three propositions (the "categorical imperatives") that specify his duty: (1) act rationally: whatever is the particular end of your action, you must want your particular end only if it can be subsumed under a universal order, that is an order in which all possible rational actions may converge; (2) as a corollary: act in a way that treats humanity—of your own person and of any other person—always as an end and never as a means; (3) act so that your will may become universal rule. By "universal rule", Kant means that law derives from the same reason that lives in every man, who is therefore obliged to observe it.[32]

This moral framework is present in Rawls' thinking, and it is necessary to understand the basis of the social contract, as envisaged by Rawls in his *A Theory of Justice*.[33] He sees this contract not in a historical sense, or arising from a supposed primitive state of nature, but arising, with "a certain level of abstraction", from a "purely hypothetical situation". It is an original position of equality, where the principles of justice are chosen behind a veil of ignorance, and are the result of an agreement or bargain between the members of the society. Here is the connection with Kant, because Rawls sees individuals as moral persons, as "rational beings with their own ends", but also "capable of a sense of justice".[34] Each person is seen by Rawls as rational and disinterested in regard to all other members of society, but this does not mean that such a person is egoistic, it just means that he does not take an interest in another's interests. He affirms two principles: "equality in the assignment of basic rights and duties; social and economic inequalities—for example inequality of wealth and authority—are just only if they result in compensating benefits for everyone, and in particular for the least advanced members of society…It may be expedient, but it is not just, that some should have less in order that others may prosper".[35] We are quite far from Pareto's optimality.

Rationality is therefore not to be considered "in the narrow sense, standard in economic theory"—he writes—that is as taking the most effective means to one's ends; rationality, according to Rawls, is rather far from the concept of utility, as generally understood. Given man's "strong and lasting benevolent impulses", the principle of utility as generally intended is "incompatible with the conception of social cooperation among equals for mutual advantage".[36]

The social contract sounds a different tune, which ends up being much more influential on the discipline of economics of his own time, in Buchanan's thinking. In its simplest and clearest form, a predominance of the individualistic position is expressed by Buchanan and Tullock, who, at the start of their major work, *The Calculus of Consent*, explicitly reject both the organic theory of the State, for which the State has "an existence, a value pattern, and a motivation independent of those individual human beings claiming membership": a view, they say, "opposed to the Western philosophical tradition"[37]; and the Marxist vision, which embodies the exploitation of a ruled by a ruling class, be it made up of owners of factors of production or aristocracies. So, having discarded both nationalism and socialism-inspired theories, "we are left with a purely individualistic concept of collectivity".[38] Their analysis is carried out in terms of "methodological individualism", which embodies a philosophical commitment and an ethical judgement,[39] and they reject any sort of class or group approach to economics.

Buchanan's (and others') constitutional economics represent a powerful attempt to build on the liberal thinking of Hayek and the Austrians, and to construct an intellectual scheme of reconciliation of individual interest with the interests of the other individuals, who are members of the same political community. This reconciliation is not based on a sense of mutual trust, which might take us back to Adam Smith. It is a reconciliation in which the State assumes a role, which is, however, only the role of guarantor. The State's role is minimal, in terms of functions to be performed, but also fundamental to permit the full realization of individuals' potentialities. Buchanan's constitutional economics theory has a strong institutional accent, as a background to his libertarian views, and in fact it is based on two pillars: the "calculus of the rational individual who makes choices" (the libertarian pillar) and the "contractarian nature of the State" (the coercive pillar).

Even though Buchanan's commentators have often insisted on the spontaneous nature of a system of market economy based on private property rights, freedom of contract and monetary stability,[40] the most intriguing aspect of Buchanan's theory is that his strong stance of free-market economy has to be reconciled with the constraints that may emerge as a result of the political process. This theoretical construction requires the close collaboration of economists, jurists and political scientists,[41] and is aimed at defining what the State ought to be (in an explicit affirmation of normative—versus positive—economics). The two pillars have to be shortly examined.

As regards the libertarian pillar, the author identifies rationality with the subjective utility pursued by the individual as a separate entity, a rationality not to be confused with some research for absolute truth, and a utility nor necessarily of a hedonistic, self-interested nature: man can be egoistic, altruistic or a combination of two. Rational choice does not mean that the individual, necessarily, makes choices according to his economic interest; it means that "the autonomous individual is...presumed to be capable of choosing any alternatives in a sufficiently orderly manner", in a scale of preferences that does not include classification between good and bad.[42] In a sort of weighting up things chosen against each other, simply, "the central rationality precept states only that an individual chooses more rather than less of goods, and less rather than more of bads".[43] (The border of what is good and what is bad is however unexplained.)

All this may appear superficially not dissimilar from Rawls' thinking, both being focussed on the individual; but the essential difference is that, while Rawls, in a Kantian way, sees a universal moral law that is derived from the common rationality of every man, Buchanan sees the individual as the only judge of his own moral behaviour.

Equally subjective is, in Buchanan, the concept of cost, as related to rational utility. "Cost is that which the decision taker sacrifices or gives up when he makes a choice. It consists in his own valuation of the enjoyment or utility that he anticipates having to forgo as a result of selection among alternative courses of action...In a theory of choice, cost must be reckoned in a utility dimension"[44]: a concept remarkably similar to the "opportunity cost" of the neo-classical economists.

The problem of choice is examined by Buchanan with reference to the single individual: the private choice, and to individuals interacting with others in an organized group: the collective choice. In both cases, the individual who makes a choice, at a cost (defined as above), looks to maximize his utility. In the case of a private choice, an exchange transaction takes place on the market; whereas in the case of collective choice, it is expressed as the exercise of political voting power.

In the private choice process, the individual makes choices within certain constraints that are put before him, that is, are exogenously determined; whereas, in the collective choice process, the choice that the individual makes is *not within, but of* constraints: these constraints are determined by the same individuals participating in the voting process. They are accepted by the individual in exchange for benefits that are anticipated against the same constraints imposed on the other members of his same collectivity.

Buchanan and Tullock examine the ethical aspect of both the private and the collective choice. In the former, that is, in a private exchange, maximum utility is reached in a market with perfect competition; while in the latter, that is, in a political process, maximum utility is obtained when unanimity is reached. (Their analysis is then aimed at establishing the limits of ethics when private exchange happens in a non-competitive market, or third parties are negatively affected; and, in a political process, when decisions are taken on a majority basis, imposing costs on dissenting voters.)

In regard to the collective choice, Buchanan contrasts "orthodox economics" [his reference is mainly to neo-classical theory] and his "constitutional economics". Orthodox economics—he writes—sees the constraints on which the voter has to express his preference, as resulting not from his own choice, but from government imposed choices: government imposes these constraints as public goods. Voters become the intellectual captives of "idealistic political philosophers, embracing variants of the Platonic or Hellenian mindset".[45] The emergence of macroeconomic theory has just reinforced this attitude, focussing the attention on macroaggregates (such as GDP, employment, price level…), and choosing for them target levels considered as objectively good. Governments have been considered able to make this choice, on advice of economists or social philosophers, in an idealistic search for the unique good.

But, Buchanan adds, from orthodox economics to socialism the step is not so difficult to climb. Quoting the philosopher John Dewey, Buchanan and Tullock write: "a significant factor in the popular support for socialism…has been the underlying faith that the shift of an activity from the realm of private to that of social choice involves the replacement of the motive of private gain by that of social good…In the political sphere the pursuit of private gain by the individual participant has been almost universally condemned as 'evil' by moral philosophers of any shade".[46]

A different direction is taken by constitutional political economy: institutional rules and constraints cannot be delegated. It is necessary to use the individual exchange paradigm, as opposed to idealistic search for the unique good. Collective choice becomes nothing else than the participatory behaviour of individual members. The selection of rules or institutions is subject to deliberative evaluations and explicit choices by members of the collectivity.[47] The very definition of public goods has to rest on a voluntary approach. Pigou's Welfare Economics, which sees government as the disinterested entity that corrects market failures in the name of a public good (Chapter 2), is completely reversed.

We might ask, on the margin of Buchanan's collective choice versus Pigou's "externalities", how the issue of climate change should be faced: only by adopting measures approved by individuals' collective choice, or by the State which would use "coercive legal devices for directing self-interest into social channels"?

To move from the libertarian pillar to the State pillar of his construction, Buchanan's philosophical underpinning is the "contractarian political philosophy" of Spinoza, Locke, but above all Hobbes, which provides justification for State coercion only with the agreement by those individuals who are subject to it. Hobbes writes: "I authorize and give up my right of governing my selfe, to this Man, or Assembly of men [the Leviathan], on the condition, that thou [the collectivity's other members] give up thy right to him, and authorize all his actions in like manner".[48] Buchanan's scheme is similar, but both the origins of the devolution of coercion to the State and the purpose of coercion are different. Hobbes sees the necessity of the devolution in the basically bad instincts of men, Buchanan seems to rely on man being good-natured. In addition, purpose of coercion is, for Buchanan, to get rid of the absolute power of the sovereign—the opposite of Hobbes' Leviathan—for the sake of individual collective choices: "[The] intellectual tradition invented the autonomous individual by shucking off the communitarian cocoon".[49] Earlier contractarians insisted on the coercion aspect, says Buchanan, because they had no idea of the efficacy of the market order. It was Adam Smith who, later, relying on market efficacy, saw the correct role for a protective minimal State.[50]

In this intellectual framework, what is the role of the political economist?[51] Buchanan starts by paying a homage to the positivist revolution and to "positive", as opposed to "normative", economics, therefore subscribing to the concept that the "positive" economist looks at what is, not to what ought to be. As a consequence, the economist's place in policy issues cannot be other than indirect. But in fact he shifts to normative economics. He sticks to the Pareto rule of "optimality": optimality in a society means that any possible change from a certain position results in some individuals being made worse off; or if we prefer, any change is optimal only if everybody is better off, or someone is better off and nobody is worse off. This is a typical case of positive economics, but is also—Buchanan writes—an ethical proposition, a value judgement.

How can this proposition—optimality as a value statement—be reconciled with Pareto's positive economics? The reconciliation is made by removing the content of the value judgement from the economist, and letting that content to the individual choice, which is, by definition, ethical.

He observes that an ambiguity remains in the content to be given to "better off" and "worse off". Buchanan's contribution to this issue is that efficiency, a position of "better off", is that position which is voluntarily chosen. While welfare economics has generally assumed that the economist-observer is omniscient and therefore able to read individual preferences, constitutional economics puts the economist in a presumption of ignorance. His efficiency criterion cannot be other than presumptive. It is only presumably that his efficiency will retain the Paretian features. "Political economy is thus positivistic in a different sense from the more narrowly conceived positive economics".[52] The political economist presents a possible change, but only if a consensus is reached, otherwise not a benefit but a harm will result. The observable behaviour of individuals as collective decision-makers, is the only test of welfare. "The political behaviour of individuals, not market performance or results, provides the criteria for testing hypotheses of political economy".[53]

No social values exist apart from individual values. The political economist makes hypotheses, concerning the values of the individuals, remaining ethically neutral. The values will be tested in the collective action of all individuals involved in the decision. The consequences of this approach are far-reaching, and the field of public finance gives scope for a fruitful implementation of the constitutional economics approach: the typical example given is State coercion on matters of taxes and public expenditure, which finds its economic legitimacy only in the process of collective choice.[54] However, this may lead to conclusions inconsistent with Pareto's optimality, and with any free-market ideological vision, even though consistent with a liberal democracy. "[I]ndividual behaviour may be fully consistent with a reduction in measured personal income or wealth". "A policy which combines progressive income taxation and public expenditure on the social services may command unanimous support even though the process involves a reduction in the measured real income of the rich".[55]

In this way we have a paradox: in the name of individualism, constitutional economics may reach conclusions quite different from those suggested by positive economists. Efficiency ends up being what emerges from individual consent, from the collective action process.

Buchanan warns economists against abandoning neutrality: their free-market stance, involving mutual gains from trade, can be presented just as a recommendation, because only individual preferences, as expressed in the collective action, have decisive relevance.

We may therefore have rules, as they have emerged from collective actions, that are not functional for a free-market economy. This is the case examined by Richard Posner, a public choice legal theorist, in respect of the American constitution (but the same analysis could be applied to others). The alignment of rules and private interest is hard to achieve particularly in the case of rules whose formulation is specially protected, because they are central to the life—not only the economic life—of a collectivity. Posner has considered the relationship between the constitution and economic growth, and its alignment with the implicit economic logic of a free market.

The important point here is that, within its broader democratic context, the constitution could well not be fully consistent with the economic libertarian view of constitutional economists. "Like any form of aggressive constitutionalism..., the economic libertarian approach [through interpretation of the constitution or its amendment] diminishes the role of democracy—potentially dramatically", writes Posner.[56] According to him, "to grasp the nature and extent of the tension between laissez-faire and democratic political or legal theory it is necessary to distinguish between two fundamental political conceptions that are sometimes confused: limited government and democratic government. The proponents of limited government want the government to be relatively powerless and, partly for this reason, are not much interested in how the people who run the government are chosen; their interest is in preserving a large sphere for private action free of government interference. The proponents of democratic government want to make sure that the government is in some sense in the hands of the people and are confident that if it is placed there it can be trusted to promote the general welfare, without having to be limited...modern economic libertarians believe that unfettered democratic government leads to the special interest state".[57]

The tension between limited government, inclined towards individualism, free exchange and trade on the one side, and democratic government on the other, inclined towards general welfare on the basis of collective action, shows how much a "classical situation" of widespread consensus on institutional structures oriented towards neoliberalism finds difficulty to emerge (later on, after the financial crisis of 2008, Posner's confidence in free markets was notably shaken).[58]

4.4 New Classical Economics

Moving to the economic counter-revolutions that reacted to the Keynesian consensus, the same libertarian stance marks an evolution of the discipline of economics, firstly involving a reassessment of the monetarist doctrine, and secondly putting a new emphasis on the rationale of individual economic behaviour in free-market economies, through highly sophisticated models. As mentioned earlier, the first approach attacked Keynes' insufficient analysis of inflation; the second, moving from the individual's rational behaviour, goes further and proclaims the "Keynesian Revolution" as a "wreckage". In this regard, the "rational expectations hypothesis-REH" and the "efficient market hypothesis-EMH" have assumed particular importance, also with far-reaching consequences for the performance of economies and financial markets. Even these two "hypotheses" rely very much on the stock of money as an essential component of their scheme, and the name of New Classical Economics can be extended to monetarism (which is not really new).

According to Johnson's approach, which interestingly mixes ideology, doctrine and convenience, the monetarist counter-attack needed to find (1) an important social problem, and (2) a theory that had to be "academically and professionally successful in replacing the previous revolutionary theory". Monetarism gained traction when inflation became a serious social concern, even in the United States with the escalation of the Vietnam war; and the quantity theory of money was regarded as a plausible scientific explanation for the extremely high inflation. This new interest implied a re-examination of that theory. The figure that was assuming a pre-eminent position was Milton Friedman; and in general the Chicago School that we have mentioned in Chapter 2 gained ground.

The "quantity theory"—in order to avoid criticism that had affected its previous formulation: that it would assume an automatic tendency to full employment (manifestly in conflict with the actual experience)—was reinstated as a way to provide an explanation, and a policy, in place of Keynesianism. Friedman's monetarism critically re-examined the theory, by selecting crucial relationships that would permit yielding results from certain variables.[59]

The chairman of the American central bank, Paul Volcker, provided the most outstanding example of what is called "practical—as distinct from theoretical—monetarism", in late 1970s, by shrinking the stock of money in the presence of a severe inflation. The inevitable recession that ensued, deep and lasting, and the unpredictable behaviour of monetary aggregates, which made it difficult to settle on a satisfactory measure of money to guide policy, led to a shift of monetary policies, not only in the United States, towards control of other variables, such as interest rates and inflation targets.[60]

Monetarism, however, attracted a renewed attention with the spread of Buchanan's and others' libertarian thinking. If, within Buchanan's thought, we put aside the theory of collective choice and its implications for the proper working of a collectivity, which is the outstanding originality of his approach, the relevant point that remains in his work is a confirmation of well-entrenched liberal ideas about the centrality of the individual, who is free to choose on the basis of his own subjective scale of preferences, a scale determined by the intention to maximize his utility, however understood. This is, in fact, the substance of neoliberalism, reaffirmed in various forms by a large number of political thinkers and economists.

In the field of the discipline of economics, individual behaviour is increasingly put at the centre of the economic analysis, and the behaviour of the whole economy is examined on the basis of individuals' rational choices, which are made using all the available information. An attempt to understand how the whole economy—a free-market economy—works on that behavioural basis, is made mathematically, in the same way as Walras or Pareto did one century before. Econometric models are built. An econometric model is a system of equations that connect certain variables deemed important to the working of a market economy. These connections are determined on the basis of agents' "rational" choices (rationality as guided by utilitarian motivations, as defined by Buchanan). The model also takes into account non-market, exogenous factors, primarily government policies, which influence and modify agents' behaviour and choices, with respect to what they would have been in their absence.

Once the equations are solved, the model yields an output, that gives a value to meaningful macroeconomic variables, such as product, employment, prices. The model eventually has to be validated by the coherence of its output with the actual experience. If this is the case, the model is "scientific" in the same sense as a model built within the physical sciences: logically coherent and experimentally confirmed. Certain economic propositions become scientifically "true", free from value statements.

It is far from our intention to give a description of the construction of these models and of the related theoretical schemes; it is rather our purpose to show that the validity—if any—of these schemes is conditional on accepting their ideological premises and on the existence of institutions whose working is functional to the theoretical scheme, so that experience can validate the predictions that the scheme aims to yield.[61]

Buchanan's rational choice can be seen as the philosophical background to two theoretical schemes, just mentioned: the "rational expectations hypothesis-REH" (Robert Lucas and Thomas Sargent are among its main exponents) and the "efficient market hypothesis-EMH" (Eugene Fama), which have become prevalent both in macroeconomics, and in explaining the behaviour of the financial markets: a theme, this last one, of overwhelming importance, given the expansion of financial supra-structures over the real structure of the economy, and the considerable disruptions that may come, and have come, from dysfunctional financial markets.

Is Buchanan's rational choice dependent on the assumption that choice is made by relying on past experience (according to which people assimilate and react to their actual experience over the years), or on current rational expectations of the evolution of the variables that account for agents' interest? The issue of expectations is central to the REH.

A paper by the Federal Reserve Bank of Minneapolis[62] gave a clear description of the new approach—rational expectations—by showing how predictions, fed into the econometric model's equations representing individuals' behaviour, yield results different from those yielded by previous methodology, not based on expectations. Take inflation estimates: people make choices of their purchases not on the basis of what inflation has been over the past years, but on how inflation is expected to evolve in the future, and in these expectations, they are affected by changes in government policies. "To accurately assess the effects of different economic policies,...a far more sophisticated modelling of people's expectations must be included in the structure of econometric models. The proposed modelling principle is based on the theory of rational expectations".[63]

The implicit assumption—that any influence by the government (or central bank) in spontaneous market behaviour disrupts expectations and therefore creates undue fluctuations in economic activity—is explained by an article in the same Review, a few months later, written by Lucas and Sargent.[64] Observing the failure of Keynesian policies based on the extensive use of monetary and fiscal tools, they wanted to "reopen the basic issues of monetary economics", recalled the pre-existing neo-classical theory, based on two behavioural postulates: that "markets clear"[65] and that agents act, make their choice, in their own interest; but added that each agent is assumed to have limited information. Therefore, agents make mistakes; but—also—everyone makes the same mistake. (It can be observed that this is a simplification that assumes that all individuals are identical, or at least that differences between them cancel each other out, so that we can conceive of a "representative agent".) On the basis of their rational expectations, a certain level of prices and output is determined. A non-market observer cannot beat the market, and the authority (the central bank), as a non-market observer, cannot act differently. An unexpected, unpredictable change in the money supply, made by the authority, changes the levels of prices and output with respect to what they would otherwise have been. This unexpected change creates business fluctuations and unanticipated shocks. Hence, what is needed is "stable rules of the game, well understood by economic agents". Activism in monetary policy or fiscal deficit financing has the "capacity to disrupt". The X-percent rule advocated by Friedman, regarding changes of the stock of money, should be followed.

This is probably the most visible, and operational, connection between Friedman's monetarism and the new "hypothesis".

The Rational Expectations Hypothesis sees macroeconomic outcomes as an aggregation of all agents' behaviour. This microeconomic basis permits to go back to the neo-classics of the turn of the nineteenth to the twentieth century, and to the Walras equilibrium (Chapter 1). Macroeconomics is rooted in mathematics; and in rigorous micro foundations. The Hypothesis is a denial of the social relations, which not only casts suspicious on any government intervention, but also denies relevance to any social connection between economic agents (individuals or firms).[66]

In financial markets, rational expectations are embedded in the prices of financial assets. Given that returns on assets are uncertain, the rational choice, which determines the asset price, cannot be made other than by relying on all information available (the EMH). An inference that could be drawn from this statement is that, if information were full, agents' forecast would be optimal and prices would be by definition correct. Since information is more or less incomplete, prices might be different from what they would otherwise be. The consequent over- or underpricing implies higher or lower returns than those resulting from the optimal forecast. In this case, however, unexplained opportunities would appear for profits, and arbitrage would make converge the choices of market participants on the optimal forecast. The market would be able to self-correct.

This is not however, according to my understanding, the correct inference that a theorist of the EMH would deduct. According to him, prices are always correct, in relation to the information available, and authorities should in any case abstain from interfering in their determination. This is an important distinction in trying to explain the causes of financial meltdowns.

The "rational expectations hypothesis" progressively gained ground and, in association with the "efficient market hypothesis", gave a significant underpinning to a specific interpretation and understanding of the behaviour of financial markets. Both proved to be extremely successful in terms of the correspondence between predictions and actual results. On this basis, innovative financial instruments were created, benefitting first of all their begetters and users.

This correspondence was facilitated by policymakers, who developed a favourable institutional environment in which this theoretical approach might have coherent results, by reducing any government interference that might alter individuals' rational expectations and constrain the spontaneous preferences of the financial market. In general, in order to ease the environmental circumstances in which rational expectations might be unhindered, a non-government intervention in the allocation of capital was pursued. In the field of monetary policy, a predictable monetary stance was pursued, and forward policy guidance by central banks (information about future monetary policy intentions[67]) was adopted. On the whole, it appears certain that over the last decades of the century, control of inflation and "sound" public finance gained increasing priority over full employment and social protection. Related to this change was the trend for the private sector debt of the economy to grow to unprecedented levels: financialization of the economy grew strongly, in particular its private component.

If we accept the view, mentioned in our Preface, that "positive" (as different from "normative") economics can qualify as a science as far as its precision, scope and conformity with experience of the predictions it yields, a question can be raised: was there any impediment that prevented the rational expectations hypothesis—and the efficient market hypothesis thesis—from forecasting, and therefore possibly preventing, the 2007–2008 collapse of the financial markets? It is worthwhile reporting the following excerpt from a book published just after the market fall:

> "Private financial markets cannot function properly unless there is enough information, reporting and disclosure both to market participants and to relevant regulators and supervisors. When investors cannot appropriately price complex new securities, they cannot properly assess the overall losses faced by financial institutions, and when they cannot know who is holding the risk for so-called toxic waste, this turns into generalized uncertainty…Thus, once lack of financial market transparency and increased opacity

of these markets became an issue, the seeds were sown for a full-blown systemic disaster."[68]

This would imply that, before the collapse, "all available information" was in fact extremely scarce, so that no market self-correction would have been possible.

But, according to Eugene Fama, this was not the issue at stake. Actually, the question I raised above—the prevention of the collapse of the financial market—is probably ill-conceived. Market prices were constantly correct, that is coherent with the available information, and Fama does not complain of a scarcity of information. He does not see in the market meltdown a market failure of the EMH, the EMH comes out of this episode pretty well; he observes that "the financial markets were a casualty of the [economic] recession, not a cause of it", but the fact is that the economic activity is "the part we don't understand"; he blamed government interference in the market: government caused the subprime crisis[69] and its "too-big-to-fail" remedies for the banking failures implicitly supported those market prices.[70]

Candide, the main character of Voltaire's eponymous novel, half-dead under the ruins of Lisbon totally destroyed by an earthquake (1755), is consoled by his companion, the philosopher Pangloss, who says that "all this is for the best; for, if there is a volcano at Lisbon, it cannot be anywhere else; for it is impossible that things should not be where they are; for all is well"[71] (the volcano in question is the economic activity).

Worthwhile noting that, already in 1997, a disenchanted Samuelson would ironically comment on "modern Lucas dogmas": "the post 1978 [the year when the REH was formulated] economic history speaks against ex post confirmation of ex ante speculations by that School".[72] There was no need for further confirmation, by the financial collapse of 2008, of a theory that was faulty indeed.

Since the concept of partial available information appears similar to that of "uncertainty", as considered by Hayek (see Chapter 2), one can wonder whether the ideological perspective is the same. Hayek does not rely on market rationality, a rational system of preferences cannot be conceived of, given the merely scattered pieces of information that agents have, but he nevertheless thinks that the price system is the most efficient way to connect those pieces. Whether we cannot rely on market's rationality (Hayek), or we can (Fama), the libertarian *Weltanschauung* is the same. In an opposite perspective, Keynes considered uncertainty in the market context: he separated risk—which is describable in terms of probabilities and therefore calculable—from uncertainty—which cannot.[73] He believed that uncertainty is at the origin of market failures, and therefore the motivation for government intervention.

4.5 A New "Classical Situation"?

We have made this short incursion into theorizing without any intention either to subscribe or to reject its content, but to show the close link between, on the one hand, an ideological underpinning—the confidence that a libertarian approach, relying on a society organized along a selfish *homo oeconomicus*, and sceptical of State intervention, can yield better results in terms of welfare (the vision as emerging from neoliberalism)—and on the other hand the construction of models that explain in a positive, neutral way, the actual behaviour of the economic system.

The neoliberal vision finds no inconsistency between the market meltdown and the core of the theory that "markets are always correct". A different view is held by those supporting a much wider role for government stimulating the economy and regulating financial markets. However, after the financial and economic disruption that followed the market meltdown of 2008 and after policy measures taken in this last direction in the aftermath of the crisis, a reverse attitude is more and more present in economic policies and market regulation. For instance, in the field of financial regulation, we see in the United Kingdom a tendency to go back to the pre-crisis "principle-based approach" as opposed to more detailed prudential regulation.

If we focus on the polyvalent meaning of "rationality", it is no wonder that the discipline of economics takes an increasing distance from being a social (moral) science, and becomes a science of individual behaviour, to be framed within the category of natural sciences. Comte's positivism seems to enjoy a full revenge. Even the "irrational behaviour" (Robert Shiller) can be subsumed under the same roof, if we see it as an attempt to understand an economic system through the motivations of human behaviour. Many decades ago, the economist George Shackle observed: "it is plain that on one side economics has a frontier with psychology, or rather, that there lies between them a no-man's land crying out to be explored and appropriated, that we might call economic physics". And he gives an example: the Keynesian propensity to consume as a function of income "rests upon foundations of individual psychology which no one so far has seen fit to explore as a psychologist".[74] Now, the study of neuroeconomics is progressing, perhaps merging economics into medical science; and the remains of political economy may be definitely abandoned.

Whether the philosophy of neoliberalism and the economic theorizing that has been prevailing at the turn of the present century—what goes under the name of New Classical Economics (essentially, a revival of the "Walrasian" Neo-classical School[75])—can be seen as a "classical situation" in a Schumpeterian sense (this is our point [c], raised above), is very doubtful, at least for a couple of reasons:

- New Keynesian approaches continue to be followed. According to one Keynesian version, given the stickiness—or rigidity—of wages, which prevents their fall even when labour resources are unemployed, it would be enough to remove that stickiness, and the economy would work efficiently, similarly to the neo-classical model. The role of government would be, in this version, an active one, but mainly aimed to restore the smooth working of the neo-classical model.

  According to another Keynesian version, possibly closer to the "original", the wage rigidity may be useful, and helps economic stabilization: lowering wages in order to restore equilibrium would mean cutting down consumers' spending, exacerbating any downturn, provoking deflation, and specifically bankruptcies if, as it was the case in the circumstances of the early 2000s, there is too much debt in the economic system.

  An echo of the controversy between monetarism, or generally the New Classical Economics on one side, and the second version Keynesianism on the other, can be heard in the current debate, inside the European Union, between a "Bundesbank-oriented" monetary policy and the anti-austerity, demand-managed policies, invoked to overcome the current stagnation. The pandemic seems to strenghten these last policies.
- After the financial crisis of 2008 and the Great Recession that followed, the sequence that links ideology, new economic theories, economic policies and financial meltdown and economic downturn could not be easily dismissed. From there, to spotting a causal connection rather than a simple sequence of events, the step was not difficult to climb. "It was not an accident that those who advocated

> the rules that led to the calamity were so blinded by their faith in free markets that they couldn't see the problems it was [they were?] creating. Economics had moved…from being a scientific discipline into becoming free market capitalism's biggest cheerleader".[76]

Since these events, there has been a strong tendency not only to re-establish Keynes in his proper role both in the history of economic thought, and—perhaps more importantly—in a truly liberal vision of the society, but also to invoke again the economic policies he advocated so successfully for a relatively long period of time. The most outstanding position in this regard is in the book *Keynes. The Return of the Master*, where Robert Skidelsky, "the" biographer of Keynes, does not hesitate to define him, with some emphasis, as "the most important economic thinker in the world".[77] My relativistic view of the whole discipline of economics, which will have emerged from these pages (and more of that in the following, final chapter), makes me uncomfortable with this sort of statements. But before that, I cannot avoid dealing with what appears to be a kind of by-product of the Great Recession, and asking what sort of economic philosophy, if any, lies behind "populism".

In the meantime, we can safely say that the discipline of economics seems unable to capture in an adequate way all the complex features of our society: we do not yet have the perfect lines of a Greek temple in our sight. This discipline makes every effort to deserve its appellation of "dismal science".

4.6 Populism as a By-Product of Neoliberalism

It may appear odd that an essay devoted to economic philosophies should deal with populism. The immediate answer to a question concerning which sort of economic thinking a populist has in mind would be a flat "none". But populism must not be fastidiously dismissed, and a more articulate answer requires us to look at:

a. the main feature that differentiates populism from liberal democracy: which is, above all, the way in which political power is acquired and exercised. In general, the former invokes some form of direct democracy, while the latter relies on representative democracy;
b. the ideological roots of populism;

c. the motivations that lie behind the rise of populism;
d. the impact of social media on populism.

A populist economic stance can be inferred once these topics have been considered.

– Populism and liberal democracy

On the acquisition and exercise of political power, both liberals' and populists' arguments are focussed on the elites, but the role of elites is seen differently:

– According to populists, the elites are necessarily set against the people. Their members use their power to promote their personal interest, with the aim to secure a gain at the expense of the people. This is today how the word "elite" is mostly used and understood by populists. Almost by definition, elites' behaviour cannot be other than "bad": they are a minority, but have the power, and they exploit the people economically as in other ways. This behaviour is viewed in the light of a conspiracy theory, and this view is self-reinforcing: representative democracy hides plots against the people. The remedy to this situation is the overturning of the elites, and a transfer of power directly to the people. In constitutional terms, the outcome of this process is to phase out, or at least marginalize, people's representation through an elected body (the parliament), and directly entrust people with the relevant decisions. The distinction between executive and legislative functions ends up being at least blurred.

  Whether political decisions are taken directly by the people itself, or entrusted to a leader appointed by the people, is a matter deserving further consideration. Even though populism can be framed within the concept of direct democracy, the very idea of direct democracy becomes vague when the leader ends up being detached from the will of the people. On the basis of a supposedly fiduciary mandate given him by the people, the leader might implicitly believe that he is superior to others in knowing what is "good" for the community, and decide accordingly.
– The liberal view also sees the elites as a group that exercises command, but also considers them as persons who—because of their

selection by the people through an electoral process, or given their specific expertise in certain fields—are constitutionally entrusted with governance of the body public. Institutionally, parliament is viewed as a body democratically elected by the citizens, not simply an executive of decisions already taken directly elsewhere. Legislative and executive functions are separated, and any potential intrusion in each other field is limited by "checks and balances". Parliament is in charge of drafting and approving laws, which the executive branch of government has the task of observing and implementing through policy action. In addition, the particular competence required for certain tasks belonging to the public sphere, implies entrusting certain persons, supposed to have that competence, with implementing those tasks: think of the judiciary or central banking, for instance. Whether parliament, or the government, or the independent authorities have or have not, in a specific case or set of circumstances, properly complied with their tasks, to the disadvantage of the people, is a matter to be looked at within the current constitutional system of representative democracy.

- Ideological roots of populist movements

Forms of populism have important philosophical fathers. We can take two thinkers, very far each other in time and place (Jean-Jacques Rousseau and James Buchanan). With them, radical direct democracy is invoked, albeit with a very different involvement of the State in the life of society. In fact, these two names are relevant because they bring us to the two strands of thought on which the entire construction of political economy was originally based: the first, based on the centrality of society as a whole, or of the State; and the second, relying on the individualistic point of view, centred on the individual as a rational agent. In addition, a third thinker comes to mind: Carl Schmitt, and his identification of the leader as dictator: his name increasingly resonates in current debates over populism.

In Rousseau's theory, the General Will is the expression of the body politic, the State, which is a moral entity and the foundation of human coexistence. *La volonté général* means that sovereignty is located in the people as a whole, and that sovereignty is indivisible. Rousseau rejected political moderation, relativism, traditionalism and enthusiasm for the British parliamentarian model, as expressed by thinkers as diverse as Montaigne, Voltaire or Hume. Rousseau's adversaries thought, on the contrary, that pure, direct democracy was the closest thing to anarchy. In the "ceaseless battle between the Revolution of the Reason and Revolution of the Will", the major strand of Rousseau's thought—the "revolution of the will"—made him an outcast in his society, and was opposed by the democratic republicans who would make the French revolution of 1789–1793.[78] At the same time, Rousseau saw dictatorship only as an extreme remedy that direct democracy may adopt in exceptional circumstances; only later would Marat and Robespierre, who held Rousseau in high regard, give a populist turn to the Rousseauian vision.[79]

The General Will, being itself the essence of the State, comes into consideration when the matter to be decided involves the interest of the whole community, and, being defined as above, has to be distinguished from the will of all. The former takes account only of the common interest, while the latter takes private interest into account, and is no more than the sum of particular wills, according to Rousseau.[80]

Rousseau's *Discourse on Political Economy*, which follows the *Social Contract*, helps to better understand how the General Will would operate in the interest of the whole community. In this regard, he defines three rules of political economy. The first says that the General Will must be followed as a sort of default solution on which the legislator has to rely. The legislator, Rousseau writes, has an infinity of details of administration and economy to care about, but he has to follow "two infallible rules": the spirit of the law [implicity, the General Will that is the origin of any law] ought to decide in particular cases that could not be foreseen; and the General Will should be explicitly consulted wherever this test fails.

The second rule is fundamental to better understanding the authority on which the General Will rests, and stresses the centrality of public education. The State has the role of public educator of citizens: "to form citizens is not the work of a day, and in order to have men, it is necessary to educate them when they are children",[81] so that they should "regard their individuality only in its relation to the body of the State and to be aware, so to speak, of their own existence merely as a part of that of the State".[82] In this way, they might come to identify themselves in some degree with this great whole, to feel themselves members of the country. Beyond any private form of education, starting from what children can receive from their fathers, education is "of still greater importance to the State".[83]

The third rule, more directly affecting the field of political economy, is that provision of public wants is an obvious inference from the General

Will, and the third essential duty of government. "If a rich man is robbed, the whole police force is immediately in motion…how different is the case of the poor man. The more humanity owes him, the more society denies him".[84] In order to levy taxes in a truly equitable and proportionate manner, the imposition ought not to be "in simple ratio to the property of the contributors, but in a compound ratio to the difference of their conditions and the superfluity of their possessions".[85]

These words made of Rousseau, for a long while, the unsurpassed hero simultaneously of the Left and of the Right, a status no other thinker had ever achieved. Rousseau's focus on the State as supreme entity, of which the General Will is the expression, meant an aversion to ideas of cosmopolitanism, universalism, and the pursuit of universal peace, which were basic components of the British philosophers of his time.

Different, and exposed two centuries later, is Buchanan's view,[86] which is largely based on the doctrine of constitutionalism we have mentioned in Sect. 4.3. He criticizes the representative system when it gives ample powers of discretion to the elected assembly, the parliament: this is typical of the situation where a political system is based on majority voting, with an open agenda. The danger is that an open-ended majoritarianism is highly vulnerable to demagogic manipulation, to what we may call the dictatorship of the majority. Another danger derives from the "open agenda", that is from the extremely wide field of action open to parliamentary decisions.[87]

Rather, Buchanan thinks that what is needed is a general agreement among all the citizens on the need "to limit the agenda for collective action": the parliament should be able to approve laws only in a limited range of matters. This does not require any agreement of preferences among the voters, it means the opposite: since no substantial consensus can be reached on most of the possible topics of choice, every person will want to agree to rules that limit political action, and therefore the range of coercion that politics necessarily involves. This is essentially a way through which individuals obtain protection against the potential extension of collectivized coercion. "[T]he constitutionalist relies exclusively on demos",[88] on the people, and in this sense direct democracy is affirmed.

As mentioned earlier, to adopt only policy decisions that are approved by unanimous consent is equivalent in principle to accepting the present distribution of wealth: it means to adopt only policies that represent "Pareto improvements".

Representative, indirect democracy has to be limited indeed in Buchanan's view, being restricted to the narrow limits imposed by collective action on the ruler: "fewer activities would be politicized under direct than under indirect democracy".[89] For instance—he adds—this system would plausibly reduce the "pork-barrel legislation", that is the trend to appropriate public expenditure for local interests, by using revenues from all taxpayers. The problem of the principal–agent relationship, which is typical of indirect, representative democracy, would be minimized under the system just described.

But Buchanan poses a further question: how to apply rules of direct democracy in collectivities where "a constitution" is already in existence, with features historically determined, far distant from the principles he advocates?[90] In this situation, direct democracy may assume a different meaning from the stylised model just described. He advocated "provisions for popular initiatives and referenda [which] can operate so as to forestall collective actions that might otherwise be implemented".[91]

Buchanan is firmly convinced that this form of direct democracy is consistent with the true essence of classical liberalism, requiring the size of the public sector in economic and social interaction be minimized. He is critical of the liberal democracy generally advocated by other liberals, enacted through a representative political system. He takes the example of a potential debate between a proposal for a supra-majority approval in parliament for tax increases, and an alternative proposal that would subject this decision to a popular referendum: socialists of any kind would oppose the first proposal on allegedly democratic principles because the minority rights would be violated; but they could not oppose the second, based as it is on the electorate itself. So—he concludes—the strength of direct democracy exercised through referenda embodies true liberalism and overcomes socialists' objections.

It is clear that intellectual positions relying, respectively, on Rousseau's and Buchanan's philosophies translate into economic ideologies of a very different kind. The first theorist relies on an all-encompassing view of an identification of the individual with the State. Are we far from Hegel's assertion—several decades after Rousseau—that it is through the State that the individual enjoys his freedom? (Chapter 1). What emerges from Rousseau's *Social Contract* and *The Discourse on Political Economy* is not only the centrality of the State in public education, but also an economic system oriented towards progressive taxation and egalitarianism, and a political and economic perspective based on national needs and interests, and distrustful of any form of globalism. Buchanan, on the contrary, sees direct democracy as linked to his constitutionalism, and as the true embodiment of a genuine liberal thought, based on an extremely reduced role for the State and, in parallel, on an ample territory for the expansion of free initiative, since the few constraints deriving from coercion by the State are themselves the result of man's collective choice.

The illustration of different philosophical approaches to direct democracy might end with Rousseau and Buchanan. But, as noted earlier, the name of Carl Schmitt is also frequently mentioned in this debate. "Chinese legal scholars, Russian nationalists, the far-right in the US and Germany, as well as the far-left in Britain and France, are all drawing on the work of the premier legal theorist of Nazi Germany", for a long time regarded "as beyond the pale".[92]

The argument that may link Schmitt to Rousseau and Buchanan is that all three exalt direct democracy over representative democracy. But Schmitt goes well beyond this contraposition, because the result of his intellectual scheme is a form of government that abandons the very concept of democracy, by cutting any permanent mandate given by the people to the leader. At the very start of the Third Reich, he writes that the new Enabling Act of 1933—which marks the beginning of Hitler's Reich—while formally presented as a change to the previous weak and "neutral" Weimar constitution, represents a radical change: the Law has been decided by the parliament only in obedience to the people's will as expressed in the political elections just held; it is in reality a popular referendum, a plebiscite, recognizing Hitler as the German people's political leader. See Chapter 2.

Dictatorship implies a "state of exception",[93] that is the suspension of law and limitation of individual liberty. In the state of exception, sovereign is he who decides on the exception; the exception separates the norm from its application, in order to preserve its substance and make it effective. The sovereign dictatorship is the organ of a constituent power. For instance, Schmitt saw this constituent power in the English Revolution of the seventeenth century, when Cromwell established a military dictatorship not answerable to any higher body, and transformed it into a genuine sovereign power, no longer delegated or provisional, but permanent and absolute.[94] Schmitt theorized dictatorship as an a-nomic regime (a regime outside the law): his state of exception means suspension of the legal state, accompanied by restrictions on personal freedom and the removal of certain fundamental rights, to establish a new order.[95]

Schmitt sets legality in opposition to legitimacy. The first achieved its highest expression in nineteenth-century liberalism, but has no effective content, as it proved impotent in Germany's Weimar Republic. The State could not anymore be limited to the application of the law, but demanded urgent, compelling decisions that could be taken only by a leader who would exercise a charismatic domination. His action would find in itself legitimacy: "the ethos of law had to make way for the pathos of action".[96]

The clash between a liberal who supports direct democracy and an extreme populist who in the end insulates the dictator's authority from control by the people that had chosen him, is well visible in Buchanan's criticism of populist dictators,[97] that is of "those who, at the same time, purport to be advocates of democracy, in some electoral sense, and fearful of the demos. Persons belonging to this group will vehemently oppose direct democracy in all forms, and they will want to restrict the role of the people to the selection of the rulers…Once electorally chosen, there is no pretence that the ruler is 'representing' the people at all…And since any ruler is implicitly modelled as doing good, there should be no reasoned basis for imposing limits or constraints on her action".[98] This view of Buchanan can be seen as an unqualified rejection of any fascist regime, if we have in mind the electoral origin of Mussolini's or Hitler's systems of government, or more recent ones.

– Causes of rise in populism

If we move from the territory of political philosophy to the motivations that are behind the rise of populism, its ascendancy is strictly connected to phases of discontent, impoverishment and class-related antagonism. In the twentieth century, we see that in times characterized by economic and social difficulties, caused by wars or deep economic crises, broad strata of the population were able to find a doctrine, a credo that would supposedly free the people from hardships and guide the people towards higher levels of well-being, social justice and an affirmation of national pride. This credo was found in nationalism, and nationalism was personified by a "Schmittian" leader who would flush out previous liberal elites from their commanding posts and cease to refer to the people for his continued authority. It is not necessary to remind here at length the birth of Fascism in Italy and National-socialism in Germany. They were both based mainly on *petite bourgeoisie* support, a class heavily hit by inflation and loss of social standing, and demoralized by the hardships of the First World War and its aftermath: a class which hoped to regain, through a dictator, a primary standing in their respective nations.

Soviet socialism can itself be seen as an extreme version of a Schmittian-type dictatorship. If we consider its political structures, the main difference in respect to the other two regimes is that Soviet socialism was the result of a working-class revolution in a still semi-feudal country, where liberal structures were in their infancy: a country battered by massive war losses, while the Bolshevik propaganda managed to turn the conflict into a shameful imperial war. But the leader unquestionably had a Schmittian standing.

Equally unquestionably, no democracy of any kind could be attributed to any of these political structures. Only countries resting on a long-standing liberal tradition, which had gradually moved towards liberal-democratic constitutional systems, were able to resist these populist tendencies.

To move to the present, what remains of the thought of those two theorists of direct democracy, in the widespread populist wave of our own days? And does Schmittian doctrine appeal to present day populists? Firstly, it appears that forms of direct democracy theorized by Buchanan—direct democracy as an instrument to achieve a "small government" and returning to the individual the decision-making power—find a very restricted audience. What might have been theorized at the height of neoliberalism, as a further step to free individuals and business from the Leviathan, has increasingly lost appeal in large strata of the population. A prediction formulated by Marxist critics when Fukuyama's essay was published sounds plausible: that "the present global triumph of liberal capitalism is unlikely to be a long-lasting affair. It says more about the weakness and exhaustion of the historical alternatives offered to it than about the intrinsic strength of liberal capitalism itself".[99]

There is, rather, a generic appeal to the State, which rests on only a few factors: stagnant or declining incomes; globalization; middle-class frustration. As a result, economic populism takes a shape defined by Barry Eichengreen in the following terms: "an approach to economics that emphasizes distribution while de-emphasizing the risks to economic stability from sharp increases in government spending, inflationary finance, and government interventions overriding the operation of the market".[100] Within the European Union, populists have questioned policies tilting towards austerity and possibly deflation.[101] Particularly in the eurozone, a wide investment programme, based on jointly guaranteed debt securities, has only very recently taken off in the midst of the pandemic; and it remains to be seen whether it is going to remain a one-off measure.

Let us consider the factors that are behind today's populism, starting from stagnant incomes, and their reputedly unequal distribution. The tail of the recent Great Recession is still wagging—not only in the European Union, but throughout liberal democracies in general—with austerity and deflationary policies that prevent substantial recovery, or rather contribute to stagnant or declining incomes, in several countries. This tendency towards a stagnant or declining output is accompanied by what several statistics indicate to be rising inequality, which has reversed a previous, opposite trend earlier in the twentieth century.[102]

It is not surprising that forms of direct democracy, which might recall the Rousseauian vision of the General Will, appears attuned to the sentiments of large strata of the population. One can however hesitate to speak, in referring to today's developments, of a well-articulated "statist" ideological view as underlying current populist trends. Beyond the confused criticism of representative democracy, is there any hint of ideological schemes of any kind, which might support coherent policy initiatives based on direct forms of democracy? It is almost jokingly that one might cite the fact that the electronic platform through which the members of the "5 stars" movement in Italy express their vote, is named after "Rousseau" (the philosopher might be turning in his grave).

On the international side, populism can be seen as a by-product of globalization. Globalization creates a "decentralised money space", not organised or controlled by a central authority. This space has geographical, economic, competitive and financial dimensions: money moves with little friction and low costs; individuals and business can buy goods and services all over this space with limited or zero barriers; the global market is consequently open to the fiercest competition; and financial assets can be purchased across borders.[103]

Globalization, with these characteristics, has overwhelmed Western capitalistic countries politically, socially and economically. With reference to this last point, it has led the entrepreneurship of those countries to move huge direct investments towards areas that have relatively skilled workforce, but are still in a backward state in terms of income and wage levels (the Asian continent comes to mind). Goods produced in those areas are exported to the advanced countries in the West, at low prices. Consequently, in these countries, the size of the economy, in particular of the industrial sector, hit by huge imports, cannot grow and often shrinks; and the bargaining power of their workforce and trade unions is consequently affected. The relative reduction of the industrial sector is not matched by a parallel reduction of the services sector, less affected by foreign competition, being more domestically oriented; but, here, it is the decentralized structure of the services sector that makes trade unions intrinsically weaker (as extreme examples, see "Uber" or "Deliveroo").

Any push for better standards of living, both in the industrial and the agricultural sectors, is frustrated by the incumbent potential presence of workers coming from the poorest regions, mainly of Africa. This low-cost workforce could possibly be considered as a positive factor by industrialists in order to regain competitiveness in the global market (and, still more, by compassionate humanitarians of the Left). But, at the same time, the pressure from immigration acts as a sort of lid on the claims of any local workforce for higher real wages. Hence, the strong anti-immigration stance taken by this workforce, and nationalism—which demands the raising of new barriers: both to goods and workers—gains ground.

Such forces can discredit representative democracy and produce a call for a leader—a Schmittian leader?—who might protect the country from opposite enemies: the constraints of economic policies aimed at stability and debt sustainability, and—globally—the erosion of market shares for domestic production and the pressure of massive immigration. Both lead to greater attention to the national interest: the former, from a Left-wing viewpoint, in the direction of greater State intervention in the economy; the latter, from a Right-wing perspective, looking for protectionism and barriers to immigration. The great protectionist of the nineteenth century, Friedrich List (Chapter 1), comes to mind, as well the German ordoliberalism (Chapter 2), in particular with reference to the EU economic policy.

A third factor in the rise of populism mentioned earlier is the frustration of the middle class. Non-economic factors must also be considered. "The old distinctions of class and economic interest have not disappeared but are increasingly overlaid by a larger and looser one—between the people who see the world from Anywhere and the people who see it from Somewhere".[104] In other words, there is often a feeling of being left behind by those who have been able to rise socially. This sense of having been left behind, is extended to people who have no specific reasons to complain from an economic point of view. Medium-income people, who tend to differentiate themselves from the "working class", have developed a sense of anger towards the elites, of exclusion from social and cultural groups that really matter in the life of a community: it is not, strictly speaking, a matter of income and wealth, but of rise to social success and meritocracy; it is a sort of social status anxiety. Our Neoliberal society, by exalting "the success" and putting certain people at the top of the social ladder—a ladder, it is worth repeating, which is not necessarily linked to well defined social classes—has inexorably generated a feeling of frustration in those large groups of population who, even though far from the bottom of the ladder in economic terms, have a feeling of not "belonging". Meritocracy is seen by those people as a fraud at the expense of the excluded.[105] Again, this is not an unprecedented development. As mentioned earlier, if going back in history we think of Italian Fascism and German Nazism, and their *petite bourgeoise* support, it is reasonable to draw compelling comparisons. And again, an increasing territory appears covered by the long and sinister shadow of Carl Schmitt. This search for a leader who might give the people a sense of social satisfaction and national pride is stronger in countries, where the liberal tradition of parliamentary democracy is weak or non-existent.

– The impact of social media

But there is another aspect of populism that deserves consideration, whose economic and social implications can be more far-reaching than those mentioned above. Let us assume that, in some way, populism can generate a sort of General Will, apparently in the Rousseauian sense. A major factor that has recently received much attention is the impact of social media. Two questions may be raised in this regard: how consensus is formed in the present era of social media; and whether there might be a hidden "Schmittian" leader who might be able to drive this consensus into directions that are far from nationalistic impulses, and rather point out to serious distortions in the market system and the political process.

The dumbing down of the mind through the use of short electronic messages, of "tweets", of too clear-cut opinions or insults (often anonymous), of "likes", of images of any kind, of emojis, is masked by their highly entertaining and fast-reaching aspects: it seems as if we never possessed such a level of freedom of expression, of instant satisfaction, and an enormous power to influence—all together—how things develop in our world: a dream of direct democracy. The fancy and infantile names given to these social networks do nothing other than increasing their attractiveness: everything is so simple, like a children's game! And we use them even when talking of the most complex issues in front of us, be they political, social or of a highly technical content, and, generally, in the total ignorance of the specific topic in question, any outcome is possible. The lack of specific expertise and competence is a matter of pride, rather than a disadvantage (a British politician, a former Cabinet member, has said recently that people have "had enough of experts"). In parallel goes the declining circulation of newspapers and other media: as we know, they can be available on the internet, but their stories are too long, and elaborate, and oblige us to spend some time on exercising our mind: it is much simpler and faster to rely on a "tweet".

This would be sufficient to motivate a critical view of these networks: the habit we have now of simplifying the most complicated issues that are before us, and therefore polarizing, to an extreme extent, different positions (even without considering the time lost in unending chats). A cost–benefit analysis should be attempted. The undoubted benefits of these networks should be assessed against the above-mentioned critical aspects. I admit that this analysis will never take place: even if we disregard its enormous unpopularity, who should be the impartial judge of the results?

In a speech given last October at Georgetown University,[106] Mark Zuckerberg, the CEO of Facebook, presented his philosophy to the audience. He placed his network in the mainstream of the American democracy, with passionate appeals to the Enlightenment, the First Amendment, the founding fathers, Martin Luther King, a Supreme Court ruling, *The New York Times*, and #MeToo (that "went viral on Facebook"). He wants "more people to share their experiences…giving everyone a voice". "Many of the stories people have shared would have been against the law to even write down". This "empowers the powerless and pushes society to be better over time…with Facebook, more than two billion people now have a greater opportunity to express themselves and help others…at scale. [This] is a new kind of force in the world…a Fifth Estate alongside the other structures of society. People no longer have to rely on traditional gatekeepers in politics and media to make their voices heard".

Facebook—Zuckerberg continues—puts people in the best possible position to face social tensions linked to massive economic change arising from globalization and new technology, to the fallout from the 2008 financial crisis, and to polarized reaction to greater migration. Facebook does its best to counteract terrorism, pornography, organized violence, interference in political elections, and not to encourage polarized contents, which lead to antagonized communities (he adds: "the most polarised voters in the last presidential elections were people least likely to use internet").

He wants to avoid the risk of "put[ting] people in danger". The users are protected by a team of 35,000 employees, provided with AI systems who can detect the risk of self-harm in minutes, being particularly focussed on people's wellbeing; while an Independent Oversight Board is available to appeal "our content decisions". His conclusion: "I believe in people".

That speech plainly sets out hesitations about traditional representative democracy. It never mentions "direct democracy" either, but rather appears to speak of the sum of certain wills. This is different from Rousseau's General Will, that can through an interpretation of "demos" be identified with the State (see above). On the other side, no support for a libertarian, Buchanan inspired liberalism is suggested.

A critical perspective, generally regarding internet, was raised some years ago by a British writer, Eliane Glaser.[107] She, distancing herself from the prevailing opinion, according to which the years following Francis Fukuyama's essay had given evidence that Fukuyama's forecast was flatly wrong (that actually history cannot end), wondered whether Fukuyama was, paradoxically, right. According to her, rather than looking at a prevalence of Western liberal democracy, Fukuyama was in reality presenting "a way of cloaking right-wing politics in benignly incontestable disguise". She pointed out to the decisive role of internet. In her view, "capitalism pretends to love free markets; in reality, it rigs markets for elites…[T]he right has systematically constructed an ideological movement that presents itself as anything but systematic, anything but ideological". Politics is presented as a matter of technological optimization, of doing a good job out of what the ever advancing technology offers us. "In a post-ideological age…the internet is either a symptom or a cause? When every single person in a train carriage is staring at a small illuminated device, it is almost a tacky vision of dystopia…digital consumerism makes us too passive to revolt…If we accept it as inevitable it will indeed lead to the end of history, in more ways than one".

To the extent that this view might lead to a depoliticized society, this sort of society might end up being an instrument of a Schmittian dictator: not any more happy to have in front of him large and vociferous gatherings of people who applaud him—as in the fascist regimes of our past—, but silent crowds that follow on their small devices his directions and unconsciously favour his own interests.

This model of society is visible clearly in David Runciman's reflections. In a still bleaker and extreme view, Runciman—in *How Democracy Ends*—presents the reader with the war that a liberal democracy constantly has to wage against excessive market corporate powers and their tendency to commingle with political institutions. Over time, and particularly in our own day, this fight has changed and become more difficult. He observes that, for the institutions of democracy, the danger of losing control of the corporate giants of the past is less critical with reference to corporate giants of today, as represented by social media networks. He writes that they "are very different beasts from Standard Oil. They monopolise many things at once. They produce stuff on which we have come to depend on our everyday life; they influence what we say to each other, by shaping what we see and hear".[108]

If this extreme interpretation were correct—a strong "if", I admit—the economic structure of society would be based on a quasi-monopolistic system, in which few corporate, social media giants would have a power of addressing our choices in a way apparently unbiased but substantially guided by themselves. This would be true not only with reference to our consumer's choices, but also to our political preferences.

In Chapter 2 of this essay, while dealing with Pigou's "externalities", the fact that social media services are provided almost free-of-charge to their consumers is mentioned as a sort of "positive externality", a consumer's surplus, measured by the market price that consumers would otherwise pay. The objection to this reasoning is that, as in many other instances, consumer needs are artificially created by the very enterprises which provide the appropriate product, and that there is on the other side a producer's surplus generated by the huge amount of data which becomes available to him.

One of the main tasks before the political class, as expressed by our representative institutions, is to face up to this impending economic and social development, and to give evidence that they look at the problem, by taking effective care of the liberal democracy that they are called to defend, and avoiding a simple impression of collusion with the powers they are called to regulate. This is the only way to redeem a representative democracy from all the accusations—often, justly raised—of having "betrayed" the people. What comes immediately to mind are some issues that are fundamental for the survival—political as well as economic—of a liberal society, and should raise consumer and regulatory attention to problems that are by now mature to be solved:

competition misconduct and antitrust legislation;
privacy protection, that is unscrupulous approach to privacy rights;
tax avoidance through exploitation of tax heavens;
role of social media as publishers. This issue is set aside by describing the network as a "platform". What this word means in legal terminology is, to me, unclear. As any publisher, social media should not ignore the responsibility for what is made public on the network.

But, above all, there is the issue of enormous concentration of economic and political power, as testified by the overwhelming share of the capital valuation of these tech companies, over the equity market's total value.

Notes

1. See De Cecco, chapter I.
2. Streek (2016, pp. 1–3).
3. See, for instance, Johnson (1965) and Levi-Faur (1997).
4. Johnson, pp. 172 and 183.
5. Fukuyama (1989).
6. p. 3.
7. Whether Hegel's admiration for Napoleon, defeating Prussia at the battle of Jena, means that he saw that event as "the end of history", is debatable. Fukuyama wrote as a political activist for the US State department rather than as a historian.
8. pp. 9 and 14–15.
9. Anyway, Schumpeter, writing in 1954, does not use this term with reference to Keynes' *General Theory*.
10. Schumpeter (1954, p. 754). It is in this sense that we have to understand the adjective "classical": nothing to do specifically with the "Classical School" of Adam Smith and other economists (even if, in fact, theirs was, in a Schumpeterian way, a "classical situation").
11. These are "classical situations", according to Schumpeter.

12. Ibidem.
13. Lucas and Sargent (1979, p. 1).
14. Keynes, *General Theory*, p. 378.
15. This factor is stressed by Heilbroner and Milberg (1995, cit, p. 57).
16. *General Theory*, p. 291.
17. See, on this last point: Leijonhufvud (1983) (the author is a half-repented Keynesian).
18. p. 5.
19. The "Phillips curve" was defined "an empirical finding in search of a theory" (James Tobin, as quoted by Heilbroner and Milberg, cit, p. 52).
20. Johnson (1971).
21. pp. 5–6.
22. For example, one of the American Keynesians, Alvin Hansen, raised the theory of "secular stagnation", to stress that an insufficiency of effective demand would always prevail, would be "structural".
23. Johnson, p. 6.
24. In Italy for instance, where inflation crossed at a point the level of 20%, a widespread comment was that democracy could not survive if inflation long remained above that rate.
25. Harvey (2007, p. 2).
26. Samuelson (1997). Somehow nicer than Samuelson, George Stigler famously wrote: "Competition is a though weed, not a delicate flower".
27. "then hibernating, as an exotic sect, in the United States and Britain" (Streek, cit, p. 154). But the British Lionel Robbins is one of them.
28. Collier (2018, p. 13).
29. Deaton (2020, p. 2).
30. *Stanford Encyclopedia of Philosophy* (plato.stanford.edu/contractaria nism).
31. "The utilitarian cause was promoted by economists; the rights cause was promoted by lawyers", writes Collier, p. 13. But this is not entirely true: Richard Posner, a jurist, was very close to Buchanan's libertarian views; Joseph Stiglitz, just to name one economist, is nearer to Rawls.
32. Kant (1981 [1785], pp. 12–13).
33. Rawls (1971).
34. p. 17.
35. p. 13.
36. p. 13.
37. But in this way they neglect, at least, G. F. Hegel.
38. Buchanan and Tullock (1965 [1962], pp. 111–112).
39. p. 266.
40. See for instance Boettke (2011).
41. Buchanan and Tullock speak of the "interdisciplinary nature of the book" (p. VI).

42. There is a Benthamian accent in this (see Chapter 1).
43. Ibidem, pp. 13–14.
44. Buchanan (1999 [1969], pp. 41–42).
45. Buchanan (1990).
46. Buchanan and Tullock, cit, p. 20.
47. Buchanan (1990, cit, pp. 4–7).
48. Hobbes's (1909 [1651], p. 132).
49. Buchanan (1990, p. 12).
50. Ibidem, p. 12.
51. Buchanan (1959).
52. p. 127.
53. p. 128.
54. Musgrave (1969).
55. Buchanan, p. 130.
56. Posner (1987, p. 21).
57. p. 22.
58. Posner (2009).
59. Milton Friedman wrote that the performance of economics as a science has to be judged by the "conformity with experience of the predictions it yields". The quantity theory was reformulated emphasizing money as an asset that can be compared to other assets, within a "portfolio analysis", an analysis of people's balance sheet, that is of the kind of assets that they want to hold. See Friedman (1968 [1964], pp. 357–359).
60. See Axelrod (2011, chapter 5) and Volcker (2018).
61. According to Milton Friedman's definition of economics as a positive discipline (see Preface).
62. Individuals were implicitly assumed as "too dumb". See Anderson (1978).
63. p. 5.
64. Lucas and Sargent, cit.
65. That is, offer of any good finds an exact correspondence with demand for it.
66. Heilbroner, Milberg, cit, pp. 81 and 83.
67. As defined by the European Central Bank.
68. Acharia et al. (2009, p. 5).
69. The crisis of loans extended to people with tarnished credit history.
70. Cassidy (2010).
71. de Voltaire(1937 [1759], p. 22).
72. Samuelson, cit.
73. Keynes (1937).
74. Shackle (1953, p. 227).
75. Because, actually, it has little to do with the Classical School of Smith or Ricardo.

76. Stiglitz (2009, p. 238).
77. Skidelsky (2009).
78. Israel (2014, p. 21). See also Kelly (2015).
79. Israel, cit, pp. 23, 216, 348 and 358.
80. Rousseau, J. J.: *The Social Contract*, cit, pp. 22–23.
81. p. 267.
82. p. 268.
83. p. 269.
84. p. 280.
85. p. 281.
86. On Buchanan's direct democracy as the antithesis of Rousseau's, see Shearmur (2010).
87. Buchanan (2001).
88. p. 237.
89. p. 238.
90. This is an issue we have already touched in Sect. 4.2, when dealing with Buchanan's concern for a constitution historically created, whose actual content can be far from the principles of a free-market economy.
91. p. 239.
92. Rachman (2019).
93. Schmitt (2013 [1921]).
94. Traverso (2016, pp. 95–96).
95. p. 238.
96. pp. 228–230.
97. However, Buchanan does not mention explicitly Schmitt (perhaps, at the time of his writing—2001—Schmitt's name wasn't so much *en vogue*).
98. Buchanan, Direct Democracy, Classical Liberalism, and Constitutional Strategy, cit, p. 236.
99. *Marxism Today*, November 1989.
100. Eichengreen (2018, p. 5).
101. It is worthwhile remembering that, in inter-war Germany, the orthodox liberal policies of chancellor Brüning implicitly favoured the electorate's tendency to incline towards the extreme Right.
102. Inequality of income, measured on the Gini coefficient

	UK	*USA*	*France*	*Italy*	*Germany*
2010	33.66	45.60	30.30	34.70	28.00
1980	25.70	37.85	32.56 (1979)	32.50	24.73 (1978)

Source ourworldindata.org

103. Pringle (2020, p. 113).

104. Goodhart (2017, pp. 3–4).
105. Kuper (2020).
106. Zuckerberg (2019).
107. Glaser (2014).
108. Runciman (2018, pp. 132–133).

References

Acharia, V., Philippon, T., Richardson, M., & Roubini, N. (2009). Prologue: A Bird's Eye View. In V. Acharya & M. Richardson (Eds.), *Restoring Financial Stability. How to Repair a Failed System* (p. 5). Hoboken: Wiley.

Anderson, P. (1978, Fall). Rational Expectations: How Important for Econometric Policy Analysis. *Federal Reserve Bank of Minneapolis Quarterly Review, 2.*

Axelrod, S. H. (2011). *Inside the Fed. Monetary Policy and Its Management, Martin Through Greenspan to Bernanke*. London: The MIT Press.

Boettke, P. (2011). Teaching Economics, Appreciating Spontaneous Order, and Economics as a Public Science. *Journal of Economic Behavior and Organization, 80,* 265–274.

Buchanan, J. (1959, October). Positive Economics, Welfare Economics, and Political Economy. *Journal of Law and Economics, II,* 124–138.

Buchanan, J. (1990). The Domain of Constitutional Economics. *Constitutional Political Economy, 1*(1), 1–18.

Buchanan, J. (1999 [1969]). *The Collected Works of James Buchanan, Vol. 6, Cost and Choice* (pp. 41–42). Indianapolis: Liberty Fund.

Buchanan, J. (2001). Direct Democracy, Classical Liberalism, and Constitutional Strategy. *Kyklos, 54*(fasc 2/3), 235–242.

Buchanan, J. M., & Tullock, G. (1965 [1962]). *The Calculus of Consent. Logical Foundations of Constitutional Democracy* (pp. 111–112). Ann Arbor: University of Michigan Press.

Cassidy, J. (2010, January 13). Interview with Eugene Fama. *The New Yorker*.

Collier, P. (2018). *The Future of Capitalism, Facing New Anxieties*. London: Allen Lane.

Deaton, A. (2020). *Inequality in Cambridge and Chicago* (p. 2). www.project-syndicate.org.

de Voltaire, J. F. (1937 [1759]). *Candide*. New York: Halcyon House.

Eichengreen, B. (2018). *The Populist Temptation. Economic Grievance and Political Reaction in the Modern Era*. Oxford: Oxford University Press.

Friedman, M. (1968 [1964]). Postwar Trends in Monetary Theory and Policy. In J. Lindauer (Eds.), *Macroeconomic Readings* (pp. 357–359). New York: The Free Press.

Fukuyama, F. (1989, Summer). The End of History? *The National Interest.*
Glaser, E. (2014, March 22). Bring back Ideology. *The Guardian.*
Goodhart, D. (2017). *The Road to Somewhere: The Populist Revolt and the Future of Politics.* London: C. Hurst & Co.
Harvey, D. (2007). *A Brief History of Neoliberalism.* Oxford: Oxford University Press.
Heilbroner, R., & Milberg, W. (1995). *The Crisis of Vision in Modern Economic Thought.* Cambridge: Cambridge University Press.
Hobbes, T. (1909 [1651]). *Leviathan.* Oxford: Oxford University Press.
Israel, J. (2014). *Revolutionary Ideas. An Intellectual History of the French Revolution from 'The Rights of Men' to Robespierre* (p. 21). Princeton: Princeton University Press.
Johnson, H. G. (1965). A Theoretical Model of Economic Nationalism in the New and Developing States. *Political Science Quarterly, LXXX*(2), 169–185.
Johnson, H. G. (1971). The Keynesian Revolution and the Monetarist Counter-Revolution. *American Economic Review, 61*(2), 1–14.
Kant. I. (1981 [1785]). *Grounding for the Metaphysics of Morals* (pp. 12–13). Indianapolis: Hackett.
Kelly, D. (2015, July 31). Review of the Book 'Politics in Commercial Society: J.-J. Rousseau and A. Smith', by I. Hont. *Financial Times.*
Keynes, J. M. (1964 [1936]). *The General Theory of Employment Interest and Money.* London: Macmillan.
Keynes, J. M. (1937). The General Theory of Employment. *The Quarterly Journal of Economics, 51*(2), 209–223.
Kuper, S. (2020, February 15–16). The Revenge of the Middle-Class Anti-elitist. *Financial Times.*
Leijonhufvud, A. (1983). *What Would Keynes Have Thought of Rational Expectations?* (Discussion Beiträge – Serie A, no 177). Universität Konstanz.
Levi-Faur, D. (1997). Economic Nationalism: From Friedrich List to Robert Reich. *Review of International Studies, 23,* 359–370.
Lucas, R., & Sargent, T. (1979, Spring). After Keynesian Macroeconomics. *Federal Reserve Bank of Minneapolis Quarterly Review, 3.*
Musgrave, R. A. (1969). *Fiscal Systems.* New Haven and London: Yale University Press.
Posner, R. (1987, November). The Constitution as an Economic Document. *George Washington Law Review, 56.*
Posner, R. (2009). *A Failure of Capitalism. The Crisis of '08 and the Descent into Depression.* Cambridge and London: Harvard University Press.
Pringle, R. (2020). *The Power of Money. How Ideas About Money Shaped the Modern World.* Cham: Palgrave Macmillan.
Rachman, G. (2019, January 12–13). Liberalism's Most Brilliant Enemy Is Back in Vogue. *Financial Times.*

Rawls, J. (1971). *A Theory of Justice*. Cambridge: The Belknap Press of the Harvard University Press.

Rousseau, J. J. (1913 [1762]). *The Social Contract and Discourses*. London: J.M. Dent.

Runciman, D. (2018). *How Democracy Ends*. London: Profile Books.

Samuelson, P. (1997, October 2) *Where Do the European and American Models Differ?* Address delivered at the Banca d'Italia, mimeo.

Schmitt, C. (2013 [1921]). *Dictatorship*. Cambridge: Polity.

Schumpeter, J. A. (1954). *History of Economic Analysis*. Oxford: Oxford University Press.

Shackle, G. L. S. (1953). *What Makes an Economist?* Liverpool: Liverpool University Press.

Shearmur, J. (2010). Preferences, Cognitivism and the Public Sphere. In C. Favor, G. Gaus, & J. Lamont (Eds.), *Essays on Philosophy, Politics and Economics*. Stanford: Stanford University Press.

Skidelsky, R. (2009). *Keynes. The Return of the Master*. London: Allen Lane.

Stiglitz, J. E. (2009). *Freefall. Free Markets and the Sinking of the Global Economy* (p. 238). London: Penguin.

Streek, W. (2016). *How Will Capitalism End?* London: Verso.

Traverso, E. (2016). *Fire and Blood. The European Civil War 1914–1945*. New York: Verso.

Volcker, P. (2018). *Keeping at It. The Quest for Sound Money and Good Government*. New York: Public Affairs.

Zuckerberg, M. (2019, October 17). Speech at Georgetown University. *Washington Post*.

CHAPTER 5

As I See It

5.1 A Liberal View

We have seen in Chapter 2 that the Italian philosopher Benedetto Croce wanted to rebuild the foundations of liberalism, convinced as he was of the inadequacy of conventional liberal theory, as it matured in the nineteenth century. This theory relied either on the Enlightenment's natural order, or on positivism's utilitarian principles.

Croce reacted against what he called "the orgy of abstract regularity", and the "most perfect equilibria of social mechanics", which were behind the theoretical construction of social scientists, and—in the field of economics—of the economists of the Classical and Neo-classical Schools: schemes that were seen as valid anywhere and always, according to the former; or as "laws" respondent to immutable regularities of the physical world, according to the latter.[1]

Croce believed that a new and persuasive ground for liberalism could be found in historicism. However, what he had in mind was the historicism neither of the dialectic Hegelian nor of the materialistic Marxist. Both of these versions want to lead to certain defined goals that are realized through the historical process: the affirmation of the State as the embodiment of rationality and liberty, or the advent of a classless society thanks to the proletarian revolution. And, for this reason, both are indeed deterministic, because consist of a historical prediction of what

A. Roselli, *Economic Philosophies*,
Palgrave Studies in Classical Liberalism,
https://doi.org/10.1007/978-3-030-53317-5_5

is going necessarily to happen: an approach to social sciences that assumes historical prediction as its principal aim.[2]

Far from any determinism of this kind, historicism means, according to Croce, that we cannot look forward to a specific societal organization that will be the final stage of human progress, a sort of permanent equilibrium in both social and economic life.

His "ideal historicism" means that the problematic situations that are in front of us, the choices that we have to make in any field of activity, are historically specific, and always require new approaches and solutions. This view can be seen as—and in a way, is—relativistic. As such, while far from determinism, it seems also to undermine any confidence in supra-historical, permanent standards, guiding us in our decisions: permanent standards that are often considered as essential to liberalism.

The central point of Croce's reflections is that historical developments are realized through institutions, policies and individual actions, but none of them should be taken as an absolute source of values that have to be indefinitely maintained. Croce's liberalism is centred on the supremacy of the individual, on his consciousness and moral capacity to act in conformity with his sense of justice (this reminds us of John Rawls, who writes of men as moral rational beings, with their own ends but capable of a sense of justice).[3] Behind our concrete behaviour, there is always "a voice that directs us towards what we must do, what is our mission and our duty: a voice that may differ for each of us, because history needs different and opposite thoughts, that history itself will take care of mediating and harmonising".[4] This view is well attuned to a common sense's definition of the liberal man, as paradoxically described by the poet Robert Frost: "a liberal is a man too broad-minded to take his own side in an argument".[5]

This means recognizing, in the light of historical awareness, political diversity and disagreements, regarding them as a source of change and growth. In this way, "Liberty – Croce writes – is not tied to any particular environment of institutions or traditions or economic conditions or anything else; all these it [liberty] can use for its own purposes as the situation and the historical process may suggest".[6] "Truth is never final, because every truth sets the premise of new intellectual stands and, with them, of new doubts, problems and new truths".[7] A liberal will never encourage the hope of achieving permanent solutions: "Who refutes or satirises apostles of universal peace and equality, does this to oppose the naïve and unsuitable means they use because of the vagueness and impossibility of their assumptions; but does not refute or satirise the honest work, pursued by good rulers at all times, to reduce in specific societies specific inequalities; or by wise policymakers, to avoid armed conflicts and wars".[8]

What may these abstract, apparently abstruse words mean in political terms? In the historical circumstances that had accompanied decades of intellectual debates about liberalism, and in the turbulent times of the century, "Croce sought to re-establish the bases of liberal pluralism and tolerance, and to show, in response to the arrogance of totalitarianism, why a measure of humility must surround political commitment".[9] In the same vein, Isaiah Berlin wrote, many years later: "The idea that there can be two sides to a question, that there may be two or more incompatible answers, any one of which could be accepted by honest, rational men – that is a very recent notion". "The merit of a free society is that it allows of a great variety of conflicting opinions without the need for suppression".[10]

How may this theorizing be relevant to the contentious field of economic ideologies and visions as discussed in this essay? As we have stressed in Chapter 2, Croce tried to elevate liberalism above any vision that may historically prevail at a specific time and place, and observed that a specific economic system can be considered as liberal if consistent with the need to affirm individual freedom and pluralism in different historical circumstances.

Croce therefore thought that the issue of economic freedom in a capitalistic system (economic liberalism, or "liberism", as we have called it earlier) might, or might not be consistent with liberalism *tout court*: the response coming only from the particular historical circumstances we live with. In the circumstances of his own time, he "sought to make [economic] liberalism more flexible by undercutting its persistent antistatism, and particularly its long-standing link to laissez-faire economics".[11]

The clash between the "liberist" economist Luigi Einaudi and Benedetto Croce on the theme of liberalism is an interesting example of a difficult dialogue between the liberal philosopher and the liberal economist. This debate went on during the 1930s, and became more direct and vehement on the pages of the *Rivista di storia economica* at the beginning of the 1940s. Croce stressed the difference between liberalism and liberism, which he saw as the doctrine of laissez-faire. Economic systems are historically specific and none of them is entitled to claim to be morally privileged and implicitly superior. Economic theory cannot be, *per se*, a theory of a liberal society.

Which inferences can we draw from adopting a liberal historical perspective—such as the one just mentioned—on the concrete economic issues before us today? It may be helpful, at this point, to recall the distinction, described at the very beginning of this essay, between a vision centred on the individual as a rational agent, and a vision of the State as the embodiment of rationality, a vision wherein the individual always ranks second. The second vision is embedded in that kind of historicism that Croce wanted to reject, and it will be evident that a Crocean approach would rule it out as antiliberal, because it denies the supremacy of the individual in all aspects of social and economic life.

Where may a balance be found? A useful distinction was made by Berlin, between negative liberty (which means: how many doors are open to me?) and positive liberty (which means: who is in charge, so that my personal development and full participation in the life of the collectivity can be realised through State intervention?). Negative liberty is measured by the absence of obstacles to doing what I want to do, while positive liberty is measured by the extent of State intervention in a country's social and economic life, and by the uses to which such intervention is put. "Uncontrolled exercise of either liberty destroys the other". In terms of negative liberty, that is with no intervention by the State at all, this unlimited liberty can be twisted and can, in the extreme, lead to the conclusion that "liberty must be equal for the tiger and the sheep" (unlimited negative liberty for the capitalist destroys the liberty of the worker, Berlin adds).[12] Positive liberty, likewise, can be twisted and lead to the authoritarian or totalitarian society. At these two extremes, liberalism is completely ruled out. Avoiding these extremes determines the degree of liberalism in society. "There must be a balance between the two [liberties], about which no clear principles can be enunciated".[13] And, in Berlin's opinion, the concept of positive liberty—even though, itself, essential "to a decent existence"—has been historically more abused and perverted that of negative liberty in the modern world.

To return to Croce, his rejection of a statist society—be it represented by the ethical State or by the Marxian proletarian State—would mean firm opposition to the extreme version of positive liberty, which is necessarily accompanied by totalitarian coercion. But if we err on the side of negative liberty, the problem is to what extent we can tilt towards it.

Herbert Stein, writing in 1990 and in a way celebrating the collapse of communism, stressed that "a note of realism has to be brought" to the celebration. The central core of capitalism is freedom, but absolute freedom is impossible, and our [American capitalism] adaptations have not all been in the same direction, some have been led by public policy, some by private behaviour. "The genius of the system is that both have been free to adapt".[14] In a similar approach, Douglass North studied the interactions of actors (individuals or groups) and institutional arrangements (organizational forms) by considering these organizations as an integral part of the economic analysis rather than a descriptive addition to the analysis.[15]

Most liberal political thinkers and economists, whatever their political and economic philosophy, would definitely agree on the idea of an "adaptive society". Society needs different strands of thought, and in the discipline of economics, the emphasis may be put in different times and places on one or the other strand:

- On the one side, individual ambition is seen as the driving force behind free market economies. State guidance would hinder and constrain individualism. This means that ample possibility must be given to the individual to pursue his own goals, so that he may succeed in his endeavours and his economic reward may be maximised, without being hindered by public constraints, at the cost of not giving priority to less favoured people. This liberal thinker believes in market incentives as a powerful instrument of growth. He will be of the opinion that a large emphasis on "negative" liberty can lead to a level of growth that raises substantially the standard of life of everybody, notwithstanding the fact that wide gaps in income and wealth distribution remain or even increase. He might also think that State intervention is often ineffective, because it may have unintended or even harmful consequences (for instance, in terms of incentives or corruption).
- On the other side, another liberal thinker—particularly when times are harsh—will look at disadvantaged strata of population, and will observe that large pools of poverty and widening inequalities call for deeper State intervention, in order to raise their level of protection, at the cost of the adoption of policies reserving an ample role to the State: a more complete fruition of "positive" liberty through ways that can include redistributive fiscal policies, stricter regulations,

public ownerships of the means of productions, and enlargements of the public safety net.

This sort of choices can well remain within the territory of liberalism. Representative democracy, on the political side, is the institutional arrangement that can properly assure the freedom to make these fundamental, but different economic choices.

5.2 Where a Liberal Would Head to, Now?

Having in mind this distinction between negative and positive liberty, one may wonder whether neoliberalism, as discussed in the previous chapter, may have led to an abuse of negative liberty. I believe that indeed it has done so.

Let us recall a few characteristics that we have considered inherent to neoliberalism. They are: labour relations based on an equal footing, irrespective of the different contractual strength of the employer and the employee; a Darwinian market organization, possibly leading to *de facto* competition suppression and emergence of rent positions, and extreme concentration of economic power; globalism in trade and capital movements that exploits labour cost arbitrage and possibly disadvantages investment and production at a regional level; neutrality of fiscal and monetary policies with respect to the behaviour of macroeconomic aggregates. In general, economic systems relying on softer regulatory structures and on retrenchment of the public sector.

Let's add that, as it is pretty obvious, in most advanced countries these features of market fundamentalism have not destroyed existing and well-consolidated structures, particularly in reference to what goes under the general denomination of Welfare State. A neoliberal would be correct in saying that the impact of the abovementioned features has been different from country to country and, on the whole, exaggerated. But the pervasive "visceral anxiety", affecting both workers and entrepreneurs alike (according to the strong words used by Paul Samuelson more than twenty years ago, see Chapter 4), has only increased.

Isaiah Berlin, looking back at the twentieth century, had ample ground, as we have seen, to comment on the abuses of positive liberty. Nationalism and totalitarianism were pretty recent experiences and, even where liberal-democratic governments were in charge, an overextension of the public safety net was a matter of debate and concern. Today, the issues at stake are different. The question is whether erring on the side of negative liberty—with the emphasis on strong private property rights, free markets and free trade—has gone too far, in the direction of what Berlin would call "pseudo-negative liberty". This sort of liberty ends up being far from liberalism, even if we adopt a definition of liberalism quite broad and encompassing different perspectives.

The relevance of this question comes out even when—setting aside the ethical aspect of liberalism—we look at the actual economic experience and ask whether it conformed to the predictions of New Classical Economics (which we may see as the theoretical background of neoliberalism). If one has in mind that the performance of "positive" economics—that is, of an economic science that aims to be independent of ethical positions—has to be judged by the conformity of experience with the predictions it yields (according to Milton Friedman, see the Preface of this essay), it is clear that the actual economic and financial experience, consistent with the schemes adopted by the theories of rational expectations and efficient markets, was not in conformity with the predictions these theories yielded.

Neoliberal policies that have long prevailed might have found a plausible legitimacy if their results had implied a general betterment of economic and social conditions. Apparently, neither occurred, in the presence of very modest rates of growth, or often stagnantion or decline in most of the advanced countries, and of inequalities in income and wealth that have only got worse. Even in the field that can be seen as a "natural territory" for an experimental verification of market efficiency theories—that is, the smooth working of financial markets—they failed, with markets' collapse with well-known consequences in terms of growth and employment (the fact that other, mostly non-Western, countries have done better in economic terms should not be attributed to those theoretical propositions. At least in one important case, that of China, its policies seem to be based on a formal homage to Marx, and in practice on a combination of sheer nationalism, political totalitarianism, and rough unrestrained capitalism, provided that it remains within the limits fixed by an unelected elite.)

It is possible to say that not only Adam Smith's vision of trust as the basis of a well-functioning free market system has been abandoned, but also Hayek's or even Buchanan's libertarian tenets of liberalism had been deprived of any ethical motivation. Here, the issue is not the liberal focus on individualism—Keynes too saw individual ambitions as a driving force of economic activity, and in fact his theory, as mentioned earlier (Chapter 2), assigned a primary role to the private entrepreneur to promote economic efficiency. The issue is rather about the general vision, or set of assumptions, underlying the theories of rational expectations and efficient markets, and about the adoption of institutional arrangements and regulatory policies consistent with them. In this regard, those theories appear as an exercise in abstract logic, whose basic assumption is the individual economic agent as guided by selfishness and unrestrained greed: an assumption that is a travesty of the view of classical liberals.

As observed in the previous chapter, we may read the current situation through what can be seen as an important by-product of neoliberalism, the widespread success of populist movements.

The decreasing share of the industrial sector and the parallel expansion of the services sector in advanced countries has been accompanied by an ample deunionization of labour, and by an increasing number of exploited workers particularly in some sectors of the economy, such as certain services and agriculture. The relative deindustrialisation is partly the result of labour cost arbitrage and consequent production delocalization. Neoliberalism has generated a strong and deep-rooted resentment against the political elites and emerging entrepreneurial classes that have put neoliberalism into practice. This resentment is the source and engine of populism, and of its generic call for more statism, and often for unsustainable economic policies.

If negative liberty has become a pseudo-liberty, a certain rebalance is needed to re-enter the field of liberalism. Negative pseudo-liberty has to be curtailed if positive liberty is to be sufficiently realized.[16] It seems to me that an appropriate, correct balance between negative and positive liberty requires, particularly under the current circumstances—I am writing these lines while the pandemic is still with us,—to carefully address specific points we have mentioned as features of neoliberalism, and to wonder which sort of approaches might be consistent with a liberal view.

About labour relations, "[g]lobalisation has moved the sweatshops that Marx and Engels and the factory inspectors of the 19th century found in Manchester to the capitalistic periphery…So the sweated workers of today [in the capitalistic periphery] and the middle-class workers in the countries of advanced capitalism, being so remote from each other spatially that they never meet,…never experience together the community and solidarity deriving from joint collective action".[17] There is only to add that the "middle-class workers" of advanced economies include also the insecure employees of the gig economy.

All this may sound old Marxism ("working men of the world unite"[18]), but in actual terms it means that, having the industrial production largely moved to the "periphery", the advanced countries' economies have become, in large part, service economies, where the dense grouping of workers in the same huge factory is less and less frequent. It is in the interest of a sound liberal economy that workforce rights are recognised and protected. The liberal man admits that there is an inherent conflict of interest between the two sides of the labour contract, and favours freely created labour unions as a common instrument of cooperation and defence, and of confrontation with the opposite party (as the "liberist" Luigi Einaudi himself stressed in his *Le lotte del lavoro*).[19] The liberal man, above all, is wary of any form of corporativism, concerned that it may favour the employer under the supreme banner of the national interest.

About open markets and globalism, it should be recognised that the origin of globalization has to be found in the envisaged opportunity to liberalize trade and capital movements, to enhance the spirit of individual enterprise, to open opportunities and to go beyond protected markets in order to reinforce competition and economic growth. The dramatic increase in international transactions that ensued has to be regarded as a positive factor for a more widespread well-being and, in a way, it may be a cause of complaint against the very fact that many areas of the world are been left behind by protectionist attitudes.

However, market openness has inevitably involved areas that have remarkably different levels of economic growth, market structures and regulation, labour skills, wages and labour protection; and governed by profoundly different political systems. Globalization has thus contributed to the adoption of broadly speaking deflationary policies to maintain competitiveness in countries that, thanks to their higher level of income and wages and of stricter labour protection, are exposed to imbalances in their foreign accounts. On the other side, it has encouraged delocalization of production for the opposite reasons. The adoption of deflationary policies and investment delocalisation are two different faces of the same phenomenon, and have been seen—with somewhat insincere resignation—as "a factual constraint residing in the nature of things that leaves you no choice".[20]

As happens when an important crisis develops in an open system—think of the 1930s—the reaction is a return to the protection of the national interest (it should however be remembered that even broad-minded liberal tinkers—Keynes is a notable example—supported barriers to trade at the start of the Great Depression, see Chapter 2: this is an issue that cannot be seen only in terms of populist rage).

It should not be taken as a necessary disadvantage that one of the possible consequences of the current difficulties of moving merchandise across the globe with the easiness to which we were all accustomed (difficulties to be ascribed both to geo-political tensions and to the current pandemic) is business's attempt to "reshore", that is to shorten and diversify long supply chains, wherever they sell their final product: either closer to their own home market, or to the far-away country which was their supplier but has by now become also a consumer market.

About the respective roles, of State and individual, in the economic system, in current specific circumstances, a question that has been raised is whether the larger role of the former is a temporary emergency or a long-term tendency, and how it should be evaluated. An enlarged role of the State is already with us, pushed by urgent motivations, be it in the form of subsidies or tax reductions for the private sector, or of increased ownership of means of production, through bail-out measures. The liberal rejects any statist view of the economic system, looks with suspicion at these often inevitable policies, is aware that this is not the best way to deal with "zombie" (insolvent) enterprises. But, beyond the emergency, one should look at a more stable public presence in specific circumstances, such as natural monopolies, or some public utilities. In a broad sense, an extended Pigouvian taxation should be imposed to reduce the often enormous negative externalities, as in the case of global warming.

The liberal man will also address the issue of the discipline of economics, and in particular of macroeconomic policies, by freeing himself from what may appear by now more as dogmas than as attempts to lead towards a more balanced well-being. Worthwhile repeating that Croce was a philosopher, not an economist.[21] And it would be misleading to identify his "ideal historicism" with any of the economic *Weltanshauungen* into which liberalism metamorphosed in the twentieth century and up to our days (Chapters 2 and 4). However, to recall Croce's liberalism and the weight of his ideal historicism may be instrumental in giving more relevance to a stream of thought, which is currently receiving renewed attention, that goes under the name of "institutionalism": a stream of thought which, by enlarging the economist's field of inquiry, might perhaps lead to a new, Schumpeterian "classical situation", still missing as we have seen.

Heilbroner and Milberg,[22] writing in the 1990s, observed that the "high theorizing" of those years attained a high degree of unreality, building models without underpinnings. They wrote that "The majority of present day economists... concentrate on capitalism as a market system, with the consequence of emphasizing its functional rather than its institutional or constitutive aspects". I think it's fair to say that they were right. These economists—they observed—do not use the broad canvas, that is the picture of the distinctive political and cultural as well as economic properties which characterize capitalism in a historical context, which is such a marked feature in the writings of figures as Smith, Mill, Marx, Veblen, Schumpeter, and Weber or also Braudel[23] (other authors, including Keynes himself, or Hyman Minsky, or Douglass North might be added). The importance of institutions is stressed by authors who think that the purely theoretical, non-institutional, non-historical accounts deprive economics of a deeper understanding of the free market economy and its success. Economic institutionalism is, in fact, the branch of the discipline that looks at the foundations of an economic system, with particular emphasis on its historical evolution. To look at the institutional side means to inquire about history, that is to look at the economy as a process in historical time, therefore at the fundamental uncertainty that characterises our future. This fits well with the responsibility of our individual, historically specific choices, stressed by Croce.

In a way, every economist who looks beyond the day-to-day working of a market is, *per se*, an institutionalist, because he has to consider the general context in which any market exchange takes place; all the more so if we move from micro to macroeconomics. Keynes himself—as mentioned above—can be read from an institutional perspective, because he, as any institutionalist, sees "economics as a broad-based social and cultural science rather than as a body of 'mathematical-logical' analysis".[24] Second, macroeconomists and institutionalists recognise the necessity of using deductive and inductive reasoning, rejecting arbitrary boundaries between pure theory and empirical analysis. Third, they also see a role for government and agree that government plays an integral part in the institutional response to real world problems. Keynes and the institutionalists have a theory of capitalist structure and institutional change, that is missing from much contemporary economic analysis.

Whether economic liberalism can be reassessed along the lines we have described, and whether the economic discipline will move by giving larger space to factors as history and institutions, remains very much to be seen. It is possible that events as the financial crisis and the Great Recession, or the current pandemic, will lead to a rethinking of economics and economic policies, in the same way as long periods of success and prosperity may lead to intellectual stagnation. These very uncertain times leave open the door to any sort of developments, and the resiliency of liberalism will be put to a severe test.

Notes

1. Croce (1922). About this article, see also Chapter 2, regarding Croce's relation with Keynes. Keynes was the editor of the series, Reconstruction in Europe, where this article was inserted).
2. This is the diminutive meaning given to historicism by Karl Popper (2002). He justly writes that "the belief in historical destiny is sheer superstition". See pp. IX and 3.
3. See Chapter 4 of this essay.
4. Croce (1922).
5. As quoted by Rachman (2020).
6. Croce (1949, pp. 93–94).
7. Croce (1922).
8. Ibidem.
9. Roberts (1987, p. 216).
10. Berlin and Jahanbegloo (1991, p. 43).
11. Roberts, p. 221.
12. Or, unlimited liberty for factory-owners or parents will allow both to employ children in the coal-mines.
13. Berlin, pp 40–43.
14. Stein (1990, pp. 5–6).
15. North (1971).
16. Berlin, p. 41.
17. Streek (2016, p. 25)
18. *Communist Manifesto.*
19. See Chapter 2.
20. Streek (2016, p. 23).
21. "To try and read as an economist Benedetto Croce's writings on the "economic science" is an embarrassing exercise, fearful of being irreverent toward an author that was the 'major controversial idol'... of all the Italian culture of the last century", wrote Giorgio Lunghini, a Marxian economist (2003, p. 185).

22. Heilbroner and Milberg (1995).
23. Heilbroner (1988, p. 50).
24. Keller (1983, p. 1088). See also Weinstein (2007) and Whelan (2012).

References

Berlin, I., & Jahanbegloo, R. (1991). *Conversations with Isaiah Berlin*. Charles Scribner's Sons.

Croce, B. (1922, August 17). A Philosopher View of Population. In *Manchester Guardian Commercial, Section 6, Reconstruction in Europe*.

Croce, B. (1949). Liberalism and Democracy. In *My Philosophy: Essays on the Moral and Political Problems of Our Time*. George Allen & Unwin.

Heilbroner, R. (1988). *Behind the Veil of Economics. Essays in the Worldly Philosophy*. New York: W. W. Norton.

Heilbroner, R., Milberg, W. (1995). *The Crisis of Vision in Modern Economic Thought*. Cambridge: Cambridge University Press.

Keller, R. (1983). Keynesian and Institutional Economics. Compatibility or Complementarity? *Journal of Economic Issues, 17*(4).

Lunghini, G. (2003). Benedetto Croce e l'economia italiana. *Economia politica, 2*(8).

North, D. (1971). Institutional Change and Economic Growth. *The Journal of Economic History, 31*(1).

Popper, K. (2002 [1957]). *The Poverty of Historicism*. Abington: Routledge.

Rachman, G. (2020, May 12). Liberals Must Prepare for a Fightback. *Financial Times*.

Roberts, D. D. (1987). *Benedetto Croce and the Uses of Historicism*. Berkeley, Los Angeles and London: University of California Press.

Stein, H. (1990, Spring). The Triumph of the Adaptive Society. *The American Economist*.

Streek, W. (2016). *How Will Capitalism End?* London and New York.

Weinstein, M. M. (2007). Institutional Bases for Capitalistic Growth—Introduction and Comments. In E. Sheshinski, R. J. Strom, & W. J. Baumol (Eds.), *Entrepreneurship, Innovation, and the Growth Mechanism of the Free-Enterprise Economies*. Princeton: Princeton University Press.

Whelan, C. (2012, May). *Post-Keynesian Institutionalism After the Great Recession* (Working Paper No. 724). Levy Economics Institute of Bard College.

Correction to: Metamorphoses of Liberalism in the Twentieth Century

Correction to:
Chapter 2 in: A. Roselli, *Economic Philosophies*, Palgrave Studies in Classical Liberalism, https://doi.org/10.1007/978-3-030-53317-5_2

The original version of this chapter was inadvertently published with an incorrect name "George Stiglitz" in chapter 2, which has now been changed to "George Stigler". The correction to the book have been updated with the changes.

The updated version of this chapter can be found at https://doi.org/10.1007/978-3-030-53317-5_2

A. Roselli, *Economic Philosophies*,
Palgrave Studies in Classical Liberalism,
https://doi.org//10.1007/978-3-030-53317-5_6

Author Index

A. Roselli, *Economic Philosophies*,
Palgrave Studies in Classical Liberalism,
https://doi.org/10.1007/978-3-030-53317-5

Subject Index

A. Roselli, *Economic Philosophies*,
Palgrave Studies in Classical Liberalism,
https://doi.org/10.1007/978-3-030-53317-5

The manufacturer's authorised representative in the EU is Springer Nature Customer Service Centre GmbH, Europaplatz 3, 69115 Heidelberg, Germany. If you have any concerns regarding our products, please contact ProductSafety@springernature.com

Printed and bound by CPI Group (UK) Ltd, Croydon, CR0 4YY
30/09/2026
02225461-0008